Borrowed Gods
and Foreign Bodies

Borrowed Gods
and Foreign Bodies

Christian Missionaries
Imagine Chinese Religion

Eric Reinders

UNIVERSITY OF CALIFORNIA PRESS

Berkeley / *Los Angeles* / *London*

University of California Press
Berkeley and Los Angeles, California

University of California Press, Ltd.
London, England

Library of Congress Cataloging-in-Publication Data

Reinders, Eric Robert.
  Borrowed gods and foreign bodies : Christian missionaries imagine
Chinese religion / Eric Reinders.
      p.   cm.
  Includes bibliographical references and index.
  ISBN 0-520-24171-1 (cloth : alk. paper)
    1. Christianity and other religions—Chinese.   2. China—Religion—
History.   I. Title: Christian missionaries imagine Chinese religion.
II. Title.
BR128.C4R45   2004
261.2'951—dc22   2004002856

Manufactured in the United States of America
14   13   12   11   10   09   08   07   06   05
10   9   8   7   6   5   4   3   2   1

Printed on Ecobook 50 containing a minimum 50% post-consumer waste,
processed chlorine free. The balance contains virgin pulp, including 25%
Forest Stewardship Council Certified for no old growth tree cutting,
processed either TCF or ECF. The sheet is acid-free and meets the
minimum requirements of ANSI/NISO Z39.48–1992 (R 1997)
(Permanence of Paper). ♾

To Mum, Dad, and Vivian

Contents

Illustrations

Acknowledgments

Thanks to: Gene Bianchi, Martin Buss, Martha Finch, William Gilders, Norman Girardot, Allan Grapard, Richard Hecht, Charles Jones, Mark Jordan, Michael C. Lazich, Li Hong, Reed Malcolm, Parimal Patil, Laura Parsons, Laurie Patton, the Philosopher Tribe, William Powell, Fabio Rambelli, Murray Rubinstein, Thomas Thangaraj, Michael Walsh, Wang Guo-hua, Sarah Warner, Zhang Zengwu, and Angela Zito.

I would like to thank the excellent staff of the Emory Department of Religion and those at the University of California Press.

Thanks to: Emory University Research Committee for a research grant, 1999; Emory College for Faculty Development Grants, 2000 and 2001; and the Emory University Institute for Comparative and International Studies for a research grant, 2000. Elements of this book appeared first in print in *Numen,* and are reprinted by permission. Excerpts from "Sai Fong" and "The Chinese Dinner" are from: *The Cricket in Times Square* by George Selden and Garth Williams, Copyright © 1960 by George Selden Thompson and Garth Williams. Copyright renewed © 1988 by George Selden Thompson. Reprinted by permission of Farrar, Straus and Giroux, LLC.

Preface

Meaning is a physiognomy.
Ludwig Wittgenstein,
Philosophical Investigations

This book is about the experiences of British Protestant missionaries in China during the nineteenth and early twentieth centuries, and about the representations of China and Chinese religion they produced. It concerns the relationship of those experiences to those representations. One immediately obvious characteristic of their writing is a hostile bias against Chinese non-Christian religions. They tended to depict Chinese "heathenism" as absurd superstition, unthinking habit, and degraded idolatry. I do not share that view, yet I do not think the missionaries were simply perverse or irrational in their various judgments about China, any more than I believe the Chinese people were perversely irrational. Rather than saying, "Well, they were missionaries after all," and leaving it at that, I am curious about the logic and sense of that bias. Trying to account for the images of Chinese religion they communicated, in this book I have explored aspects of their religious identity, their assumptions about religion, and their ideas of the fundamental nature of different civilizations. But most of all I have tried to locate their images of China in their lived, embodied experiences in China, especially since they spoke to other Britons on the authority of having "been there." No other group of people went to China in such large numbers, lived among the Chinese, spoke the language, argued in the streets, and wrote so much about their experiences. Missionaries introduced "the West" to China, and introduced "China" to the West. In some ways they were a very noble group of people. They went to save souls — not to buy and sell like traders, not to posture with the ruling elite like diplomats, not to point guns like soldiers, and not to leave after a month like tourists. They spent much of their lives in small-town China, village China, among the illiterate population. Many missionaries came to know China truly at the grass roots. They were there before any professional anthropologists. The missionaries I discuss represent a group of mostly quite well-educated, prolific letter-writers (as were so many Victorians), prolific book- and tract-publishers, and active public speakers. They had a large audience, via society publications, sermons, and exhibitions. In these and other ways, their subject positions made them a unique and influential group of agents in the history of "East–West" interactions.

In the title, "Borrowed Gods" refers to the appropriation of other peoples' religions, such as for the purpose of creating an Other-image with which to contrast a self-image. "Foreign bodies" calls attention to the bodily strangeness between foreigners and natives, which surely conditioned their representations of each other. British bodies and Chinese bodies were mutually foreign. This book investigates how the fact of their bodily foreignness influenced or even created certain Western images of the Chinese.

I hope that this study may stimulate more discussion of the general dynamics of long-distance intercultural understanding conceived as a bodily process and discussion of the significance of "being there" (with its sense of immediacy and its authority to speak). Standing eye to eye with the Other is valuable but ambiguous. How does cultural knowledge condition foreign experiences, and how do foreign experiences create textual representations which are then intelligible to those at home? With these questions in mind, it is worth examining the case of Protestant missions to China, especially as the historical memory of the China mission is still contested.

In the literature for understanding Christian missions to China, we find publications from churches, which tend to present idealized images of missionaries and positive views of their missions as narratives of the Holy Spirit in operation. The negative images in this book are in contrast to the overriding tone of missionary hagiography. Though I have come to admire some of them, I do not imagine missionaries as the great heroes of hagiography, valiant and pure but also rather two-dimensional. Yet I do not intend that this book should be taken as a simple condemnation

of missionaries, despite my calling attention to some of their pronouncements which today strike me (and I assume many of the readers
of this book) as egregiously arrogant, racist, smugly dismissive, and otherwise "Victorian" in the worst sense. Missionaries are often treated as
forerunners of colonial conquest, avatars of Imperial ambition, in service
of the foreign office and unambiguously loyal to Britannia. These are also
stereotypes. I do not imagine them as innocent bystanders, uninvolved
with the abuses of a semi-colonized China. But they certainly have a bad
reputation in some circles. At times the negative images surface in the
news. In 2000 the Vatican canonized eighty-seven Chinese Christians and
thirty-three European missionaries who had died in the Boxer Rebellion
of 1900 and in other anti-Christian violence. The government of the
People's Republic of China issued strongly worded statements that the
canonizations were a humiliation to China and a glorification of colonialism. "Some Catholic missionaries were the very perpetrators and
accomplices in the colonialist and imperialist invasion of China," read an
official statement. Clearly, sometimes they were, but isolated from other
views, these criticisms become emotional stereotypes which are of no
more help in understanding their lives than the church hagiographies.

In his book *The Deathly Embrace: Orientalism and Asian American
Identity,* Sheng-mei Ma wrote: "In order to retire racist stereotypes, one
is obliged to first evoke them; in order to construct ethnicity, one must
first destroy what is falsely reported as one's ethnic identity. Both result
in an unwitting reiteration of Orientalist images."[1] According to this view,
by recounting anecdotes of what we now call racism, I am in a way per-
petuating such images — as did Ma himself in *The Deathly Embrace.*
Given the history of violence directed against "foreigners" of every
kind — and the history of colonial condescension toward the "natives" —
almost any talk of "foreigners" and "natives" can be provocative.

To judge — to say whether something is good or bad — is often a way
of ending conversation. Very broadly speaking, I have tried to set aside
moral judgment when studying phenomena already richly coated in
value judgments. Rather, I have tried to articulate the logic of those value
judgments in terms of social practices, bodily experiences, and material
cultures.

My interest in the bodily experience of being foreign is autobio-
graphical. I remember being quite fascinated by the strange effects of
being a foreigner, an American (by passport) in England; a Briton (by culture) in Thailand, China, and America. In Asia, I was often told that the

English are gentlemen, and I thought of the crowd at the Nottingham Forest Football Club. If one begins to catalogue any given group's misconceptions of other groups, the list is practically endless, turning out to be less a list of truths and errors and more an itinerary of the imagination. "Correcting" those errors becomes an endless process, and in the end you have to pick your battles.

CHAPTER I

Borrowed Gods

Idols of Islington

The first thing visitors to the Great Missionary Exhibition of 1909 saw was a large Chinese arch. A narrow Chinese street ran two hundred feet from the arch to the stage in the Chinese Guest Room at the far end. This "very realistic" representation of Chinese life included displays of Products, Home Life, Industries, a Chemist Shop, an Opium Den, a Cobbler, "a typical Chinese inn — the kind with which missionaries often have to be content," two more archways, a pagoda, and a "temple with its idols and other appurtenances."[1] Nearby were Chinese Shops in the Foreign Market. The *tableau vivant* was completed by a cast of English "shopkeepers in Chinese dress"[2] in an area designated "Natives" on the map (see Fig. 1).

During its run from June 8 to July 3 (except Sundays), perhaps as many as a quarter of a million Britons visited "Africa and the East": "the largest and most comprehensive missionary exhibition that has ever been organized."[3] The *Times* described the exhibition as "a great museum of curiosities and rarities of every description . . . illustrating native arts, industries, and even superstitions and cruelties."[4]

This exhibition was promoted through churches and advertised in train stations, but probably the biggest advertising expense was the announcement on the front page of the *Times* throughout the month of June 1909. Readers of the newspaper had a number of other options for entertainment and edification that month. As a spectacle, "Africa and the East" had to compete with such special attractions as the fireworks

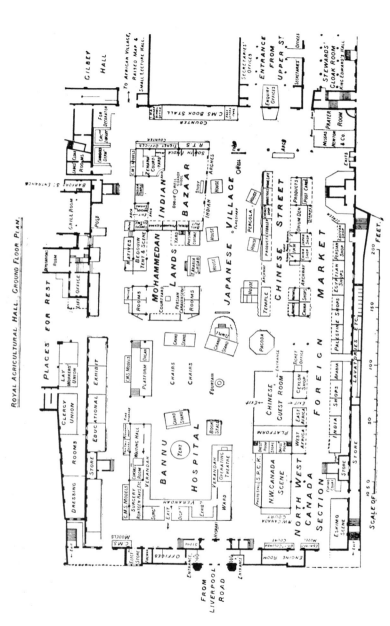

FIGURE 1. "Royal Agricultural Hall. Ground Floor Plan." *Church Missionary Gleaner*, June 1909, 93.

display at the Crystal Palace, the International Horse Show at Olympia, and the Ladies' Kennel Association show. "The Golden West Exhibition" in Earl's Court featured bronco-busting, the San Francisco earthquake, and the Black Hawk massacre. The new building of the Victoria and Albert Museum was opened that month, displaying a fraction of the gathered wealth of the Empire. Anglican congregations throughout England would also have been aware of the English Church Pageant, which reenacted dramatic episodes from Church history. Evangelicals of the Anglican Church Missionary Society (CMS) were at the same time celebrating its 120th anniversary. Yet even in this crowded field of worthy events to attend, the exhibition was a success.

The Church Missionary Society had done much more than fabricate an authentic replica of China, there in the Royal Agricultural Hall in North London, and populated it with would-be Chinese with British accents. They had arranged other attractions in the main hall: an Eskimo scene, a Shinto shrine, a CMS hospital in northwest India, an Indian bazaar with its temple and shrine of Kali, and an African village. There was also a large, three-dimensional, topographic map of Uganda. These attractions had the jumbled taxonomy and visual appeal which made this exhibition kin to the better-known colonial displays such as the Great Exhibition of 1851 and the Victoria and Albert Museum.

For publicity purposes, the organizers printed 105,000 copies of an "Explanatory Statement," and half a million "prospectuses" for clergy to insert into their parish magazines. A large (sixty by forty inches) full color poster was produced showing three maps: Africa, China, India (see Fig. 2).[5] Standing behind these maps, hands reaching out, are three men, representing the respective native peoples, appealing to Christendom. These posters were widely exhibited on church notice-boards throughout England. Smaller bills were distributed on railway platforms and billboards.

The exhibition represented the pooling of many resources. There were requests in the *Church Missionary Gleaner* for the loan of "curios to which special significance is attached, or relics, etc., which have associations with missionary heroes of the past or with martyred converts."[6] There were also requests for foreign picture postcards and stamps. The response to a request for needlework was so great that the February 1909 issue of the *Gleaner* asked for such contributions to cease. The Prince of Wales's model of the Golden Temple at Amritsar was on display, as was a model of the Heathen Girls' Boarding School at Fuzhou. In addition, objects from Africa, India, China, and Japan were on sale, including the "charm-

FIGURE 2. Advertisement for the exhibition "Africa and the East," June 8–July 3, 1909. *Church Missionary Gleaner,* March 1909, 48.

ing cocoa-nut ware made by Chinese Christians, the delicate carving of which must be seen to be appreciated."[7] The shops were sponsored and staffed by parishes throughout England, each having sent 20 pounds toward the purchase of goods from the mission fields represented.

The Archbishop of Canterbury (and CMS president) Randall Thomas Davidson opened the event. He said that visitors to the exhibition "understood now something about those people who were still in childhood, to whom [the missionaries] were allowed to bear the message."[8] Every day of the exhibition opened with a featured speaker. Speakers included prominent leaders of missionary organizations, retired colonial administrators, and high-ranking church dignitaries.[9]

Many thousands of less-renowned people participated in the display: eight thousand members of the Church of England served as stewards, sharing the four hundred costumes (six hundred, according to the *Times*[10]) that ranged "from the simple bark-cloth wrapper worn by the poorest of the Baganda to the elaborate silk embroidered robes worn by the Chinese aristocratic lady."[11] Three hundred missionaries home on furlough or ex-missionaries were in attendance to lecture or comment, and over four hundred volunteers staffed the four empty shops nearby that had been converted to tea rooms.

As they retrieved their hats and umbrellas from the cloak room, visitors noticed the Prayer Room, and some entered. It contained a map of the world, "a Bible on every seat," and "the familiar text shining out from the green baize-covered wall, 'Pray ye the Lord of the harvest that He will send forth labourers.'"[12] The room was set up to facilitate not only prayers for the conversion of the world, but also personal Calls to the mission field. Indeed, at the World Missionary Conference the following year it was reported that between fifty and one hundred of those who attended the Exhibition had offered themselves for mission service, forty-six of whom were ultimately accepted.[13]

With all the colorful costumes, "curiosities and rarities," the exhibition must have been fun. However, the organizers might have balked at a comparison to the "Golden West Exhibition" or to a fireworks display. Though these entertainments shared space with "Africa and the East" on the front page of the *Times,* the organizers sought to put such events into discrete categories. They emphasized "the educative value of the Exhibition: that it will not be a place of mere entertainment,"[14] but rather "a truly consecrated place."[15] Accordingly, "very great pains are being taken to lift the work to a high spiritual level. A card of *Rules for Costume Wearers* has been specially prepared" exhorting the stewards that "they are doing [this work] as part of their work for God. . . . Nothing must be done or worn for mere display; no attempt must be made to colour the face or the eyebrows by costume wearers, and anything likely to lower our ideal of this work must be avoided. Each wearer should be able to use the dress for real missionary work reverently and prayerfully."[16]

The insistence that the Exhibition was serious education rather than entertaining display reveals the inherent tensions between, on the one hand, the need to draw an audience and make the mission field vivid or even exciting, and, on the other, the dangers of deceiving the audience with illusion and exoticism for its own sake. It was one thing to put on a costume and pretend to be someone else in a theater — in a clear framework of consciously produced fiction. But these actors were there to tell the truth. Victorian and Edwardian missionary culture encouraged an aesthetic of sincerity and plainness, in opposition to the façade which they believed characterized Roman Catholicism, heathen religion and foreign cultures in general. The organizers were suspicious of visual ritualism and ideologically nervous about "mere entertainment."

Gilbert and Sullivan's *The Mikado* (premiered 1885) and many other displays of the Victorian imagination of East Asia had long established the "Chinese Street" or "Japanese Village" as grounds for amusement. To guard against this latent frivolity, stewards in particular were expected to educate themselves about the mission field they represented, by attending training sessions and reading instructional literature. For public consumption, a series of new books were published for the event: four sixpenny books on missionary themes; four large penny illustrated books (*Heroes of the Holy War, A Chinese Hero and Other Stories, Women of Other Lands, Doctors' Doings in Far-Off Lands*); six penny illustrated booklets, including *Little Honourable Eldest Son*; a penny book, *The Story of the C.M.S.*; and the *Guide to the Exhibition* (sixpence). The CMS had a large book stall at the exhibition.

As is clear from the publications list, particular efforts were made to appeal to children, who were thought to need particular guidance in distinguishing true from false. Publicity before the event had "infus[ed] the minds of boys and girls with eager anticipation; so much so, that we hear of children who for many weeks past have been saving pocket-money towards their railway fares!" (special railway excursions had been arranged).[17] The CMS's annual Children's Services were cancelled so as not to compete. The exhibition catered to children with special meetings and "Ten Minutes' Talks." A Summer School was held in an annex of the exhibition building, daily except Saturday, with such themes as "Prayer and Missions," "Modern Thought and Missions," "The Literature of Missions," "The Church and Missions," and "The Demand of Missions." Follow-up reports on the exhibition appeared in the CMS children's magazine, *The Round World,* in the summer of 1909.

The exhibition was thus a huge undertaking which served to populate and furnish China in the British imagination. By November, the *Gleaner* had judged "Africa and the East" a success. The exhibition had expounded "aims far higher than mere financial ones"; nonetheless, it had come out 1,000 pounds in the black, with another 1,000 pounds worth of costumes and unsold goods.[18]

Portions of the exhibition, including the Chinese Street, went on display in Oxford for ten days that November. Seven hundred fifty costumed stewards were involved. A "replica" of the exhibition was displayed in Liverpool in October 1909. The following summer, the exhibits from London were shown in Birmingham, and similar exhibits opened in Macclesfield, Limerick, and Cork.[19] Perhaps inspired by the Chinese Street, the Church of England Zenana Society produced a "miniature Chinese Street for children to paint and set up," including a city gate, shops, "an opium den, an idol shrine, and a Christian Day School" (price: one shilling and sixpence).[20] The Chinese street became a child's toy.

Considering the estimates of attendance in multiple locations, plus the numbers of people involved as stewards and so on, perhaps as many as half a million Britons eventually gazed at that Chinese idol temple first constructed in Islington. Londoners could stare at a Chinese idol, or wander past it on their way to the tea rooms — whether at "Africa and the East" or, for that matter, at the Victoria and Albert museum. So far out of their contexts, these images of deified Chinese must have seemed lonely specimens, exotic perhaps, or tawdry, but in any case, remote from any reasonable religiosity. Standing before those alien idols — those borrowed gods — in London, how did they imagine the original temple context of this icon? How did they imagine the religiosity of the Chinese, bowing before their icons so far away in Peking? Curious visitors would have been informed that the Chinese heathen, "in his blindness," believes this carved thing has a life inside it, but for Londoners it was only a cultural artifact, or an artistic object, or a "curiosity." It could not say what else it was, nor what it used to be in China. It had a mouth, but it could not speak.

The Idols Speak

The popular books produced for the exhibition, and the steady stream of other books and magazines published by the various missionary organizations, depicted not only the noble work of their missionaries, but also — necessarily — non-Christian religion. The judgmental qualities of missionary reportage could be explicit or implicit, blatant or subtle. Their writings mixed praise and blame, scorn and pity, positive and negative evaluations. In various ways, missionary ethnography became one of the foundations of Western Sinology, Religious Studies, and Anthropology. Modern, secular readers are forced to negotiate this mixture of factual description and moral judgments, and to consider the subject position of the missionary. When secular academics have read the missionary records, we have tended to either edit out the value judgments to see what can be salvaged from the religious bias of the missionaries, or we have seen nothing but bias.

In general, popular Chinese religion was described as the antithesis of familiar monotheistic order. The Anglican missionary Mary Darley began a long list of all their deities, including: "The God of War," "The Five Grains Fairy," "The Kitchen Gods," "The God of Musicians, Actors, Pugilists," "The King of Hades," "The Tall and Short Demons," "The Fox

Devil," "The Small-pox and Measles Demon-goddess," "The Many-headed Buddha," and many others.[21] The sheer number of these gods, with their quaint divisions of labor and archaic titles, must have conjured for Victorians a bewildering polytheistic phantasmagoria. How chaotic, how preposterous, and how exotic it must have seemed to readers in Surrey!

And how sinister: some missionaries' descriptions of Chinese temples read like episodes from the works of writer Sax Rohmer (whose literary character, Fu Man-chu, appeared in 1913). The missionary W. E. Hipwell, for example, wrote of his visit to a temple of the "Dragon Mother," where "the centre of attraction for all is the brazen image of the goddess, before which the people, mostly women, were bowing in abject devotion." During a festival there,

I entered the temple for a few moments, but was compelled to withdraw quickly, on account of the horror by which I was overwhelmed as I watched those before the idol who with intense fervour besought the blessings which they desired. One woman was specially conspicuous in constraining others to greater earnestness as they practiced their offerings, incense, and prayers. The place was reeking with sickening smoke, and horrible because of the almost manifest presence of the devil, glorying over these multitudes thus enslaved by him.[22]

Darley's book, *Cameos of the Chinese City,* describes processions, "in which the devils and demons of hell, in horrible image form, are fearfully in evidence."[23] Naturally, to make sense of it all, missionaries and their readers often drew Biblical analogies: unconverted China was Babylon, Babel, or Sodom. In the midst of Darley's account of festivals and processions, she comments by quoting a well-known Bible quotation: "And they called on the name of Baal . . . saying, O Baal, answer us; but there was no voice, nor any that answered."[24] The reference here, from 1 Kings 18:26, recalled to Darley's readers the dramatic contest between Elijah and the 450 prophets of Baal, who "cried aloud, and cut themselves after their manner with knives and lancets, till the blood gushed out upon them" (1 Kings 18:28). The reference to Elijah construed the Christianization of China as a great contest, in some sense the exact same battle that had been fought since Elijah, or even since the serpent in Eden.

Most Protestant categorizations of the religions of the world were ultimately quite simple: there was the true religion, and then there was idolatry. The term *idolatry* could be applied to any and all non-Protestants, including Chinese Buddhists, Catholics, and the prophets of Baal. Theologically, idolatry was the worship of anything other than the true God, and the term could be used in relatively abstract ways but most often had a very tangible, visible reference: people bowing to an object. Obeisance was the most crucial focus of the Protestant problematization of ritual. But what status did the missionaries assign to these objects of Chinese devotion, the icons, or as they named them, the idols?

Let me briefly interject a note on terminology. I use *image* as a general term for the statues and paintings of human or humanoid figures in temples and on altars, most of which are also considered *icons,* that is, holy images — in ritual terms, images which are objects of obeisance. *Idol* is an inherently pejorative term for someone else's icons, icons wrongly conceived and "worshipped." Due to its pervasive use in missionary writings, I use the term without quotation marks, but it should always be understood as "so-called." The same is true of *idolatry* and *heathen,* which do not name any person's own religiosity but rather someone else's wrong religion and (in this case) the Victorian imagination of non-Christian (sometimes specifically non-Protestant) religion.

We usually think of the Protestant attitude toward idols as materialistic because a great deal of iconoclastic rhetoric emphasizes the raw materiality of the icons: this icon is just a piece of wood. The missionaries in China often preached on the folly of idolatry by highlighting the inanimate nature of the icon's body, especially its inability to perceive or respond. Missionaries paraphrased such Biblical passages as Psalm 115:

> Their idols are silver and gold,
>   the work of men's hands.
> They have mouths, but do not speak;
>   eyes, but do not see.
> They have ears, but do not hear;
>   noses, but do not smell.
> They have hands, but do not feel;
>   feet, but do not walk;
>   and they do not make a sound in their throat.
> Those who make them are like them;
>   so are all who trust in them.

Certainly, amid the shuffling crowds in the Royal Agricultural Hall, the statues of other people's gods must have seemed as powerless and easily objectified as the furniture in the Chinese inn or the cocoa-nut ware. It would seem absurd to believe that this *thing* was ever alive. But from the mission field we see a different view of the idols. After her account of the Satanic cults of China, Mary Darley ends her chapter entitled "Heathenism in Kien-Ning" with an initially conventional Christian critique: "It is said that in the central rest-house of a village some men were intently listening to two of their fellow countrymen preaching the Gospel; towards the close of their exhortation they turned to the rest-house shrine, in which was the idol of Spirit Tu-Cu. 'See this work of men's hands,' they said, 'this image you worship and serve. Can it speak, or hear or see? Can it answer to your call?' To this the men smiled as answer, and nodded in agreement."

But behind the backs of the traveling preachers, something else appears — that work of men's hands suddenly hears, sees, speaks, and acts:

When the preachers had gone on their way, they still sat on, and discussed, not only the words they had heard, but also the idol before them. Then one of their number stood and, pointing towards the shrine, declaimed in satirical scorn, to the amusement of his companions, "Yes, you are made of wood: your mouth, is it able to speak; your ears to hear from afar; your eyes, are they good for seeing; were you by wind blown down, how long would you lie where you fell?" The words were yet on his lips when suddenly, smitten with terrible pains, they rolled on the ground in agony, calling on "heaven and earth" to save them. They crawled to the idol's feet and craved his pardon for having despised him by laughter and words. Later, the Tu-Cu spirit entered into a man and spoke through him with authority.

"Those strangers serve the true God, the God Whom I greatly fear; over those who belong to Him I have no power at all. For me they have no respect; they count me a lifeless thing, only remembering my image, forgetting that I am spirit; and so when they call me deaf and dumb, blind and unable to move, I accept what they say in silence. But *you* who serve me, *you* whom I help to protect, to shame and reproach me before them, to revile me amongst yourselves! For this my wrath is towards you, and chastisement was due."[25]

The idol is not mere wood and stone, not "a lifeless thing," but has consciousness and agency. Here, the contrast is not between the heathens who are deluded into thinking a material object has consciousness and the Christians who know it as only inanimate matter. Rather the contrast is between the heathens who are under the power of a cruel spirit in the icon ("Satan's seat"[26]) and the Christians who have gained a kind of immunity or magical protection from the spirit's power. When the Christians say the icon cannot speak or act, in this story, at least, they are wrong. The idol cannot speak to or harm *them*. The idol can, however, attack non-Christians. Fear, not love, was thought to be the basis of Chinese popular religion.

Two icons, appearing in the imaginations of early-twentieth-century missionaries and their supporters. One was visible and inert and no one bowed to it any more. The other appeared in a missionary's story, but it was alive and people bowed down before it. Whatever power or life contained in the idol of Islington was neutralized as much by its distance from the cultural normality of its audience as by the theology of idolatry. It was no more than an artifact, very decidedly dead. But the Church Missionary Society valued and took care of it for another reason: though it was false, it had a role in telling the truth — the truth about its own falsity. The idol of Islington's message was not primarily that Christianity was true, but that heathenism is false. Both of these idols had some kind of power, at least to reveal the truth, though by doing so they damned themselves.

The Spirit Tu-Cu of Kien-Ning also testified to the superior power of a God who made Christians impervious to his demonic power while he continued to bully his followers for their lack of respect. Mary Darley distanced herself slightly from the story with the words, "It is said . . . ." But the idol in her story was alive and kicking. Tu-Cu specifically admitted the greater power of the Christian's god, but in doing so — by speaking and acting — he contradicted some of the Biblical rhetoric of idols, as if to rephrase Psalm 115: they have mouths, and they do indeed speak; they have eyes and can see. Even though the story about him was published in England, within the story Tu-Cu was in his native place. For its readers, the story was set on the other side of the world, and that great distance probably helped readers suspend their disbelief, or take the story with a grain of salt. If it were true, it might represent the communication of a minor demon, a case of possession far off and rarely seen in England since Christianization. At worst, Christianity got a begrudging endorsement from a rival deity, or from a denizen of Hell.

Silence of Another Race

Already we have seen Western missionaries giving a voice to a heathen god, creating educational displays of Chinese culture, public space, and spirituality (or a lack thereof), and helping the good folk of England to picture Chinese bodies. These representations were authoritative in tone, and validated by the advice and presence of many who could claim to know the Chinese. But how sure were they that they knew the Chinese? There was certainly a Western tradition, of the Chinese, in particular, as a people no outsider could ever know. Cultural boundaries led some Western visitors to more or less despair of ever truly *knowing* a Chinese person. For some, we can never see through the mask: "What thoughts about us pass behind those inscrutable yellow faces with their fathomless almond eyes, which regard us with such pleasant smiles, and welcome us so courteously?"[27] Here, comprehension seems to penetrate no deeper than the surface, making even the surface inscrutable. For others, even if we can see through the mask, the mind behind it is unintelligible: "The Chinaman's mind is a profound and inexplicable puzzle that many have vainly endeavoured to solve. He is a mystery not only to the foreigner, who has been trained to more open methods of thought, but also to his own countrymen."[28] Even the Chinese don't understand the Chinese.

Some visitors were aware that this perceived inscrutability was a quality of the visitor's own perception and saw that the idea of the "inscrutable Chinese" was related to other, more offensive and dangerous stereotypes. Sarah Pike Conger wrote:

The locked and barred doors of centuries are little by little swinging ajar, and the world looks through into a house — a home — all China's own. At first, as we look we see nothing but confusion; we see no method, and everything seems to be done backwards; we see customs without meaning, education without value, religion without a redeeming feature; we are amused at the people, at their styles of clothes, of wearing their hair; at their modes of locomotion; their process of tilling the soil; their ancestor worship; their attitudes toward women. We ridicule their amusements, and doubt their sincerity in all things. In fact, we deride, belittle, and woefully underrate everything Chinese. We feel that with the banner of progress in our hands, with superior knowledge and wisdom in our minds, and determination in our hearts, a reformation must come to this household that God has forsaken.[29]

Of course, Conger went on to refute this kind of view and stuck up for the Chinese to her American readers. Still, she also despaired of ever reaching true understanding:

Oh, this strange, strange old country! Its hidden meaning I cannot find. I wish that I could know what these Chinese think. I look at them and wonder what is under the calm surface. Sometimes I see them unobserved and they are merry, full of fun, and have innate grace. In everything our standpoints and modes of action differ. We seem to be travelling in different directions — growing farther apart. Will the time ever come when we shall be of one mind?[30]

Conger apparently considered being "of one mind" a good thing. But whose mind?

Many missionaries developed deep friendships with a few Chinese converts, and we should not diminish the degree of that mutual understanding. Yet, as in many writings about remote cultures, we find evidence of a pervasive essentializing, that is, the use of generalizations about "the Chinese" or "the Chinese mind" as if the Chinese were all "of one mind." Such blanket statements homogenize millions of people into a single voice and a single mind. No culture is unanimous. Under scrutiny, monolithic narratives of ethnicity or nationhood fragment into multiple voices, and the single answer reveals itself as an ideological construct. When "inscrutability" is built into the supposed cultural essence, it seems further to absolve one of the need to make an effort to understand.

China of the Imagination

My earliest memory of exposure to "China" was the book *The Cricket in Times Square* by George Selden. A boy called Mario, who sells newspapers in a New York subway, finds a cricket, called Chester. Mario seeks a house (or cage) for Chester in Chinatown. He finds a run-down shop with a sign that reads "SAI FONG — CHINESE NOVELTIES," and in smaller letters "also do hand laundry."[31] Sai Fong is the owner of the shop, and he conforms to a common stereotype of older Chinese men: he is wise but childlike, his clothes sporting dragons embroidered onto silk, and he smokes a "long white clay pipe." He speaks pidgin English. "You got clicket?" Seeing the cricket, he cries "'Oh velly good!' . . . He suddenly became very lively, almost dancing a jig on the sidewalk. 'You got clicket! Eee hee hee! Velly good! You got clicket! Hee hee!'"[32] Later, Mario meets Sai Fong's "Velly old fliend here — know evelything about clickets." The old friend bows to Mario; Mario isn't sure what to do but bows back; the Chinese man bows back again. "They might have gone on bowing all night if Sai Fong hadn't said something in Chinese to his friend."[33] In the book's accompanying illustration (see Fig. 3), we see one of the quintessential Western images of the Chinese. The old friend also bows deeply to Chester Cricket, who in turn bows back.

These images might accurately be considered stereotypes, and yet, like so many stereotypical images, they are not simply invented out of nothing. Some shops in American Chinatowns are indeed cluttered with "novelties," and traditionally minded Chinese do bow, though not to children or insects. Still, *this* image of the Chinese was the one selected. In *Marginal Sights: Staging the Chinese in America,* James Moy analyzes pho-

FIGURE 3. Illustration by Garth Williams in
George Selden, *The Cricket in Times Square*, 85.

tographs of San Francisco's Chinatown taken by Arnold Genthe (1869–
1942) to show how Genthe systematically erased white people, cropping
the photos to show only those Chinese who looked "stereotypical" and
"unassimilated." English signage was also erased and replaced with
Chinese.[34] These examples reveal a compulsion to represent even a neigh-
borhood of San Francisco as another world. Genthe's fascination with the
forbidden mystery of Chinatown was almost compulsive — "I would go
again and again"[35] — a compulsion echoed by Sax Rohmer's white adventurers, who also enter that exciting *other world*. This exoticization, which
made Chinese space simultaneously remote and attractive, has been ana-
lyzed by literary critics such as Moy and Sheng-mei Ma, and in more general terms, by critics of "Orientalism." The selectivity and editing of
Genthe's Chinatown has been rendered visible and obvious by Moy's
analysis, but any such analysis is always vastly outnumbered by the innumerable representations which pass without analysis, even without
thought. Genthe's camera-eye stands as a concrete example of what we all
do when imagining any place or people.

Empire of Signs seems to be a book about Japan, but Roland Barthes admitted right up front that his book is not about the objective reality of Japan at all, but about his imagination of Japan. He wrote: "Imagine a fictive nation . . . in no way claiming to represent or to analyze reality itself," and then "isolate . . . a certain number of features . . . [to form] a system. It is this system which I shall call: Japan."[36] So "Japan," in this book, is a fictive system of features in the author's imagination. Rather than "lovingly gazing toward an Oriental essence,"[37] *Empire of Signs* is a contribution to a "history of our own obscurity."[38] Barthes's playfulness should not obscure the basic honesty of these remarks about himself and his subject position as a foreigner. A lot is "lost" in translation, but experience is far more than words and conscious meaning. While the voices speak unintelligibly, bodies share the same room, smell the same smells, and most of all, perform. The body of the unintelligible Other assumes importance in the reportage of foreign visitors, especially during the early moments of a visit and in formative periods of intercultural imagination. Roland Barthes recognized and celebrated this fact on a visit to Japan: "To make a date (by gestures, drawings on paper, proper names) may take an hour, but during that hour, for a message which would be abolished in an instant if it were to be spoken . . . , it is the other's entire body which has been known, savored, received, and which has displayed (to no real purpose) its own narrative, its own text."[39] Few foreign visitors are quite so self-reflective or enamored of linguistic unintelligibility. Usually, the lack of shared language is regarded as an annoyance or an obstacle, or a reason to "tune out."

The influence of direct physical proximity is known as the "contact hypothesis" in social psychology: the idea that stereotypes break down when people meet — when their mutual awareness is more embodied than is possible through text and image. While Conger despaired of truly understanding the Chinese, she was nonetheless freely "amused at the people, at their styles of *clothes,* of wearing their *hair;* at their modes of *locomotion;* . . . their ancestor *worship.*" And: "I *look at them* and wonder what is under the calm surface." While the rational mind of the Other may not be evident, their bodies apparently are. Bodies are more immediately perceivable to any foreigner fresh off the boat. This sense of immediacy is still a fantasy: the foreign body is *ultimately* no more and no less inscrutable than the mind. However, because bodies are *apparently* and *relatively* immediate to visual perception, representations of the human body become crucial depictions of the foreign, carrying potent messages about the foreigners' culture.

Barthes alerts us to two aspects of being in a foreign culture: first, that whatever name we give to that foreign culture — "Japan," "China" — we name a "system" of our imagination; and second, that the absence of a shared language forces the foreigner and native to "know, savor, receive, and display" each others' bodies in a heightened way. Being forced to communicate without benefit of a shared language draws attention to "messages" that have been communicated body to body already, under the radar of thought. The unintelligibility, which to a greater or lesser degree we all experience when encountering unfamiliar systems of meaning, disconnects us from a solid sense of obvious fact. When nothing (or rather, so much less) is self-evident or predictable, we have to speculate, guess, fill in the gaps. Sometimes we do so with great confidence, and so we write books about the inner meanings of foreign life.

Clearly, we must place the missionaries' representations of Chinese religions in the larger context of the Western imagination of China. By my use of "imagined" and "imagination" I do not mean that Westerners simply "made up," or invented, China, any more than they "accurately" recorded China from their direct perceptions in ideologically neutral terms. As Sinologists and historians we have our own reasons for wishing to distinguish between fact and fiction, our own investment in epistemological norms and discursive practices, but on the whole, our knowledge of the Other (cultures, places, eras, peoples, events) is an ambiguous blend of images verifiable through the contested canons of disciplinary truth — images which, if pressed, we would acknowledge as anecdotal, intuitive, or even unjustified. It is in this sense that we always imagine the Other, and, in fact, we imagine ourselves. The imagination is, however, historical and local. Certain stereotypical or preconceived images gained currency in the nineteenth-century imagination and are still accepted and reproduced: the Mystic East contrasted to the violent and spiritually bankrupt West; the Inscrutable Chinese, the kowtowing civil servant, the vampiric missionary, the opium-smoking coolie. Knowledge as imagination is not mere daydreaming but always appears in tandem with power. Imagination of the Other is the basis of action and orientation toward the Other, and our physical and material practices generate our images of the Other.[40]

It may be misleading to call imagination a "system" at all, since imagining is also a practice, and practices have a particular way of working that is not the logic of a system of abstract knowledge. In my thinking here, I am following Pierre Bourdieu, who wrote at length on the habitual norms of practice (including the practices of thought, speech, and representation), which he called *habitus*. Rather than picturing culture as a coherent system of knowledge which individuals approximate imperfectly (often getting things wrong or leaving gaps), Bourdieu, and Wittgenstein before him, turned our attention to actual usage. In daily life, we respond to things — a ball thrown in a game, a strategic move in an argument, a particular tone of voice, the movement of cars in traffic — in a strategic, expedient way, following rules as they suit us, but without making conscious reference to all the relevant rules, moves, or interpretations — which, in any case, we can never have in mind in their totality. This "practical sense" is like the "feel for the game" which allows a great soccer player to react, fully engaged but without conscious calculation; it is the "air of a solider," discussed in Foucault's *Discipline and Punish,* which lets others see a soldier's training even when he is in mufti. The habitus allows us to function in society and negotiate with material structures in the world without thinking too much about them, without needing to "reinvent the wheel" at every moment, and without having to know the whole "system" at once. Most of the time, in our native space, we behave normally and naturally with very little effort. But the fact that our behavior is ultimately unnatural becomes very clear when we find ourselves among people who behave differently (except that we tend to see "their" behavior as abnormal or unnatural, because "our" behavior is more ingrained, embodied, and invisible).

Missionaries found themselves in such situations, when their own "natural" behavior was suddenly contrasted to a whole other way of life and total disengagement was not an option. The logic of habitus is usually invisible, precisely because it seems natural, just the way things are, normal, or commonsensical. But when "everything seems to be done backwards,"[41] the fact of foreignness that surrounded the missionary threatened to unveil these apparently self-evident ways of behaving. In a way, the theoretical dimension of this book is the articulation, in historical terms, of these three terms: "body" (or more technically, habitus), "imagination," and "the Other."

The Plot Structure of Missions

Victorians imagined Chinese religion as idolatrous, and, above all, as *of the flesh*. Though a few missionaries laid the foundations for more sympathetic views, the religions of China, as they appeared in missionary writings, were unappealing and self-evidently absurd. If that was the case, why did the Chinese not reject their traditional religions and accept

Christianity? Though the strident tone softened during the early twentieth century, the missionary enterprise always assumed that the Gospel was a clearly superior commodity entering a vast untapped but restricted market and lacking only adequate infrastructure for distribution and marketing. Missionary publications were constantly raising funds to support their workers and recruiting new workers for the mission field. Given the absurdity and the horror of Chinese religions in missionary accounts, it was perhaps puzzling to the missionaries that more Chinese did not accept the Gospel more readily, especially given the evangelical focus on the great power of the Word. Missionaries like Charles (or Karl) Gützlaff, who claimed that their preaching tours had converted masses of Chinese, presented a problem to the more realistic missionary organizations. Clearly, merely hearing the Gospel did not necessarily effect any change. Yet if Chinese religious life was so awful (and the Gospel so true), why did the Chinese not want to change? If only the Word could reach the millions of Chinese who had yet to hear it, why would they not believe?

One explanation of the Chinese resistance to conversion could be found in the theological anthropology of the missions: man as fallen, and hence proud, confused, sinful, and alienated from God. "Of the flesh." In this sense, the Chinese rejection of the Gospel was no different from anyone else's, though there were extenuating circumstances, such as Chinese culture itself.

Chinese culture was a second challenge to the missions. The relatively small numbers of converts could be blamed on the Imperial state's barriers to missions, such as restrictions on travel. Many of these legal barriers were lifted, especially after 1911, but in a more diffuse way, the grip of their rigid heathen culture constituted a barrier: the necessity of the ancestral cult, fear of idols, and conservative peer pressure. These ingrained and internalized forces were thought to have immobilized the Chinese. Their resistance to change caused stagnation and a failure of imagination. Hence, a consistent theme in missionary discourse was the sense of the Chinese acting mechanically, without thought or free will. These political, psychological, and cultural barriers could be avoided or overturned, but English Christians did not always support the unfolding opportunities.

Hence, another possible reason for low conversion rates was economic and logistical. Missionary publications continually asked for donations and lamented the small numbers of missionaries in the field compared to the vast "untouched" population in the "interior." Missionaries needed funding, and the nature of their funding made it necessary for them to write home, to their sponsoring societies; and for the societies to publish edited versions of the letters from missionaries. Mission societies had to be public relations machines and active publishers in order to draw funds from churchgoers and philanthropists to support the presence of foreigners in China, whose primary occupation was to convert the natives from false religion (or no religion) to Christianity. Many churches supported individual missionaries, and many other people went to China more or less independently or with private sponsorship.

All of these obstacles (and others) were explicitly recognized by the missionaries. But implicitly, the simultaneous messages (of the worthlessness of Chinese religion and the low rate of conversions) can be seen as a part of the fundamental *plot structure* of the missions. There had to be misery and evil, which endured in order to justify the good mission. A too rapid acceptance of the message would have undermined the mission's support just as much as a total lack of success. With a reasonable number of conversions, the mission could be justified, but too many conversions might warrant a withdrawal from the field and leaving the native church alone. Many missionaries were very clear that Chinese could convert Chinese better than foreign missionaries, and they pushed for a native church. In itself, this idea was not controversial, but to say it too often and too loudly to the churches back home would have dried up funding. Starting early in the twentieth century there were discussions in print debating the continued necessity of foreign missions in China.

Conversion rates did increase sharply during the nineteenth century, largely due to native ministry. Among foreign missions, the gradual nativization of the church occurred parallel to the gradually increasing acceptance of a model of missions known as the social gospel, a shift in emphasis away from public evangelization and less talk of Hell for the unconverted. The historian Terence Thomas remarks on the effect of liberalization on missions in this period: "It is not too difficult to see that if any doubts were ever entertained as to whether the heathen were destined for perdition the cutting edge of missionary preaching would be blunted. Indeed this is something that began to happen in the late nineteenth century and became even more prevalent in the twentieth century. The more liberal the missionary became the less successful the mission seemed to become."[42] Though the rhetoric thereby lost some of its hellfire, the missions thrived on a sense of horror at the fate of the unconverted in this or the next world. Still, stories about the unremitting belligerence of the heathens would not have encouraged Britons to fund more missionary work. Missionary publications always included more inspiring stories of success, of natives transformed by the Gospel, and the missionary societies held out the promise of reaching sincere Chinese souls thirsting for the truth. Like the figures in the poster for "Africa and the East" (see Fig. 2), these Chinese were holding out their hands to English Christians.

Outline of the Book

In the following chapter, I briefly survey modern Chinese history as it pertains to Protestant missionaries in the nineteenth and early twentieth centuries. Chapters 3 and 4 examine the underlying metaphors of body and mind in missionary (and other popular) accounts of China. I argue that these metaphors cohere as a unit because they consistently present the Chinese as relatively mindless; the corollary is that Westerners — those who produced these representations of Chinese — were therefore relatively mindful, and furthermore, rational, vigorous, clearheaded, modern, adult, and masculine. In missionary accounts, the undifferentiated mass of Chinese bodies was contrasted to the few Protestant individuals.

Recognizing mental acuity, rationality, and intellect in another culture inevitably begins with the observation of bodily appearance, but soon moves to spoken communication and texts. For Victorian Protestants, "rationality" was evidenced by explanatory words or the ability to articulate in words the motives behind actions. Part of their identity as Protestants was a rejection of the use of incomprehensible Latin in favor of the vernacular and a return to the Book. The place to find evidence of the greatness of a civilization, the missionaries assumed, was in that civilization's great books, and many Chinese agreed. Missionaries looked for rationality in the Chinese language, "the home of meaning."[43] They found the Chinese language uniquely difficult to learn and tended to interpret these difficulties as obstacles set before them by Satan. Furthermore, most of the English they heard spoken by Chinese was pidgin, which they thought was grating or comical, but in any case incorrect (see Chapter 5). They wrote of Chinese speech as defective or even literally meaningless — particularly in the case of Buddhist mantras. The semantic blank that mantras presented to Protestants was compounded by the mantras' spiritual impotence (see Chapter 6). The view that mantras were "empty ritual" must be seen in terms of Protestant anti-Catholicism — another theme of this book. Their legacy of anti-Catholicism gave missionaries ways of perceiving Chinese bodies, rituals, and sacred objects.

How did Protestant anti-Catholicism manifest itself in missionary accounts of China? Most commonly, this occurred in the repeated assertion of the similarity of Catholicism and Chinese religions. The most emphatic connection made was that of the bow — and the folly of their bows. In Chapter 7, I outline the homology of Catholic and Chinese heathen obeisance and show how the history of debate on Chinese obeisance was reinvoked in the simultaneous condemnation of both Catholic and Chinese "idolatry." In contrast to the quintessentially prostrate Other, the Protestant should not bow any more deeply than the bent knee (kneeling with torso erect). This basic postural contrast informed not only representations of China but also the lived experiences of missionaries and converts. Chapter 8 describes this dis-obeisance, this very deliberate refusal to bow, as a constitutive part of Victorian Protestant identity. In the chapter I explore the reasons why deep obeisance was so viscerally repellant to so many Britons.

Chapter 9 draws together some of the themes of the preceding chapters through a commentary on the story of Goon, showing how missionaries imagined the possible redemption of the damned in China. With some sense of the ways that the Chinese body was invested with meaning, I then examine five other aspects of bodily experience related to missions in the subsequent chapters: Christian meat-eating and anti-Buddhist polemics; the smells of missionaries and of China; the foreignness and public spectacle of missionary bodies; the missionaries' experience of being at the center of a large crowd's attention; and their efforts to disguise themselves as Chinese to avoid that "dangerous" gaze. This disguise brings us back full circle to the "shopkeepers in Chinese dress" we saw in Islington, walking down the Chinese streets, under the archways, past the opium den, and into the temple of idols.

CHAPTER 2

Missions in Chinese History

Western missionaries had been reaching out to Chinese for several centuries before the Great Missionary Exhibition. This book focuses on images of the Chinese and of Chinese religion represented by Protestant missionaries and other Western travelers, from the first arrival of a Protestant missionary in China (Robert Morrison, 1807) through to the large-scale disruption of the missionary presence in the 1930s. I am particularly interested in the middle of that period, the 1850s through to around 1914, during which missions to China had their greatest momentum. Though Queen Victoria reigned from 1837 to 1901, and the time scope of this book adds three decades to either side of the sixty-four years of her reign, I use the term "Victorian" in a loose sense to refer to this larger time frame.

China was not a blank slate for missionaries arriving in the nineteenth century. Most relevant to Victorian missionaries, the Catholic presence in China during the sixteenth and seventeenth centuries was well known, as were the debates over Imperial ritual. In this chapter, I shall briefly consider some of the legacy of Western awareness of China prior to 1807, then summarize political and cultural developments, particularly as they affected Protestant missions. This chapter concludes with a sketch of the lives and cultural influences of missionaries to China.

Rites and Roots

In Europe before the thirteenth century China was unknown or only vaguely known, far beyond any territory of relevance. The earliest detailed accounts of China, such as that of Marco Polo (1254–1324), were greeted with skepticism; it was hard for Europeans to believe his evaluation of East Asia as being so civilized. The reports of Catholic missionaries to the Mongol empire also had little impact. Western influence in China would increase with the establishment of more reliable and direct sea routes from Europe to China via the Cape of Good Hope in the sixteenth century. The opening of sea routes to China was the start of a long and tense relationship between China and the great naval powers.

In the sixteenth through eighteenth centuries, hundreds of Catholic missionaries were sent to China. The best known was the Italian Jesuit Matteo Ricci (1552–1610), who arrived in Macao in 1582. In general, the Jesuit strategy was not to focus on numbers of converts but to convert members of the elite so as to secure prestige and status in China. Ricci gained the attention of the Chinese authorities not primarily by expounding the Christian gospel, but through more broadly "cultural" means: through his published work *Jiaoyoulun* (*Disquisition on Friendship*), by composing and playing music for the emperor, by expounding Western science and technology, and by introducing European clocks, a map of the world, and scholastic mnemonic techniques. His intention was to gain a powerful audience, bridge the cultural differences, introduce Christianity, and convert the Chinese beginning with the official class "downwards." Meanwhile, other Jesuits, but more commonly, Franciscans and Dominicans, worked the more rustic corners of the mission field.

Western missionary monks — their dress, social roles, celibacy, and strange diet — were immediately comprehensible to the Chinese, largely because the monks were assumed to be more or less like Buddhist and Daoist clerics. When the Jesuits first arrived, they adopted the robes of Buddhist monks — a logical choice. A native category already existed for celibate, robed ritual experts, and initially the Jesuits made full use of this resemblance. They even took Buddhist names. The analogy was particularly strong because both Buddhism and Christianity arrived from "the West" replete with monastic institutions and a foreign pantheon. But the Jesuits soon realized that monks had low status, so Ricci and his cohort became literati. In the process, Ricci came to see in the Chinese classics not only a religious/ritual/ethical system of great beauty and subtlety, but also the prefiguration of Christ — God at work in the heathen cultures, preparing the ground for the Gospel. These early missionaries learned the Neo-Confucian classics, and Ricci absorbed the Neo-Confucian classification of religions divided into three "isms": Daoism, Confucianism, and Buddhism. One might add to these "three teachings" *(sanjiao)*, another category, "heterodoxy" (*xiejiao*), which identified a wide variety of other people's religions. Ricci opposed Buddhism and Daoism, but felt that the Christian gospel was compatible with the Confucian classics and with the best of literati culture. He felt that the cult of Confucius, and the family ancestor cult, could be reconciled to Christianity. Rituals of respect to Kongzi (or "Confucius") were very important to the literati class; in fact, they were legally mandated. Ricci argued to his ecclesiastic superiors in Europe that these rituals were gestures of respect only, and not idolatry: the Chinese were not "worshipping" Kongzi in order to get something from him. Ricci picked up on certain voices of the more secular-minded literati class, who themselves defined these rituals in very un-worshipful terms, claiming that bowing to the plaque of Kongzi was no more than bowing to one's ruler or to one's parents. This was a tricky business, of course. In this same period, accusations of idolatry were being made in Europe against the Catholic Church and the Church's own Counter-Reformation was reducing the number and role of its own icons, so it would have been impossible to condone any act of idolatry. An extended and complex controversy went on, known to later generations as the Rites debate. In 1704, then 1715, and finally in 1742, the Vatican declared the debate over: such rituals were simply incompatible with Christianity. The Vatican's rejection of these bows was due to the stated nature of their objects — bowing to the emperor was acceptable, but bowing to a name-board of Confucius or of one's ancestors was deemed idolatry.

Catholic missions declined in the mid-eighteenth century. As much as they Sinicized themselves, the missionaries were still prelates, and the literati had a long-standing bias against celibate monks. Chinese anti-Catholics drew on a subgenre of literature consisting of writings denouncing Buddhist celibacy as unnatural, unproductive, and alien to Chinese antiquity. Buddhist writings against Christianity also grew sharper during the seventeenth century. The Jesuits tolerated and rationalized the ancestral cult in a very particular way — until Rome put its foot down. The petering out of Jesuit missions in China was also a result of ecclesiastical politics in which "China" became a strategic pawn. In the second half of the seventeenth century, "the opposition to their missionary practice visibly ceased to be objective in character. The criticism and condemnation of the missionary practice instituted by Ricci became increasingly nothing more than a weapon in the hands of the enemies of the Jesuit Order in Europe, who neither understood anything of the circumstances in China, nor possessed any understanding or interest in the Chinese mission as such."[1]

During the eighteenth century, there was widespread European interest in the exotic aesthetics of China, labeled under the broad category of Chinoiserie.[2] Best known for its Ming ceramics and certain motifs in painting and theater, Chinoiserie was also significant in certain utopian, Romantic, and rationalist philosophies and literatures. Voltaire, for example, saw in China evidence of a universal religion of reason. The teachings of Confucius were placed on a par (almost) with the Bible — which was scandalous to Protestant theologians. Ironically, Jesuit accounts of China served as a criticism of the Christian church because such a high civilization had been created without divine revelation. The Romantic admiration of China and the idealized Jesuit accounts were undermined by the reports of merchants, though the merchants usually knew nothing of China's higher culture. The more thorough dismissal of China coincided with a Eurocentric revival of interest in Greek and Roman culture, a growing interest in Science, and colonial expansion. Just as "China" had served as a foil to criticize aspects of European societies, in time the derogatory accounts of China served to flatter Europe by contrast.

Because early images of China had been monopolized by Jesuits, the debunking of idealized images of China was at the same time a critique of Catholicism. As Peyrefitte commented on the British Protestant George Lord Macartney and his peers, "They set about to destroy this myth irrevocably, denouncing the writings of the Catholic missionaries as pure fabrication. . . . They came to believe that the supposedly incomparable model [of Chinese civilization] was in fact fossilized by ritual and steeped in vanity."[3] By demonstrating idolatry, absurdity, and clerical parasitism in Chinese religion, anti-Catholics simultaneously imputed those qualities to Rome. In anti-Catholic tracts the "Papists" were compared to Chinese idolaters; and in English works on China, Chinese religion was consistently viewed as identical to Catholicism. Furthermore, the Protestant narrative of Christian history was superimposed onto Chinese history: a degeneration from an original pure community to institutional idolatry, followed by (at least the possibility of) a Reformation. Protestant history pictured Christianity as having fallen from a bright early moment into centuries of ritualism until it had been purified in the Reformation. Protestant historians referred to the Reformation as a waking up, as light having fallen upon a darkened world, as a dawn. "Western Europe awoke at the Reformation, but Eastern Asia slept on till our own day."[4] The sad lapse into the sensuality of mere ritual, for which Protestants also found evidence in Old Testament anti-idolatry, was generalized as a universal human weakness.

Missionaries disagreed on the possibility of true divine revelation outside of the Bible, and hence disagreed in their evaluations of Chinese religion, even in the question of its categorization as "religion." Many missionaries took the stance that God had revealed Himself to the ancient Chinese, and in the present to a smaller number of Chinese with unusually spiritual natures. Chinese religion was still considered a subordinate religiosity, analogized to the subordination of the Old Testament to the New (at least in certain doctrinal questions), or of Catholicism to Protestantism (especially by virtue of the latter's rejection of "idolatry").

Protestant Missions in Chinese History

The transition from the Ming to the Qing (ca. 1644) had caused a rupture in trade and diplomacy, but by 1685 various European powers had established bases in the ports of South China. From 1760 until the mid-nineteenth century these were concentrated in Canton. Missionaries were not allowed into China, and the movements of all Westerners were closely administered and restricted. Missions had never been totally erased in China, but the period from the 1630s to early in the nineteenth century was unusually difficult for Catholic missionaries, and their numbers were low.

When missions recommenced in larger numbers during the nineteenth century, the missionaries found themselves in a very different China. The early missions had had very little political power behind them; the new missionaries had cannons behind them, and considerably more trade. The earlier missions had been spread very thin. The newer missions, both Protestant and Catholic, gradually traveled inland and into the villages. The missionaries very consciously tried to "penetrate" into the fine grain of China. This made missionaries vulnerable and sometimes impossible to protect. During the decline of the Qing, the inevitable deaths of Christian priests were used as rationalizations for military actions. Chinese Christians in trouble argued that they were being persecuted for their religion and claimed rights of extraterritoriality (that is, certain exemptions from the full jurisdiction of Chinese law, as if they were foreigners). The military and economic power of the nations that sponsored the missionary presence in China changed the nature of the mission field.

One of the most troubling aspects of the British missionaries' relationship to their nation was the importation of opium. In the late eighteenth century the British set up a triangular trade, selling Indian opium to China

FIGURE 4. "Chinese Opium-smokers." *Church Missionary Gleaner,* October 1850, 73.

to buy tea and sell it in England. The East India Company monopolized this trade until 1834, when Parliament revoked its monopoly. In 1819 opium traffic increased. Missionary societies depicted the sad debauchery of opium addiction (see Fig. 4). The Qing government tried to ban the sale of opium, with limited success. In 1839 Imperial commissioner Lin Zexu made some progress in a dramatic fashion, by seizing and destroying opium in Canton. This act was used to justify British military force, which soon escalated into the first Opium War. British warships attacked Canton and gained reparations. The Chinese military forces were not equipped or trained to deal with superior Western weaponry and ships.

Some missionaries were strongly critical of certain British practices, such as the opium trade, and disapproved of the aggressive Western tactics, but whatever the degree of personal complicity, Victorian missions were always deeply implicated with the long, painful period of China's humiliation. Christianity has not lost its association with the territorial concessions, the indemnities, and the unequal treaties. The British navy seized a series of ports and forced the Qing to agree to the Treaty of Nanking (1842). This treaty, and subsequent agreements soon after, ceded Hong Kong to Great Britain, established the treaty-port system, and gave Western powers greater rights and privileges in diplomacy and trade. Right of access to Canton was soon resisted locally, and anti-foreign tensions continued to rise, especially in South China. A second Opium War was provoked by the Chinese seizure in 1856 of the *Arrow*, a Chinese ship flying the British flag. An Anglo–French force occupied Canton and then sailed up the coast to Dagu and Tianjin. In 1860, in the midst of the Taiping rebellion, the allied forces captured Beijing, forcing the Emperor to flee. The British troops destroyed and looted the Imperial summer palace, the Yuanming-yuan. Diplomatic agreements following this humiliation extended foreign rights, such as the rights of missionaries to evangelize in China. The 1860s saw a sharp increase in the numbers of missionaries to China.

In the 1860s the government responded by establishing the Zongli yamen (Office for General Management) to deal with foreign affairs, and some efforts were made to learn more about Westerners. Schools were established for teaching foreign languages and a Chinese diplomatic mission traveled to America, England, and Germany. Western-influenced industrialization also began in the 1860s, initially focusing on arms, machinery, and shipbuilding. Many of these efforts toward learning from the West and industrializing were stymied by half-hearted implementation, disdain for foreigners, reversals of government policy, and by the Imperial Court's isolation.

A series of rebellions engulfed much of China during the latter half of the nineteenth century. The worst of these was the aforementioned Taiping Rebellion, started by Hong Xiuquan (1813–1864). Hong and his followers began to make territorial claims in 1851 and the extent of the rebellion expanded. By 1853 the Taipings controlled Nanking and almost half of China. An expedition further northward to take Beijing collapsed, and the rebellion was crushed soon after, in 1864. Hong had had some contact with Western missionaries, and there were clear Christian elements in the Taiping religion. Early Western observers sometimes optimistically believed the rebellion to be Christian — until the details of Taiping theology became clear. Hong believed himself the second son of God, younger brother of Jesus. Missionaries were happy to see the Taipings destroying so many Buddhist and Daoist temples, gleefully noting the iconoclasm, but they balked at the extent of the killing in this particularly bloody civil war. Briefly though, before the blasphemy and bloodshed were clear, the Taipings were seen obscurely as "a miracle of what the dissemination of the Scriptures unaided by instruction had performed."[5] The evidence of this miracle was primarily their attacks on

Buddhist and Daoist temples, as well as their suppression of brothels, gambling, and alcohol.

Overlapping with the Taiping Rebellion, the Nian Rebellion raged in Shandong, Anhui, and Henan; Muslim rebellions occurred in Yunnan, Shaanxi, and Gansu; and Western armies looted the capital. With their own Imperial troops stretched to the breaking point, the Qing had to rely heavily on local militias, as well as Chinese mercenaries that in some cases were armed and led by Westerners. This reliance on provincial power further weakened the influence of the central regime. China's traditional tribute states of East Turkistan, Tibet, Nepal, Burma, Vietnam, Korea, and Japan began to ignore or challenge the Qing. Japan and China fought for influence in Korea, with the Japanese gaining the upper hand during naval battles in 1894. As a result, Taiwan was ceded to Japan. The incremental process of Japanese influence and occupation eventually led to its control of Korea after 1910, and most of North China in the 1930s and 1940s. The Sino-Japanese War also triggered a rush for territorial concessions as Western nations competed to occupy or claim control of larger parts of China. The Qing government continued to shrink and fragment, and reformist movements within the Qing government were generally suppressed by the Empress Dowager Cixi and other conservatives.

Although missionaries were given rights to travel and evangelize, the central government was deliberately lax in letting local officials know of this policy, so that many local officials persecuted or harassed Christians. Missionaries sometimes had to go over the heads of the local officials, who received begrudging orders to protect the foreigners. Meanwhile, the anti-foreign sentiment became increasingly intermingled with specifically anti-Christian sentiment. Anti-Christian riots occurred sporadically, destroying churches and mission compounds. Some of the missionary accounts describe the Chinese mobs as utterly unruly and animalistic, while other accounts noted signs of leadership behind them: during the Wu-shih-shan case of 1878, for example, missionaries and converts had almost finished a new college, "when it was deliberately destroyed by a riotous mob led on by jealous mandarins."[6] In any case, such riots were often incited or orchestrated by agitators. Placards exhorted people to burn the houses of the foreign devils and to pull down the houses of men who had sold the missionaries land.

The church literature is voluminous on killed missionaries and (much less so) killed Chinese converts. While missionary organizations did not want to deter their readers from undertaking foreign missions, the deaths of missionaries were undoubtedly good for raising funds and rallying readers to the cause. However, public sympathy was never unanimous, and British hostility to missions was fueled by such deaths, especially when they led to further military expenditures and disruption of trade. (We must remember that missionary publications were also pitched at those back home who felt missions were a dangerous annoyance or at least a waste of money.) It was therefore very important to refigure murdered missionaries as martyrs. Following a massacre in Guzheng, an 1895 Resolution of the Church Missionary Society's General Committee included rhetoric of "the blood of the martyrs" becoming "the seed of the church."[7] The *Gleaner* and other publications gave space to various forms of commemoration, such as pictures of the martyrs' graves.

This popular anger against Westerners, Christians, and indeed against the ineffectual Manchu rulers reached its peak in the Boxer Rebellion of ca. 1900. The Boxers, more properly called the Yihequan (Righteous and Harmonious Fists), were militia groups with some of the characteristics of secret societies. They fomented anti-foreign sentiment and attacked Christian churches, Chinese converts, and missionaries. The Qing government was concerned about the current of anti-Manchu hostility among the Boxers but sympathetic with their anti-foreignism, and soon threw its support behind the Boxers. Nineteen thousand allied troops eventually marched on Beijing to rescue the besieged Westerners there, and once again to destroy and loot the Emperor's new summer palace by way of punishment. The Western powers further claimed a huge indemnity. The siege of Peking was widely reported in England, and many of the survivors wrote books about their experiences.

The Qing dynasty formally ended in 1911, but political unity was elusive. The Nationalists (Guomindang, or KMT) won a majority of seats in the first elected Parliament, but its president, the former governor-general of Zhili, Yuan Shikai, tried to become instead the first emperor of a new dynasty, dissolving Parliament in 1914. He died in 1916. Sun Yat-sen (1866–1925)and others formed a rival government in South China, but again, the real power was in the hands of military men. China remained fragmented until the Communists took control and established the People's Republic of China in 1949. During the first half of the twentieth century, China was in more or less continual warfare, among warlords, rival governments, and the Japanese.

Missionaries wrote of the 1911 Revolution as a great movement toward progress and a rare opportunity for evangelizing. The indemnities and the unequal treaties were seen as remnants of the previous dynasty's folly, which had weighed down China's efforts to modernize. Support grew for debt forgiveness and more equitable trade. Anti-Westernism went out of fashion, but hostility to Japan took its place.

World War I allowed Japan to seize the former German claims in China, but these invasive moves provoked a widespread popular resentment and resistance. Boycotts of Japanese products were attempted. Anti-Japanese sentiment was also mixed with disillusionment with the republican government and a thorough critical reevaluation of China's own heritage. During the late Qing, many Chinese had studied in Europe, America, and Japan, absorbing not only technological skills but Western notions of individual liberty, science, and Marxism. In China, thousands of modern-style schools had been created, sometimes taking over Buddhist and Daoist temples. The changing policy made some missionaries view the new national or provincial governments as allies. One missionary wrote in 1912, "With regard to idolatry, I think it is not too much to say that it has received its death-blow nationally, though individually and locally there is apparently as much as ever."[8] The provincial administration of Yuan Shikai was particularly active in converting temples to schools as part of modernizing campaigns in collaboration with rural elites. However, the idea of the separation of church and state also took root, so that from 1924 preaching Christian doctrine in schools was limited. The New Culture Movement was iconoclastic toward China's own history, especially the legacies of Confucianism, the Imperial system, and traditional religions. Vernacular literature replaced writing in classical Chinese. Much of this intellectual and political turbulence was identified as the May Fourth Movement, named after the date in 1919 of a protest against Japanese gains in the Versailles Peace Conference. The Chinese Communist Party (CCP) was formed soon after. Initially, it consisted of a group of urban intellectuals, but eventually, under Mao Zedong's leadership, it became a peasant-based guerilla force and then the government of China in 1949.

With the austerities imposed by World War I, missions to China gradually declined. Missionaries left North China in great numbers in the 1920s under political pressure from the Japanese, and those remaining were later expelled by the Communists in the late 1940s and early 1950s. Many of them went to Taiwan with the Nationalist Government (KMT), or to Hong Kong and other Han-Chinese diaspora communities. It was not until the 1980s that Protestant missions to mainland China resumed in significant numbers.

This is the historical frame of reference for the missionary culture explored in this book. The time period of the study begins in 1807, when

Robert Morrison arrived in China as the first Protestant missionary designated for the China mission. This period includes the gradual build-up of missions throughout the Victorian period and into the early twentieth century, until the dwindling of the missionary presence during the 1930s. Given the different narratives available from such other sources as Catholics, other Protestant denominations, interdenominational missions, and non-Britons, some readers may perhaps feel that "British Protestant Missionary Culture, 1807–1937" is too narrow a topic as an object of study, although other readers may feel I have stretched my generalizations. The tone of missionary rhetoric changed in this period from a relatively strident evangelical urgency, epitomized by the lone missionary addressing a vast population of heathens, as did Paul in the book of Acts, to the more pastoral commitment to the Social Gospel as the native Church grew and native Christians assumed more leadership roles. Very loosely, one can date the transition, which was a shift in emphasis rather than any complete rupture, to the turn of the century. Some aspects of missionary culture were specific, but there were also generic aspects, common attitudes and shared discourses, among different Protestant groups. Churchmen read the works of other visitors, and there was frequent communication among Protestant denominations. Protestants in China often decried the sectarian boundaries that had become so habitual in Europe, and in the twentieth century Chinese Christians urged Protestant unity, rejecting the denominationalism and sectarianism which had its roots in a history alien to them. In China, there was a shared culture and permeable boundaries between different groups with different agendas. Thus, I include such non-missionaries as Robert Fortune, Archibald Conquhoun, and even a widely-read Catholic, Evariste Régis Huc in this study, because CMS missionaries probably read them as well.

Early Western Study of Chinese Religion

Images formed in the early moments of contact between peoples tend to enter popular and scholarly usage as elements in a repertoire of imagined Others. Some of the images established during the earliest period of representations of China (roughly from Marco Polo to the fading of the Jesuit presence) remained active in the imaginations of Victorian missionaries and continue into the present day. But Western publications on China before ca. 1800 were sparse compared to the sheer uncoordinated volume of reportage produced by Western Europeans in the global diaspora of the nineteenth century.

The second half of the nineteenth century saw a tremendous burst of serious reportage about China, by missionaries, diplomats, merchants, adventurers, and soldiers.[9] Though China had been of interest to a few academics, the study of Chinese religion was dominated by missionaries. Nonetheless, with some exceptions, Victorian academics were Eurocentric. In France, where certain universalist traditions persisted, and where Chinoiserie had been stronger, the College de France established in 1818 a chair in Languages and Literatures of China and the Manchu Tartars — language and literature, not science or art or religion. Academic Sinology was heavily philological, or if historical, then it mainly concerned relations of the West to the Chinese and Mongols. Europe learned of Chinese religions primarily through the missions.

During the Qing, the most respectable subject matter for Western Sinologists (missionary or otherwise) was Chinese classical literature, which most closely approximated the cultural position of the classical Greek philosophers for Europeans. Certainly, native intellectuals presented the Five Books and the works of Confucius and Mencius as exemplary treasures of wisdom and most-worthy objects of study. The study of China's classical texts dated back to the Jesuit presence in China and was taken up by a small number of Protestant missionaries — usually those in treaty ports rather than remote villages. James Legge (1815–1897) became the first professor of Sinology in England. He worked with Max Müller (1823–1900) to include a number of classical Confucian and Daoist texts in the multivolume Sacred Books of the East series.

The study of what was worthy in Chinese religion was for many years almost entirely a textual matter. Disparities between the ideas of the classical texts and observed practices in Chinese temples were explained as degeneration. In Hastings's *Encyclopaedia of Religion and Ethics* (1916), for example, most of the article on Daoism concerns the ideas of the *Daodejing,* and only as an afterthought is "popular Taoism" mentioned, "which is not unfairly described as a mass of superstitious magic . . . [which has] yielded to the love of the marvelous."[10] In this view, the Daoism of the majority of Chinese resulted from an "inrush of superstition," a "deterioration."

Since Buddhist texts in Sanskrit or Pali were thought to represent more closely "original" (hence, "purer") Buddhism, the study of Chinese Buddhism was not a high priority. However, especially after the Qing, a few Westerners studied Chinese Buddhism more sympathetically.[11] These titles stand out for their focus and scholarly qualities, but of course a great many books have been written about China in the last two hundred years. It seems that most of these were travelogues; or they were surveys drawing heavily from other travelogues. One finds a wide variety of interests pursued, and frequent amateurism. In the midst of descriptions of chopsticks, diplomatic negotiations, coolies, and farming techniques, one finds a few pages here and there on visits to monasteries. These accounts vary widely and resist generalization, but may collectively represent a more important voice for the Western imagination of Chinese religion than all the works of scholars.

Some of the study of Chinese Buddhism was clearly motivated by the desire to convert Buddhists to Christianity, or at least to place Buddhist teachings in the larger frame of Christian revelation. The Pure Land school was of particular interest because of its devotionalism and its doctrine of a heaven-like future existence. Joseph Edkins (1823–1905) was especially interested in the Pure Land school, as was the progressive Baptist Timothy Richard (1837–1919). Having participated in the World Parliament of Religions of 1893, he collaborated with a lay Buddhist scholar, Yang Wenhui (1837–1911), in search of some kind of Buddhist-Christian synthesis.

In the 1920s the missionary Karl Ludwig Reichelt (1877–1952) helped set up a Christian mission to the Buddhists and was more ready to praise Chinese Buddhism than the vast majority of missionaries. His allies included Lewis Hodous and Johannes Prip-Møller. Reichelt worked to create a "Christianized Buddhism," taking Buddhism seriously but still working to show Buddhists that the culmination of their religion was Jesus. He had some success converting Buddhist monks, first in Nanjing and later in Hong Kong. He was criticized by some Buddhists and many conservative Christians, especially neo-conservatives who rejected inculturation and emphasized the unique and separate revelation of the Bible. There were always those who felt that the idea that God had revealed Himself in non-Christian cultures was too close to an abandonment of Christian identity. There were a few Westerners who accepted Buddhism, such as B. L. Broughton, the first Briton to take the bodhisattva ordination in 1933, John Blofeld, and Ananda Jennings. Such travelers usually had little in common culturally with missionaries, who in turn probably never read their books.

As there developed an academic study of Chinese religions whose intellectual agenda diverged from missionary goals, and as Chinese religions themselves began to be presented as spiritual paths by Buddhist or Daoist missionaries to the West, the missionary context of knowledge about China was apparently lost. During the twentieth century, the missionary voice has been recalled in academic writing as a mixed blessing at best, a mish-mash of unique eyewitness reportage and hostile judgments. Those who promote Asian religions as spiritual paths have dismissed or ignored the missionaries, since the accounts seem biased and their righteous hostility may be irritating.

Readers who do not come to the missionary record in search of evidence of the Holy Spirit have had to negotiate this mixture of elements and try to compensate for the judgmental tone. Much of the time, the value-judgments in missionary writings are quite obvious. For example, most of Arthur Elwin's article "Idols' Souls," which appeared in the April 1903 *Church Missionary Gleaner*, is a quite creditable piece of ethnographic description, more or less free of judgment. He describes icon consecration and includes a photograph of the talisman used in the process. This short descriptive piece surely came from a moment of genuine curiosity, but it was framed in the article by a Biblical condemnation of idolatry and by its location in the pages of the *Gleaner*. In a much larger sense, Elwin's moment of neutral description was further framed by its cultural position as a product of the missions. Analogously, despite its location in the Great Missionary Exhibition of 1909, the Chinese idol might still tell us something about Chinese religion, but more likely it speaks to us now of its captivity. To understand the larger cultural frame requires us to consider the subject position of the missionary, to explore the presuppositions brought to that moment of observation (and representation), and to point our questions toward the lived experiences of the missionaries.

Missionary Lives

The British and Foreign Bible Society was founded in 1804 to evangelize those parts of the world as yet unreached by missionary societies such as the Society for Promoting Christian Knowledge (founded 1698) and the Society for the Propagation of the Gospel in Foreign Parts (1701), which had concentrated on distributing Bibles to European Catholics. The BFBS gradually expanded the geographic range of Bible distribution. From its regional base in Shanghai, it maintained a network of subagents, depots, native colporteurs, and Bible women. In 1899–1900, for example, the organization distributed 4,698 Bibles, 33,074 New Testaments, and 805,553 Biblical selections in China.[12]

Another important missionary society was the Church Missionary Society for Africa and the East, publishers of the *Church Missionary Gleaner*. The CMS was founded in 1799 by members of the Eclectic

Society (an Anglican evangelical society), with the explicit intention to evangelize Africa and Asia. It began sending missionaries out as early as 1802. From 1814 the CMS was active in India, and in China from 1845. A "sister" organization, the Church of England Zenana Missionary Society, active in China from 1883, worked in close cooperation with but was institutionally distinct from the CMS, which formed its own Women's Department in 1895. In 1902 the CMS managed 1,276 missionaries (over two hundred of them in China), with an income of 327,000 pounds. The numbers of missionaries in the field grew slowly during the nineteenth century, but there was a surge in missionary numbers after 1880, with a further increase of female missionaries, especially after 1890. Hence, the period ca. 1880–1914 may be considered the peak of missionary activity in China.

The uncoordinated proliferation of missionary groups in China has been called the "anarchy of Protestant evangelism."[13] Also active in the nineteenth and twentieth centuries in China were the London Missionary Society, the China Inland Mission, the China Evangelization Society, the American Board of Commissioners for Foreign Missions, the American Baptist Missionary Union, the Missionary Society of the Methodist Episcopal Church in the United States, the Foreign Mission of the Presbyterian Church in Ireland, the Protestant Episcopal Church of America Missionary Board, the Board of Foreign Missions of the Presbyterian Church of the U.S.A., the Society for the Propagation of the Gospel, the United Free Church of Scotland, the Wesleyan Methodist Missionary Society, the Presbyterian Church of England, the Friends' Foreign Missionary Association, the Scandinavian Mission Alliance of North America, and many others.

Each of these organizations had slightly different means of financially supporting their missions in China, and hence different funding problems linked to political and economic conditions in Europe or America. Each society had a line of publications and relationships with churches at home. The various Protestant societies were often ecumenical, but there were occasional squabbles over territory and jurisdiction. The many societies established a multitude of sites and groups of all shapes and sizes: stations, chapels, churches, hospitals, schools. Cities afforded a concentration of potential converts, but the image of the unreached millions who had never even heard the Gospel, and the joys of itinerating, led to a very wide dispersal among the villages.

Most of the CMS missionaries were college educated, and they had often been involved with individual churches and other church organizations such as student evangelical fellowships. They spoke of having received a call from God, of having been called to the mission field to preach the gospel to the unconverted. Experienced missionaries, home on furlough, visited churches and gave public talks on their particular mission field, and undoubtedly the missionary's hardships were attractive. Not only were the locations exotic, but the very presentation of the mission as a narrative placed the missionary in the position of the hero.

Alternatively, service to the church could be in the form of training for the priesthood and ministering to a parish, or of working in the offices of church organizations. Some preached first to British congregations before hearing the call to foreign missions. In fact, the earliest missionary societies were domestic in scope; only later did they expand into foreign missions, first in Europe (especially among Catholics) and then gradually in the various colonies. (Both in popular usage since the nineteenth century and in this book, the term "missionary" means foreign missionary.) A few CMS missionaries held appointments to English parishes while on furlough and even retained those positions in absentia while back in China. To ensure that volunteers were fit for the task and indeed called by God, a system of probation developed, which required the more-senior missionaries to evaluate new arrivals, for a period of some years, if necessary. According to a probation form, criteria for evaluation included "teaching in accordance with C.M.S. principles," "zeal and eagerness in his missionary work," language study, and "understanding, and adapting himself to, the customs, thoughts, and character of the people to whom he is sent."[14] A missionary's health was constantly monitored as well.

Most beginning missionaries were unmarried, and many missionaries were married in the field. Some men conducted long-distance courtships with possible partners back in England, with the expectation that their new wives would join them in China. Many left for China shortly after marrying. More often, missionaries married other missionaries, though it was sometimes considered advisable to hold off marriage for two years in the field. Rarely, there were marriages between white missionaries and Chinese converts, as, for example, the apparently uncontroversial marriage of George L. MacKay to a Taiwanese woman, or the more contentious marriage in 1898 of Anna Jacobsen and Zheng Xiuji of the China Inland Mission. White men marrying Chinese women was always more socially acceptable than white women marrying Chinese men. Travel and residence in China were usually arranged to avoid unmarried men and women being together. More preferable was the pairing of unmarried women to married couples or groups of women. Ideally, newly arrived missionaries would travel with native converts and servants.

The journey to China was a large investment, and missionary societies each had various means of recruiting, screening, and selecting volunteers. The pay was never good, though the cost of living in China was low. Missionaries of modest means in England found themselves with multiple servants in China. Missionaries returned to Britain periodically for several months "on furlough," to recover their health and reconnect with home culture, but such breaks from the field might be years apart. While at home, the missionary was expected to promote missions by giving talks, showing slides, answering questions, and helping with missionary publications. Many missionaries were "invalided to England" and served in various church positions at home. Naturally, after decades in China, retirement in England was regarded as a mixed blessing, and some old China hands felt they were slighted upon their return. Archdeacon Arthur Evans Moule complained to the CMS that his valuable language abilities were destined "to be buried, wrapped in a napkin tied with red tape, in my Rectory garden, and not rather at hand for the Master's use, if He wants it."[15]

Anglican evangelicals emphasized Biblical faith, personal conversion, piety, and the specifically Protestant heritage of the Church of England. They were generally favorable to evangelism and missions. They are also known as "low churchmen" because they placed a relatively "low" value on the priesthood, the sacraments, and church ritual, in contrast to members of the "high church," which emphasized Anglicanism's more Catholic heritage. In the nineteenth century, evangelicals were opposed to groups such as the Oxford Movement, also known as the Tractarians, who taught this type of Anglo-Catholicism and included some who later converted to the Roman confession. The anti-Catholicism which pervaded the CMS is a recurring theme in this book. An early group of wealthy evangelicals, the Clapham Sect, was active in the late eighteenth and early nineteenth centuries, but the evangelical attitude was, more importantly, a broadly popular movement. In many respects, missionaries were very much in tune with the cluster of values and attitudes sometimes called the "Victorian ethos" or "Victorian morality." In general, these terms refer to an emphasis on religious belief, on civic and moral responsibility, and on willpower. Respect for law, earnestness, and plain directness in social interactions were valued. Though such a broad generalization is hard to define with precision, we have seen examples of this sensibility and we will see many more.

CHAPTER 3

Metaphors of Mindlessness

Foreign Images of the Native Body

Missionaries were often educated by other Westerners about the Chinese before they arrived in China, but they usually began their serious language study in China, and in the meantime they were well aware of their inability to communicate with the native people. The language barrier,

> I may add, at least doubles our labour in every thing we have to do. We cannot ask for any thing to be brought to us. If we desire the attendant's help at all, and do not entirely procure the article ourselves, we must at least walk right up to it and say, "Bring this." . . . Our commonest communications with our native attendants — for of course we *endeavour* to communicate with them — take such an excessive time, that all business is magnified, mole-hills become mountains.[1]

The near-total mismatching of languages led to the need for physical demonstration — touching objects. In contrast to the immediacy of the pointing finger, the obvious lack of a common language made most Chinese speech-acts impenetrable and rendered their own words and even some gestures powerless. On the other hand, bodies were always and immediately visible. Many Westerners with no previous language training began writing their expert books on the Chinese as soon as they stepped off the boat (if not sooner). New arrivals could not understand what was being *said*, and knew it; but they could write about what they *saw* of the Chinese people, and what they saw was bodies. This chapter shows how the Chinese were represented as mindless (in varying degrees and through various metaphors), and therefore, simultaneously, "body-ful."

39

I take it as a general axiom that the linguistic (and body-gestural) differences between natives and newly arrived foreigners make it difficult for any foreigner to perceive good reasoning in the natives, and vice-versa. Inevitably, the body is used more expressively, more for communication. The body of the Other is observed more closely for messages which cannot be communicated by words. Eye contact, gesticulation, and total body gesture become more pronounced and emphatic. One has to mime, act out, pretend, repeating the same message several times, while at the same time guessing at the meaning of a hand wave or facial expression.

Whereas for Barthes the display of the body is "to no real purpose," Victorians were freer to assign specific moral meanings to the body. According to Marjorie Morgan, they were particularly prone to viewing the human body as a legible object. As she writes about a slightly earlier period:

In the late eighteenth and early nineteenth centuries, people did not yet believe in an intangible, unconscious realm. All forms of invisible reality, including character, emotions and truth had, in their opinion, corresponding visible manifestations that were easily perceived. In fact, they invested the whole material world with a chain of significant hidden, spiritual implications. With regard to people, the most minute details of physical appearance were thought to betray the innermost recesses of the heart and mind.[2]

A body's appearance was a reasonable indicator of a person's inner character. It was thus easy for missionaries to move from bound foot to bound mind, from long hair to effeminacy, from dirty bodies to sinful souls. These shifts from the physical to the spiritual might strike us as merely metaphorical, but they may have been intended as more than metaphorical, or (we might say) more deeply metaphorical. As Wittgenstein wrote — though with an entirely different theoretical agenda — "The human body is the best picture of the human soul."[3]

Quite simply, and without qualification: "The Chinese mind is not logical."[4] The Chinese were called "inscrutable," but in fact this incomprehensibility is not a characteristic of the Chinese at all. When we cannot understand the rationality of others, we tend to displace that misunderstanding from the subject (us) to the object (them). Nor is it simply a characteristic of the foreign observer, though it is the foreigner who says the Chinese are inscrutable, the foreigner who cannot understand. As the modern hermeneutic tradition has stressed, understanding lies in the interaction between native and foreign, and this is just as true for *mis*understanding or the despairing failure to understand. Even when the other language has been learned, the deep epistemic reasoning behind activities may still be invisible or obscure. We have a tendency to fail to recognize "rationality" as culturally relative, as *our* rationality. When we can perceive no rationality, it is very easy to think there is none, or that the foreign rationality is flawed. This attitude toward the foreign mind appears in various metaphors of mindlessness which pervade, especially, the earlier-nineteenth-century reportage on China.

In this chapter we examine how Chinese bodies were represented and how the Chinese were represented as bodies. The "mindlessness" of the Chinese in early Anglophone Sinology appears in a wide range of metaphors — the Chinese as diseased, atrophied, feeble, blind, mentally deficient, in a stupor, drugged, sleeping, dead, childlike, and as animals — all metaphors which share the common thread of a weakness or lack of consciousness and a "higher reason" (defined, of course, within a Western, Victorian framework). Given the dominant Victorian gender construction of women as more emotional than rational, it is also worth considering a number of related images of the Chinese as feminized. The Chinese were sometimes also viewed as a dense, homogenous mass of bodies; as unemotional and unimaginative; as liars with no "higher" moral conscience; as entirely materialistic or bodily, even in their religion; as babblers, speaking and listening to incoherent gibberish or "pure noise." Chinese bodies in the performance of ritual received attention as flailing performers of a meaningless sham; as prisoners of an oppressive regimen of courtesy; and quintessentially as bending or groveling in the form of a kowtow, all images that are explored in subsequent chapters.

Diseased, Atrophied, and Feeble

We begin with a widespread view: the general stagnation of Chinese civilization. The idea of China as timeless and unchanging until it received a stimulus from the West was widely assumed in missionary reportage: "The Chinese have been a self-satisfied and conceited people, filled with vain ideas of their superiority to other nations, and pursuing the same habits of life, religiously and socially, which they had received from their forefathers, without feeling the need of alteration or improvement."[5]

According to this view, China had remained stationary for at least two millennia. Even when missionaries, merchants, and adventurers recorded some degree of praise for Chinese culture, the greatness was often in the remote past. The celebrated traveler Evariste Régis Huc (1813–1860) remarked: "This nation, which at so early a period attained so remarkable a degree of civilization, has remained stationary and made no progress for centuries."[6] Chinese civilization was ancient but stunted. "China is a land of millennial ruts."[7]

Such complacent inactivity had led inevitably to a rotten and filthy condition: "China is a stagnant pool. It needs only to stir it, to be convinced how foul it is."[8] Even the European peasant is cleaner than the Chinese peasant, according to S. Wells Williams: "Filth and misery appear everywhere to be concomitants of heathenism; a Christian peasant strives to make his poverty clean and wholesome, while a heathen is content to live in such wretchedness and mire as put the more cleanly beasts of the forests to blush."[9] Even animals are embarrassed by the human filth of heathen China.

Like the diplomats and traders who felt continually constrained by the imperial government's isolationist policies, missionaries felt that the Qing government, and the entire Confucian governmental system, must assume particular blame for this stagnation. S. Wells Williams commented: "The *vis inertioe* of this fossilized body which rules China seems sometimes to me to be the only obstacle to the advance of this country towards a high condition of civilization."[10] This atrophied condition justified harsh medicine, to be administered by the West. In 1858 Williams commented with grim humor on Chinese ignorance of Western military power: "I am afraid that nothing short of the Society for the Diffusion of Cannon Balls will give them the useful knowledge they now require to realize their own helplessness."[11] (The humorous reference here is to organizations such as the Society for the Diffusion of Useful Knowledge, founded in 1834.)

Even the massive violence of the Taiping Rebellion was but a temporary stimulation to the more natural state of inertia: "A mighty movement has taken place amongst the Chinese themselves. That there should be a rebellion in China is nothing wonderful. Rebellions in China . . . have been ordinary occurrences. They seemed to be short-lived disturbances of the inert mass, which soon subsided, and all became stagnant and monotonous as before."[12]

Whereas Western violence could fundamentally change China, China's own "indigenous" violence did not have that capacity. The West was regarded as the only source of the sustained activity of progress, while China inevitably tended to entropy. Though many commentators praised the Chinese as peaceful and industrious, they generally viewed the habits of the Chinese as prone to laziness and poverty, apathy and lethargy. As one would expect from all this, "China is in a diseased state."[13] One can sense the real health problems of foreigners living in China behind the extensive use of disease as a metaphor for culture. The Church Missionary Society archives reveal the toll on missionaries' lives in the extensive documentation from medical examinations, in the system of furlough, and in the terse entries in the missionary registers: "retired in consequence of broken health," "shattered health," "medical Board not recommending return to China," "died of typhoid fever."

The stagnant and diseased condition of China was inevitably tied to its heathenism:

Every thing about him is pestilential with the rank malaria of heathenism. Nowhere on earth does the Christian more need to be perpetually clad in the whole armour of God, that he may be able to stand and withstand. Contact with filth does not promote cleanliness. An infected atmosphere does not promote health. They whose duties lie in such surroundings, should not spare to use preventatives, disinfectants and correctives. Habitual and long continued contact with the low impurities and immoralities of heathenism, tends to impair the acuteness and delicacy of moral perceptions, and the purity of Christian taste.[14]

Disease, like sin, was in the entire atmosphere. Though most Protestants did not go as far as the Christian Scientists in the moralization of illness, nonetheless, for most Victorians illness had moral implications, and the language of illness and immorality inevitably blended. Conversely, walking and other vigorous activity had moral connotations. A reaction of disgust to slums, and especially to the foul air of slums, pervades Victorian reform literature, not to mention novels. The fear of airborne disease intermingled with the desire to contain the slum's other contagions — prostitution, venereal disease, criminality, and sewage. Exposure to the bourgeois gaze (discipline and surveillance, as well as policing) was conceived as a large part of the solution to slums, for reasons explored by Michel Foucault in *Discipline and Punish*: visibility led to a sense of being watched, a self no longer able to vanish from authority, which was the emerging mode of subjectification.

The Chinese self-confinement was not only a matter of walls and windows but of "breeding." Their refined civilization, precisely at its highest points, was their trap: "The Chinese of the upper classes encase themselves in polite insincerity: this is their armour."[15] Non-Christian religious observances were reported on as if they were symptoms of illness. George Smith wrote about a visit to a Buddhist monastery, "I was disturbed at an early hour by a priest groaning in the ante-room, and uttering doleful sounds, as he prostrated his body before the hideous idol."[16]

Satan in the Atmosphere

"By a law of nature when a thing becomes stagnant it soon grows corrupt. The same law holds good among men,"[17] wrote the missionary R. H. Graves in 1877. By contrast, "Faith partakes in the *general quickening* of the faculties excited and developed by aggressive work. In our bodies the quickening of one function involves the quickening of others — if the flow of the blood be quickened by vigorous exercise, the appetite is improved, the power of digestion is increased, the limbs grow strong and the brain is clear. So it is in our souls."[18]

The causal sequence of exercise — appetite — digestion — limbs — brain — soul linked body movement to spiritual condition. The unhealthy stagnation of the Chinese was contrasted with the middle-class Victorian penchant for exercise and fresh air. Lack of exercise or fresh air assumed meaning as metaphors for a dire spiritual condition: visiting a large temple, "we felt the very power of Satan in the atmosphere, making it quite a relief to be outside in God's free air once more."[19] The *Gleaner* lamented that the "higher classes live so shut up in their own premises, surrounded by high walls. . . . A Chinaman has no idea of walking about for health and recreation."[20] In the following anecdote by the missionary Mabel Pantin, published in 1903, we see the overlapping associations of Jesus, Christianity, Western influence, modern health practices, doses of medicine, and fresh air:

When we go over to give the evening doses we find every window in the hospital fast closed, and the first thing I do is to make for the windows and let in a little air. The Chinese reason for closing all windows at night is to keep the evil spirits out. One evening when I opened a window, and someone asked, "Why do *kuniongs* [unmarried female missionaries] always open windows?" this old lady, who was called *A-ci* (Big sister), replied, "Oh, don't you know? They do it to let Jesus in." Though she was hardly right, yet her explanation so exactly showed the difference between their dark superstitions and our faith in a living Saviour, the Giver of light and life, to be *let in* at all times and never to be feared.[21]

Here, Pantin reported on a Chinese understanding — that the spirit Jesus flies in through the open window — which she treats as a misunderstanding and yet one that is quaintly insightful. While she obviously does not think of Jesus as a wind-borne spirit, she aligns Jesus with fresh air, light, and open windows. The idea that evil spirits and illness fly in on the wind has a long history in China, as does the practice of confining the ill. By contrast, the medical missionaries were informed by a radically different medical etiology. Victorian health reformers took "miasmas" very seriously, as bad-smelling air was associated with diseases such as cholera. John MacGowan found it "astonishing" that living amid the "evil smells"[22] of densely packed Chinese cities — smells "such as would knock off the head of a water buffalo"[23] — did not cause massive plagues. Especially after the Crimean War, it was widely felt that the foreign "climate" of the Crimea killed more soldiers than the enemy's guns did. By contrast, the fresh air of public parks, as well as modern sewerage systems, were viewed as cures for disease in London. In order to avoid "making the sick repeatedly breathe their own hot, humid, putrescing atmosphere,"[24] Florence Nightingale's influential *Notes on Nursing* (1859) was distinctly pro-ventilation: "The choice is between pure night air from without and foul night air from within. Most people prefer the latter. An unaccountable choice. What will they say if it is proved to be true that fully one-half of all disease we suffer from is occasioned by people sleeping with their windows shut? . . . Windows are made to open; doors are made to shut."[25]

Christian doctors and nurses put these rules into practice in the ventilation of their hospitals, but the priority of fresh air was also a metaphor of salvation. The missionary May Griggs discusses the smooth running of a Christian educational program, adding: "Unless there is this spirit of co-operation and encouragement a spirit of inertia and despondency seems to chloroform them. It is largely due to the deadening influence of heathenism. The oxygen of fellowship in prayer and work counteracts it."[26] Heathenism is chloroform, Christianity is oxygen.

The attitude toward fresh air obviously went beyond opening windows. Many reports contrasted British walking with Chinese riding: "Our walking on shore seemed to puzzle them, for they could not comprehend why people should walk when they paid for being carried."[27] We are not told how the writer knew the meaning of this puzzlement, but this kind of particular observation was rapidly generalized. In China, as in Victorian England, public or private transport tended to consist of carriages. For a small number of more wealthy people, these included palanquins, smaller carriages, and private vehicles; for the upwards of fifteen, thirty, or a hundred less wealthy people, these included larger carriages, buses, trolleys, trains, and ferry-boats. For a Caucasian to be in China already implied some wealth and status, which was confirmed by their tendency to have dealings with government officials and by their independent income from England. Seeing them walk any distance would certainly have seemed a little odd, like a Chinese ambassador taking a Greyhound bus, or a millionaire's family hitchhiking.

Missionaries were influenced by the Christian Manliness and Rational Recreation movements, which valorized hearty outdoor exercise as not only healthy but morally superior. English visitors, even missionaries, did a lot of sightseeing and hill-climbing. A great deal of the pleasure of itinerating was the hiking and sightseeing. Itinerating was "the cream of the work," as Mary Darley explained, not only for its physical pleasures but also for its spiritual value: "There is no other work which provides the same scope for keeping under the body, to bring it into subjection."[28] Indeed, missionaries were able to leave us so many detailed reports of life within the Buddhist temples in large part because they frequently lodged in them, while itinerating, or just as often, when traveling for fun. Like all sightseers, they tended to climb to higher elevations. When irritated with his Chinese servant, Robert Fortune would punish him by obliging him to take long walks — long walks appearing here as a form of punishment. His method of getting away from crowds of Chinese was to climb any steep hill, "as they are generally too lazy to follow far where much exertion is required."[29] Perhaps, after all, they were not quite so curious to look at Robert Fortune. (The Western ascent to higher ground mimics the vertical logic of Westerner's attitudes toward obeisance, discussed in Chapter 7.)

In addition to fresh air and vigorous exercise, sunshine was thought to be a healing and invigorating influence. Despite its abundant sunshine, the continent of Africa was most routinely thought of as "dark" — as in Henry Stanley's famous *In Darkest Africa* (1840) and numerous other titles — but England's own industrial cities were also depicted as sunless, by Charles Dickens and Friedrich Engels, and by various social reformers, such as the adherents of Rational Recreation. Florence Nightingale associated a lack of sunlight with genetic decay: "Where is the shady side of deep valleys, there is cretinism. Where are cellars and the un-sunned sides of narrow streets, there is the degeneracy and weakliness of the human race — mind and body equally degenerating."[30] Yet China was represented as more overcrowded and much denser than European cities: millions of Chinese "are found huddled together in lanes from five to nine feet wide, where an European could not freely breathe."[31]

Mentally Deficient, in a Stupor

If the "quickening" of the body led to clarity of the mind, it is not surprising that the perceived inertia of Chinese bodies was also attributed to their minds. The motif of stupor or dim stupidity is remarkably pervasive in nineteenth-century accounts of China, as if to emphasize the supposedly mindless and timeless routine of the Chinese. The hardest thing, the missionary Thomas M'Clatchie reported in 1851, was to make people *"think"* about the issues. "If our preaching stirred up opposition, there would be much ground for hope; but the great difficulty is to make those with whom we come in contact, and especially those of the more respectable class, *think* on those subjects which we bring before them. Chinese etiquette generally leads a respectable man to profess a perfect assent to every statement made."[32]

Though gathering a crowd was apparently quite easy, many missionaries complained of the difficulty of getting listeners to respond. In Chapter 6, I will discuss in more detail the Western frustration with what the missionaries perceived as a rigid façade of courtesy, which they interpreted as seeking to preserve harmony even at the cost of real communication or debate. And in Chapter 12, we will see missionaries annoyed when their audiences showed interest, not in the Gospel, but only in their foreign bodies — eyes, noses, beards, buttons, and boots. For the moment, let us note the missionaries' suspicions that the Chinese mind behind that façade would not or could not think properly. MacGowan asserted, "The Chinese mind is wanting in lucidity,"[33] with a "turbidity" and "haziness of thought."[34] An 1861 report from Canton describes a crowd listening to a sermon: "Some have thought and character written on their faces, bespeaking for them talents and acquirements of no mean order. The countenances of others would *almost deny the existence of thought,* while too many have stamped upon them the certain signs of degrading vice."[35]

S. Wells Williams agreed with this view: "The torpor of mind in heathen countries is inconceivable to one who has all his life lived in a Christian land. . . . I could willingly dispute all day long with them, but there is none who thinks enough to carry on a dispute, none who defends his religion or his customs. . . . They generally and chiefly act because their ancestors did so."[36]

An unwillingness to engage in debate was consistently interpreted as a complete inability to do so, as a kind of culture-wide lack of mental energy or as a profound disinterest in seeking truth. Many missionaries were distressed by what they perceived as spiritual and intellectual deadness, since their passionate condemnations of idolatry elicited little response. "The general impression I got of the people was that their minds are an utter blank in matters of spiritual religion."[37]

Some missionaries and other writers focused in particular on the supposed mental vacuum of Buddhist monks. Robert Fortune noted: "They are generally an imbecile race, and shamefully ignorant of everything but the simple forms of their religion."[38]

Never in all my travels in China had I met with such poor specimens of the human race as these same priests. They had that vacant stare about them which indicated want of intellect, or at least, a mind of a very low order indeed. They did nothing all day long but loll on chairs or stools, and gaze upon the ground, or into space, or at the people who were working, and then they did not appear to see what was going on, but kept looking on and on notwithstanding.[39]

The notion of religious professionals being ignorant of their own religion except for the "forms" suggests assumptions about ritual that were common in anti-Catholic thought, which will be discussed further in Chapters 6 and 7. Most commonly in Protestant reportage the monks and nuns are seen practicing devotional rituals, their "dreary worship" more or less public and immediately visible to visitors: "We were struck with the dull, unintellectual countenances of the priests, as we met them with their rosaries in their hands, busy at the wearisome task of repeating incessantly the name of their god, 'O mi doo veh' [Pinyin: Amituo-Fo]."[40]

Any visitor could see obeisance practices, but some visitors became aware of a less obvious Buddhist practice, seated meditation. Western visitors and missionaries were, in varying degrees, aware of the basic mechanisms of Buddhist meditation. Practices of *samadhi* (Ch. *ding,* which implies stilling or emptying the mind, in extended periods of quiet sitting, without thought or desire), and ideas of *sunyata* ("emptiness," or "void") must have seemed fortuitous metaphors of stunted mental development or deliberate mental blankness. The monks who meditated "place[d] their religion in absolute mental abstraction, tending to that perfection which shall fit them to be absorbed into that something which, as they say, faith can conceive, but words cannot describe."[41] In Buddhism, wrote Charles Gützlaff, "the summit of happiness — [is] to be swallowed up in nonentity. . . . The way they mark as the shortest that leads to happiness is, perfect silence, utter apathy of feeling, and entire cessation from thought and action. As soon as a man ceases to be man by becoming as unfeeling as a stone, he enters the portals of happiness."[42] For evangelicals, the center of culture was religion, the root of China's problems was its heathenism, and at the heart of at least the Buddhist form of heathenism was a deliberate cultivation of (what seemed to be) mental nihilism.

John Francis Davis evaluated Buddhist spirituality thus:

Their notion of total abstraction, or quietism, seems to aim at getting rid of all passions, even of thought itself, and ceasing to be urged by any human desires; a species of mental annihilation. Certainly, to judge by its effects on the priests, the practice of Budhism [*sic*] appears to have a most debasing influence. They have, nearly all of them, an expression approaching to idiocy, which is probably acquired in that dreamy state in which one of their most famous professors is said to have passed nine years, with his eyes fixed upon a wall![43]

One can easily understand the skepticism of a generation of missionaries raised on the Victorian work ethic, Christian Manliness, and Rational Recreation. Indeed, the practice of emptying the mind of all thought and "just sitting" for hours on end would seem to have been custom-made for their derision. "They get as near to their ideal as possible by sitting cross-legged for hours together, trying to think about nothing. That seems to be easier to the Chinese mind than it would be to the English!"[44] (Because the Chinese more naturally have no thoughts, apparently.)

Another metaphor for the Chinese mind was the bonsai tree. "These dwarfed trees, of which the Chinese are so fond, are they not emblems of the Chinese mind? How different would its growth be, brought under the elevating influences of Christianity!"[45] Almost fifty years later, the analogy was alive and well: "The mind of a Chinese woman often reminds one of their favorite ornamental trees, grown in a tiny pot, kept all their lives in a narrow courtyard, twisted and bent into fantastic shapes, where new growth or expansion is almost impossible."[46] The trees are dwarfed because of the tiny pot they grow in; metaphorically, the "tiny pot" is the restricted cultural space available to the Chinese — its trade protectionism, isolationism, the various walls it builds around itself. Within such a small range of cultural possibilities, cut off from "the world," the Chinese mentality has knotted in on itself and has failed to grow. The tree's roots are not stunted accidentally, but deliberately, and indeed as part of a hobby of refinement and taste, as a great art and a spiritual practice.

The stunted roots of Chinese plants were regarded as symptomatic of China's culture, but they were at least benign. More passionate ire was aroused by the stunting of Chinese feet, or footbinding. Missionaries referred to unbound feet as "Christian feet." A girl "with a very bad leg, says she is going to unbind her feet and be a 'real Christian.'"[47] Certainly, the bound foot was used as a metaphor for minds: "Christendom has long enough wept over the bound feet of the yellow babies and the bound minds of their mothers."[48] While there were Chinese critics of foot-binding independent of missionary influence, there can be no doubt that missionaries were instrumental in ending the practice. Anti-footbinding societies were founded in the late Qing, especially in the cities, and reformers like Kang Youwei and Liang Qichao argued that the fate of China depended on women's physical strength.

Finally, blindness was a pervasive metaphor of mental incapacity. As in so many other contexts, poor eyesight and/or surrounding darkness functioned as metaphors for intellectual or spiritual weakness. The inability to see (a truth) was often depicted as a darkness of the surrounding environment: "Alas! poor China is in midnight darkness."[49] As Thomas M'Clatchie claimed (blurring the distinction between blindness and being in the dark), "The Chinese are dark indeed."[50] An 1863 communication from A. E. Moule developed the metaphor: "China is a dark land; gross darkness covers the people: and benign and placid as the Buddhist idols and Buddhist priests appear, what cruelty is worse than that of spending one's life in rendering deeper the black cloud of error which shrouds the land, and in riveting more firmly the chains which Satan has bound round the millions of China."[51]

Drugged

The *Church Missionary Gleaner* printed a picture of "Chinese Opium-smokers"[52] (Fig. 4), showing seven men, some with shirts wide open, lounging around in a frivolous and drunken state and seemingly enjoying themselves. One man in the picture is asleep or passed out. Despite the drunken cheer of this picture, opium addicts were usually depicted in more lurid, pitiful terms. They were "known by their sunken cheeks, their glassy watery eyes, their idiotic look, and vacant laugh."[53] Missionary publications were very vocal against opium, and they described the misery and death of opium smokers in ghastly detail. Opium dens were seen as the proverbial dens of iniquity, perhaps quite stylish among the rich but inevitably more awful as the drug sapped the addict's finances.

Buddhist and Daoist temples and their inhabitants were depicted in similarly depressing terms, an analogy made clearer in this 1919 case by the proximity of poppies:

A dark, grimy temple . . . Just behind there is an opium field. Inside the temple is an altar covered with dust and candle grease; the large idols — dim, dusty, and shabby — fade away in the gloom of the shrine, their faces devoid of expression, huge in size and immense in their helplessness. . . . With a wailing, sad, hopeless drone, with postures eloquent of laziness and unbelief, he [a priest] performs evensong, the onlookers apparently indifferent to the service.[54]

Images of opium addiction resonated with the dominant image of Chinese religious life: dark, grimy, dim, dusty, and shabby, fading away in the gloom of the shrine; faces devoid of expression, helpless, wailing, sad, hopeless, lazy, unbelieving, and indifferent. Rather than providing aid to those addicted to opium, Chinese religion was seen as irrelevant, having no capacity to improve the morals or lifestyles of addicts. In contrast, a cure for this addiction was associated with Christianity. W. C. White described a 1906 visit of one Dr. Wilkinson and others to a village in Fuzhou, where they conducted a large treatment of opium addicts with the support of the village elders. As Wilkinson dispensed pharmaceuticals, White held services and preached. Hence, curing opium was an opportunity for preaching and conversion. The missionaries set up in the middle of the patients in the big ancestral hall, and "we took turns at the preaching. . . . Of the seventy-nine, as far as we could make out, forty-three had definitely decided to become Christians."[55]

Missionaries were faced with a paradox and a moral quandary, since their own nation had to bear the responsibility for importing opium, despite the opposition of the Chinese government. Missionaries had to concede that England had used military force to enable the opium trade. Missionaries had always seen "this deathful drug"[56] as a deeply moral and theological issue which challenged their own national identity. A poem by Martin F. Tupper appeared in the *Gleaner* in 1856:

> Yonder vast industrious realm
>   We, at lucre's bated breath,
> Like a torrent overwhelm
>   With the very juice of death;
> China, poisoned to the core,
>   Pleads to God against our spell
> English commerce dares to pour
>   O'er her people drugged by hell![57]

"Christian men . . . have always deeply felt that a national sin had been committed."[58] The *Gleaner* and other missionary publications were consistently against opium, blaming both the British merchants and smugglers, and Chinese officers, for failing to stop the smuggling. Opium had been introduced into China "from without" through the "covetousness of Europeans, and the lust of the Natives for the drug."[59] Another target of blame was the addict himself. In one account, a Chinese teacher told

William Russell that as long as Westerners brought opium to China, the preachers would be wasting their time. Finally, after a long harangue, Russell says, "Remember in every trade there must be two parties, the buyer as well as the seller."[60]

Some of the Chinese acknowledged the peaceful message of the Gospels but urged missionaries to challenge their own countrymen on this issue. Missionaries did just that, and generally rejoiced at the rise of an anti-opium movement in England.

Sleeping

Sleeping and dreaming appear in Protestant representations of China as the "sleeping dragon," a pervasive metaphor consistent with other metaphors of mindlessness. If, as we have seen, China was in "darkness," their natural state would seem to have been slumber, when conscious thought and individual will are dormant. Sleep is at least healthier than an opium stupor or rotting stagnation. Though the Taiping Rebellion momentarily disturbed the Chinese "dream of self-complacency and sensuality,"[61] it was not until the break-up of the Qing state in the late nineteenth and early twentieth centuries that Western accounts of China emphasized the motif of China waking, and then always in terms of its openness to Christianity, trade, Western influences, industry, women's rights, and science. Nonetheless, the resiliency of the metaphor of waking, in a flow of rhetoric about China since the late Qing, gives the impression of a nation always waking up but never quite awake. Even today, we read of China as the "next world power."

In a historical correlation of the spread of Protestantism and rising from slumber, Louis Byrde wrote in 1907: "Western Europe awoke at the Reformation, but Eastern Asia slept on till our own day. Now, however, even the 'antiquated' empire of China is rapidly awakening."[62] As an existential condition, slumber was Catholic, Chinese, and antiquated, and idolaters lived their lives hovering over sleep:

> Unheeding sit the monks below,
> And mutter prayers to senseless clay:
> LORD, wilt Thou open their slumbrous eyes,
> And hasten the dawn of eternal day?[63]

To the extent that such references to physical inactivity, half-hearted ritual speech, and nighttime sleep were applied to the religious culture as a whole, we can read them as metaphors. There is, however, little sense of metaphor in Robert Fortune's remarks: "A great proportion of the northern Chinese seem to be in a sleepy or dreaming state, from which it is difficult to awaken them. . . . [They gaze at foreigners] with a sort of stupid dreaming eye; . . . drawn there by some strange mesmeric influence over which they have no control."[64] They "stare as though riveted by a magic spell,"[65] lost in "that dreamy state which I have already noticed as a characteristic feature in the Chinese race."[66] Despite the qualifiers "seem to be" and "sort of," clearly Fortune was describing what he considered his honest perceptions of at least some Chinese as a people without normal waking consciousness. He particularly applied this image to certain Buddhist priests: "They seemed to be in a kind of dreamy, mesmeric state; their eyes indeed are open, but apparently they see nothing that is going on around them."[67]

The "magic spell" which put the Chinese into a "dreamy state" was, in some popular Chinese anecdotes, cast by the foreigners themselves. Mary Darley noted a revival of stories about missionaries who threw a "'sleeping medicine' . . . in people's faces as they walked in the open street, causing them to sleep for days or 'to death.'"[68]

Dead

There were many evaluations of China as a dead culture, and of the people as spiritually dead. Of course, the living death of the non-Christian was a consistent theme of the New Testament: "For the wages of sin is death" (Romans 6:23). In Paul's view, death is not what happens to the body at the end of life, but the true condition of the body before its redemption. Paul equated death with the body and its sensual pleasures. The human spirit embraces death to the extent that it identifies the self with the "flesh" and is controlled by the body's desires. With this kind of theological background, it is hardly surprising to read S. Wells Williams description of China as "such a valley of dry bones."[69] Other missionaries agreed: "China is *dead — terribly* dead."[70]

Victorian evangelicals picked up on these themes. In this single lifetime on Earth, conversion and baptism are especially urgent as death approaches. The imaginations of some writers seem to have reeled at the horrifying prospect of such a vast empire of non-Christians dying in such vast numbers. In his poem, "The Voice of the Brother's Blood," H. Grattan Guinness gives the sheer quantity of deaths as a reason for increased support for sending to China those "workers" who have heard the call:

> They have heard from the far-off East
>   The voice of the heathen's blood;
> A million a month in China
>   Are dying without God!
> . . . .
>
> Is it nought that one out of every three,
>   Of all the human race,
> Should in China die, having never heard
>   The Gospel of God's grace? [71]

Each of the seven verses ends with the same refrain about that "million a month, dying without God."

Outside of missionary circles, much of the reportage on China came from observers of (and participants in) the many wars, rebellions, and lesser skirmishes, so that the China of the Victorian imagination was indeed a bloody place. A Captain Loch wrote that when he and his men broke down the walls and stormed one city, there was a frenzy of mass hysterical suicide. In one house they saw "twenty bodies of women and young girls, some hanging, others extended on the floor."[72] In one of Robert Fortune's more lurid passages, he described the aftermath of mass executions in connection with the Shanghai Rebellion as a "field of blood. . . . Here hundreds of headless bodies scarcely covered, or only with an inch or two of earth, lay in a state of decomposition, and the stench from them filled and polluted the air."[73] Even the *Church Missionary Gleaner* carried a description of heaps of corpses, hacked and mangled.[74] Some accounts of China seem to have fixated on grotesque spectacles of death, or seem inured of it. "Very frequently you will see dead bodies lying by the side of the busy roadway."[75] Missionaries paused to view the charnel houses at the edges of some cities and wrote home of the awful heaps of bodies: "The bodies are carried to a common pit without the city walls, into which all those that are living, as well as those that are dead, are said to be thrown promiscuously."[76]

Even in times of peace, Chinese corpses appeared in the missionary representations. One report describes emaciated and sick beggars and corpses lying on the street, then went on: "Within three or four yards of a corpse, a company of noisy gamblers were boisterously pursuing their nefarious vocation. Such is the baneful spell of Paganism! . . . Even within sight of Buddhist altars, . . . we beheld the spectacle of death."[77]

Missionaries gained a reputation for taking in those who were near to death, which unfortunately led to accusations of murder and of the use of human organs (see Chapter 10 on the purported Western desire for Chinese bodies). A significant number of conversion stories deal with Chinese people close to death, and with the rush of concern to convert them in time. The noisy, public funeral processions were thus unavoidable reminders of the missionaries' failure to save Chinese souls. As eye-catching and public manifestations of heathenism, funerals and graves were described repeatedly and often in some detail: "China seems to be one vast graveyard. Many, many graves, anywhere and everywhere, lay along our route to the city."[78]

Due to the calendrical system of auspicious days for important events such as burials, bodies were not always buried immediately after death, and Western accounts dwelled on the large numbers of unburied bodies: in 1830 there were "reported to be ten thousand coffined bodies in Canton, not interred."[79] We thus see the spectacle of China littered with death: vast graveyards, heaps of coffins, corpses exposed. Robert Fortune often encountered these graveyards because he wandered the mountainsides looking for plant specimens: "On one hill-side on the island of Chusan skulls and bones are lying about in all directions, and more than once, when wandering through the long brushwood in this place, I have been entangled by getting my feet through the lid of a coffin."[80]

Apparently, Chinese culture seemed entangled in coffins as well, in its near-universal practice of the ancestral cults, described as the worship of the dead. This "ancestor worship" was "one particular form of idolatry which they are very tenacious of," and which "will be one of the last strongholds that will yield to the spiritual weapons of the soldiers of Christ."[81] John MacGowan asserted, "The dead to-day all over China hold the living within their grip."[82]

While missionaries tended to favor what we now call "family values," few missionaries saw the ancestral cult as merely comparable to the normal remembrance of the dead among English Christians. While some acknowledged the virtue of respectful remembrance of one's beloved parents, the ancestral cult was seen as significantly more sinister and idolatrous. As an 1854 article in the *Gleaner* explained, "It is the working of the same corrupt principle which leads the Chinese to worship the ancestral tablet, and the corrupt Romanist or Greek Christian to bow themselves before images and pictures, and invoke the aid of the Virgin and the Saints."[83]

Childlike

The ancestral cult assumes that the relationship of father and son survives death. Some Western observers have speculated that the Chinese are unable to ever leave behind their subject position as children and thus can never become adults. If the ancestor cult is a continual denial of the real death of the father, the son is always a child, trapping him in what Alain Peyrefitte much later called "psychic infantilism."[84]

Aside from the specific case of ancestral cult practice, missionaries wrote of adult Chinese as children in a variety of ways. Sometimes in rather broad terms the Chinese were, for better or worse, simply child-like: "They are grown-up children and I fear quite beyond teaching."[85] The Chinese people "must be treated as children."[86] The "multitudes . . . come around us on the ship with all the ingenuousness and docility of children."[87]

Once again the underdeveloped mental power suggested by this perceived infantilism was linked to religion. "Idolaters may be men of education, skilled in art and science, but in religion they must be vacant as babes."[88] Even after their rejection of idolatry, the newly converted Chinese Christians were described as "baby Christians."[89] Edith Couche wrote: "Our difficulties do not end when our converts hand us their idols and say they have no further use for them. Does a mother's care cease when her little son has taken his first two tottering steps?"[90]

In what ways were the Christian converts like children to the Western missionaries? Childhood socialization is the inculcation of a habitus, and in China, Christianity as a habitus required re-inculturation in Chinese minds and bodies. One who aspires to but has not yet embodied a culture is often analogized to a child.

Feminine

According to an 1874 report, the (Daoist, or Buddhist) priest's mind is "a strange compound of fanaticism and imposture, and it is his policy to keep his followers in a gross and credulous state, the women especially, who, in all countries, are easy captives to superstition."[91] Missionaries frequently regarded women (in China, and in fact, everywhere) as more inclined to idolatry than men, just as, in a more positive sense, women were considered more naturally inclined to piety.

Most reports of temple activities mentioned or even stressed that the majority of devotees were women, who visited the temples most conscientiously, often bowing to the female deities: "The centre of attraction for all is the brazen image of the goddess, before which the people, mostly women, were bowing in abject devotion."[92] The lowest class of religious practitioners, consisting "almost entirely" of old women, was "the vulgar, whose devotion can rise no higher than the sensual ceremonies, who strike their foreheads upon the steps of the temples."[93] The devoted women also protected the images against damage.

In one case, the reverse was true: in a Daoist temple in Shandong, "the scarcity of women and children made each temple compound seem a congress of adult males, and the mixture of Fourth of July boyishness and fishwife credulity with which these men solemnly carried out their superstitious antics would have seemed even more out of place but for their girlish cues [sic] and their generally simple, almost childlike manners."[94]

In their solemn religious acts, the men are like little boys and girls or women, simple and credulous in their "antics." In this remark, published in 1923, the "adult males" had their ages reduced, their gender changed, and their religious and civil rituals were regarded as child's play. Rhetorically, men become girls. The symbolic feminization of the idolater has a long history in anti-Catholic polemics and in descriptions of worshipping Chinese — and always in connection with their obeisance.

One aspect of the Victorian missionaries' system of values that is worth noting here in a little more detail is their widespread masculinist qualities. The ethos of the missionaries was strongly influenced by the Christian Manliness (or "Muscular Christianity") movement,[95] a broadbased cultural movement which associated physical strength with spiritual strength, vigorous activity with religious certainty, and masculinity with Protestantism. In the view of Christian Manliness novelist and essayist Charles Kingsley (1819–1875), the Reformation was a pivotal moment of union between true religion and "Primeval Teutonic energy."[96] Though not every missionary agreed with Kingsley in detail, from the 1850s calls for a re-masculinized Christianity were common. Although individual male missionaries could be personally nonviolent, this kind of masculinity always implied the capacity for violence, including violence on their own bodies. In a culture which was busy using its physical (industrial, material, military) strength to subdue the "weaker" peoples, a fetishization of the robust was also a spiritual justification of conquest. To willingly endure pain or privation for the cause of spreading the Gospel was to "bear the cross" — to share in Jesus' struggle. Hence we find missionaries in China voicing this masculinist religiosity: "Christianity is essentially aggressive and revolutionary."[97] Some missionaries were proud of their robustness. S. Wells Williams enjoyed showing off his muscular strength as compared to the Chinese. His son wrote: "In later years he often referred, for example, to his being able to lift and shoulder a box which two Chinamen could hardly carry, and in his wherry on the river he used to enjoy 'pulling round' his side of the boat, in great glee at his companion's unsuccessful efforts at holding his own against him."[98]

The missionaries' attitudes toward the ideal body were also influenced by a widespread debate in the 1830s and 1840s on recreation for the urban working classes, a movement named "Rational Recreation." Drawing for its support from the temperance movement and from many churches, Rational Recreation was directed against drunkenness and brawling, and instead viewed games — from board games to rugby — as inevitably conducive to morality. Game-playing teaches rules within cooperation; it also teaches there is always a winner and a loser. Games are also the basis of many spatial metaphors used by missionaries and academic alike — field, sides, territory — and often imply capitalist principles, such as exchange, profit, scarcity, and bookkeeping. The Churches tried to claim leadership in such recreations: "In games, the rhetoric of recreation and religion tended to become one."[99] Many of the CMS missionaries had attended public schools, which famously valued athletic virtues.

Team sports in particular came to be regarded as an invaluable training ground for a life in service of the Empire, and images of the ideal man represented him as liking his sport good and rough. In more than seventy best-selling boys' adventure books, George A. Henty (1832–1902) praised boxing and other sports as the basis for Imperial greatness. In his *With the Allies to Pekin,* the hero, Rex Bateman, states that good scholars make poor soldiers, whereas good sportsmen can conquer any army.[100] Rex kills dozens of Chinese in the Boxer Rebellion, to the praise of the girls: "It is wonderful that you two should have killed twelve of them in two minutes."[101] An essay by Henty made the religious connection to manliness explicit: "True heroism is inseparable from true Christianity, and as a step towards the former I would urge, most strongly and urgently the practice of the latter."[102] Victorian writers tried to balance the image of Jesus turning the other cheek with their cultural valorization of assertive pugnacity. The Christian Manliness movement struggled with the image of Christianity as weak, feminine, or effeminate. Missionary work seemed to present an ideal model of Christian courage and mercy combined, since missionaries faced hardships and dangers but did so out of their commitment to Christ. Missionary work required a courage "that will even roll up sleeves and lend a vigorous helping hand to those in need."[103]

The best-selling writer Samuel Smiles (1812–1904), whose books extolled the virtues of vigorous work and exercise, viewed idleness as perhaps the worst sin in his extended paeans to British industriousness, exploration, and stamina.[104] Physical inactivity not only weakened the body: "The mind itself grows sickly and distempered, the pursuit of knowledge itself is impeded, and manhood becomes withered, twisted, and stunted."[105] This grotesque specter appeared possible to Smiles and many evangelicals as a potential lapse among Protestants, and as an actual condition of Chinese heathens.

This "effete" Chinese religion contrasted with Christian Manliness, including the view that "the kingdom of Christ can be set up only by aggressive work. Missionary work is aggressive work."[106] During the 1860s and 1870s, at the height of the movement in England against Ritualists — seen as crypto-Papists — the association of Catholicism and femininity was explicit. Ritualists were viewed by critics as silly, effeminate, babyish, and sensual, as "effeminate fanatics . . . sentimental ladies and womanish men," or as Sabine Baring-Gould put it, "not conspicuously virile men who delight in tinsel and paper flowers."[107] In the same period, there was a shift in popular British attitudes toward the military. Not only could the soldier be a good Christian, but contrary to previous views, the best soldiers were Christian and the military was an appropriate model for Christian identity. Sabine Baring-Gould wrote the hymn "Onward, Christian Soldiers" in 1864, and military rhetoric, practices, and symbols were widely diffused in society. The Crimean War (1853–56), and then the Indian Mutiny (1857), became the settings for a new hagiographic image, the soldier-saint, such as Hedley Vicars or Henry Havelock. Many factors refigured masculinity in mid-century Britain: the movement against Anglo-Catholicism, the overlapping phenomena of the Christian Manliness and Rational Recreation movements, the rise of mass participation in sports, the expansion of the Empire, and the adulation of the soldier.

Many Victorians held the view that women are naturally emotional and beautiful, whereas men are (or should be) rational and strong. Women were viewed (relative to men) as irrational and weak, while men were, by contrast, unemotional and not beautiful (plain, unadorned, and not vain). As the Victorian moralist Samuel Smiles put it, "Man is the brain, but woman is the heart of humanity; he its judgement, she its feeling; he its strength, she its grace, ornament, and solace."[108] In a less complimentary way, women were often represented as inherently more interested in the display of beauty and as happier with subordinate roles; hence their attraction to Ritualism, which was characterized as a "female movement." This kind of gender distinction assumed the existence of male and female spheres which should not be confused. Hence, Victorians often focused with disapproval on the blurring of gender distinctions that existed in China. J. R. Wolfe described how the Chinese would give a boy a girl's name, and even dress the boy in girl's clothing, so as to avoid premature death: "I have seen boys grow up almost to the age of manhood in females' dress, and treated in every way by their parents as if they were girls, and all this in order to outwit the devil, and save the boy from his fangs."[109] The use of the queue was also seen to feminize the Chinese: "Long hair . . . was never intended for men. When the tartars forced the queue upon the Chinese, there must have been the ulterior purpose, born of Satan himself, to deaden the sensibilities of the conquered race."[110] Western writers often commented on the hair style of Chinese men during the Qing, which involved shaving the hair above the forehead to enlarge the forehead and a long queue which was braided and hung down the back (see Figs. 5, 6, and 7). Foreigners ridiculed the queue, or regarded it as an abomination. Along with bound feet on women, long hair on men was regarded as a deformity and an outrage against nature. Victorians were undoubtedly aware of Paul's opinion on gendered coiffure: "Doth not even nature itself teach you, that, if a man have long hair, it is a shame unto him? But if a woman have long hair, it is a glory to her: for her hair is given her for a covering" (I Cor. 11:14–15). In Chapter 13 I will return to the queue, since some Western missionaries actually adopted it as a disguise.

For the missionaries, the real and imagined homosexuality of the Chinese suggested Biblical parallels, and homosexual desire was associated with idolatry. Gazing across a plain in Fujian, one unnamed missionary remarked that it was "like the plain of Sodom, well-watered everywhere, but the men wicked and sinners before the Lord exceedingly."[111] And missionaries referred to the New Testament, particularly to Paul's description of the heathen in Romans 1:24–28,which describes them as having unclean hearts and as practicing idolatry: they "worshipped and served the creature more than the Creator." But more to the point, they "dishonour their own bodies between themselves"; "even their women did change the natural use into that which is against nature"; and "the men, leaving the natural use of the women, burned in their lust one toward another."

The missionaries' indictment of homosexuality in China undoubtedly had a number of resonant associations for the readers of the *Church Missionary Gleaner*. In their imagination, the combination of homosexuality and idolatrous religious practice probably evoked Protestant stereotypes of Catholic priests and Anglo-Catholics as homosexuals. Among the evangelical Victorians who supported and read about missions to China, probably homosexuality evoked another set of associations: an urban and urbane refinement tainted by a sensual sin of the flesh that was epitomized by Oscar Wilde (1854–1900).

Metaphors of Mindlessness

Such metaphors should be seen in terms of Victorian and subsequent Western ideas about mind, body, and the relations of mind and body. Obviously, in the case of missionaries, but also pervasively throughout society, their strong sense of dualism was heavily informed by the Bible. Mind/body dualism was a strong tendency in Reformation theology, indicating strongly dualistic attitudes toward the body and mind, spirit and matter, and informing missionaries' views of ritual, and specifically, "idolatrous" obeisance to images and rulers. "Whether it be the minister at home or the Missionary abroad, the flesh must be crucified."[112] However, religious life did not by itself create mind/body dualism; it was also a product of the Industrial Revolution, radical changes in medicine, and colonial expansion. Neither was Victorian mind/body dualism ever unanimous or stable, but rather it was polyvocal and nuanced in terms of gender, class, occupation, location, and ethnicity.

Some of the metaphors cited in this chapter can clearly be read simply as metaphors, intended as such. We do not imagine anyone really thought that the Chinese literally never moved or that they were all drugged. There are testimonials to the erudition, courtesy, refinement, and common sense of many individual Chinese, though in some cases one wonders if the overall effect of praising one Chinese official was to treat him as the exception that proved the rule. What these metaphors have in common is the way in which each of them presents a basic contrast:

diseased	healthy
atrophied	dynamic
feeble	strong
stagnant	fresh
mentally deficient	mentally whole and healthy
in a stupor	alert, clearheaded, sober
drugged	sober, clearheaded
asleep	awake

dead	alive
childlike, childish	adult, mature
feminine	masculine

Other binaries of categorization could be added to this list. In the next chapter, for example, we consider:

sensual	cerebral
materialistic	spiritual
dense, homogenous	individual, individuated

Also, in different contexts, ancient/modern, past/future; bowing/not-bowing, and heathen/Christian. For the missionaries and for many in England, China's heathenism was at the heart of all its troubles, of all its decrepit technology, its ineffectual culture, and the dire misery of the population. These clusters of associations would sometimes have been obvious to readers in England, and sometimes they would have "resonated" in implicit or subconscious ways.

The column of positive qualities is, by implication, a kind of self-image for those who wrote and agreed with Church publications, a mirror for an identity drawn tightly around certain social and religious issues in China — against opium and foot-binding, and for promoting missions and ultimately, of course, converting the heathen. The missionaries were not the only sources of information about China available to people in England, but I believe they were extremely influential in molding popular Victorian attitudes to China. While some of the rhetoric softened in the early twentieth century, many of the basic images persisted — and still do. Within a framework of strong mind-body dualism, with the mind or soul considered superior, nineteenth- and twentieth-century missionaries construed the Chinese as distinctly lacking in the power of their minds and as naturally more focused on their bodies. That Victorian missionaries should perceive the Chinese as distinctly more bodily than the Victorians themselves is perhaps hardly surprising, given the latter's self-image as a more rational people and given the degree to which their judgments were confirmed by their rapid Imperial expansion and industrial-technological superiority. Furthermore, one may speculate that the supposed Chinese obsession with their bodies was in fact an effect of the missionaries' consciousness of their own bodies and those of the Chinese, a consciousness heightened by the discomforts of being foreign.

CHAPTER 4

Gods of the Lump

The Chinese are, in the metaphors of Victorian reportage, women, children, asleep, and so on. Bodily metaphors present a specific kind of body, as was seen in the previous chapter. Other stereotypical distinctions are more abstract but still based on homologies applied to the body of the Other. Victorian writers in China drew broad contrasts that were less literal and more existential. The Chinese/Western contrast was also mapped as sensual and cerebral, materialistic and spiritual, homogeneous and individual. Such contrasts were used as the basic binaries for commenting on Chinese ideas of heaven, on population density, immigration, crowd behavior, even on the faces glimpsed from a speeding sedan-chair. The Chinese practicing their religion were described, in particular, as crowds of materialists absorbed in the world of their bodily senses. Even the vigor of Chinese religious practices was explained as sensual, materialistic, and herd-like.

Belly Religion

There was a natural sense of urgency in mission work. Missionaries often felt frustrated by Chinese listeners who fixated on some trivial detail rather than attending to the missionaries' sermons, and some missionaries were particularly crestfallen when potential converts asked about money. Christiana Taylor relates how she told some listeners "how vain and useless their idols are," only to have one listener declare, "This doc-

trine is very good, but if we follow it how much money will you give us?"[1]
The speaker may have been joking, or very poor. The suspicion that converts might have ulterior motives led to an entire system of tests and
measures of sincerity designed to screen out "rice Christians." (see
Chapter 10). Evariste Huc wrote: "The Chinese is so completely absorbed
in temporal interests, in the *things that fall under his sense,* that *his whole life
is only materialism* put in action. Lucre is the sole object on which his eyes
are constantly fixed."[2] Llewelyn Lloyd phrased it still more bluntly:
"Money is the god of the Chinese."[3]

Thomas M'Clatchie reported a conversation in which a Chinese man
asked him if foreigners worshipped their ancestors, at which point
another Chinese man interjected: "Why should you imagine that foreigners worship ancestors? They have *plenty of money,* and therefore need
not do so!"[4] The image here is of a culture where religious devotion is
undertaken solely for the sake of money, where piety is always a bribe.
This view of Chinese religion as "materialism in action" was very common. The Chinese were thought to approach their deities as they
approached other people, such as diplomats or traders or gangsters: with
ritual politeness, followed by a bargaining process.

The supposed avarice of the "earthly minded" Chinese was inevitably
associated with the absence of any concern for or even conception of a
Christian heaven and its eternal reward: "Instead of God they have many
idols, to whom they make prayers and offerings, in the hope of obtain-
ing a larger share of this world's goods, which is all they care for. The
world is every thing to them, and they have no desire beyond it."[5] Mary
Darley wrote: "The Chinese Heaven's hall is no correct Nirvana, but a
place of bliss, where one may sit and do nothing for ever, feasting continually and living luxuriously, with money to spend in abundance."[6]

Since it is clear that a good number of the missionaries frequently visited Buddhist or Daoist temples, statements such as these certainly make
one wonder what they were thinking when they saw the temple's depictions of various hells and heavens. But even the finest temple can confirm
a judgment that its builders had no taste. If the unconverted Chinese were
seen as a people "whose God is their belly,"[7] perhaps the obese and grinning image of Budai (Maitreya) at the front of many Buddhist temples
(and seen today, also, in the lobbies of many Chinese restaurants) must
have confirmed this supposed idolization of gluttony. Given the pervasive
materialism, sensuality and body-centered mentality supposedly characterizing the culture as a whole and Chinese religion especially, the sensual
inactivity of the Chinese even accounted for their mass participation in

festivals: "With a people fond of sloth and addicted to sensuality; it is not to be wondered at that feast days should be popular."[8] Like the inhabitants of the well-watered plain of Sodom, the Chinese were imagined as captives to their senses, addicted to their sensuality, obsessed with their worldly desires. The heathen Chinese were "almost brought to the level of the brute creation."[9]

A Dense, Homogenous Mass

In some accounts — especially those by recent arrivals to China — the Chinese are represented as a dense mass of bodies, more or less homogenous. Here, the swarthy physicality of many Chinese bodies melded into one body, "the multitude composing 'the lump'."[10] S. Wells Williams remarked on the difference between sitting at home discoursing on the Chinese and actually being there amid the concreteness of bodies: "It is much easier loving the souls of the heathen in the abstract in America than it is here in the concrete, encompassed as they are with such dirty bodies, speaking forth their foul language and vile natures, and exhibiting every evidence of their depravity."[11]

Chinese cities were indeed more densely populated than European cities, a density remarked upon by many observers. Already in Victorian England there were explicit concerns with the increasing overcrowding in cities, and especially with the density of the working class. The linked associations of bad air, illness, venereal disease, social ills, mental weakness, poverty, drunkenness, incest, and immorality were well established in Victorian writing about the densest parts of London, Manchester, and other cities. In terms of city planning, Charles Dickens's characters had become almost synonymous with densely packed Victorian ghettoes. Yet the cities of China must surely have seemed even denser to the foreigners, who were so often the center of attention for crowds, or less often, the victims of mobs. The density of crowded bodies is experienced largely in the spatial imagination, and not having a feel for the native sense of space can make an outsider feel claustrophobic, or that others threaten to intrude on one's "personal space."

Whereas prolonged interaction inevitably helps one to perceive distinguishing features and individual personalities, newly arrived foreigners often have difficulty in distinguishing the individuality of natives. It is a significant step to attribute to the natives that lack of individuality, but one that is constantly taken. S. Wells Williams looked out at the Chinese on the streets from his hastening sedan-chair: "On the whole their putty-like faces have rather a dismal sameness, I must confess; for candor forces the confession that there really has not been much beauty distributed among the Chinese."[12] Chinese facial identity was thus to Williams a dull gray sameness.

Various reports in the *Gleaner* describe the excursions of missionaries and the large crowds that come to see them, like "swarms of bees." The insect metaphor appears in many forms — for example, when viewing the city walls of Beijing: "The labor of heaping up such mounds is comfortable to one's notions of Chinese ant-like toil."[13]

The great physical population-mass could, however, be mobilized by the Chinese curiosity about Westerners, and missionary accounts teem with anecdotes about them being suddenly surrounded by huge crowds. Visitors to China wrote of "the dull roar of the mass of the people,"[14] of the "uproarious babblement."[15] Missionaries and travelers were virtually unanimous in reporting the inordinate attention they attracted, which generally took the form of being stared at. Thomas Blakiston wrote: "We were most terribly mobbed. The people were not usually uncivil, but they wished to 'makey look see'."[16] Being stared at can be unnerving, especially when language or dialect differences make communication difficult. Some writers joked about themselves as animals in a zoo or members of a traveling peep-show. While on furlough in England, Mary Darley put a cheerful gloss on this useful (to the preacher) but often aggravating phenomenon: "'Did you have any difficulty in getting close to the people?' is a question asked us quite frequently. 'No, not at all! Our only difficulty was ever getting away from them.' 'Oh!'"[17]

In China, getting away from the natives was only possible for Europeans if they clustered in small enclaves, in the clubs of Hong Kong and Shanghai. However, the native gaze could be averted. Robert Fortune went to great lengths to disguise himself as a Chinese as he traveled in areas technically forbidden to Westerners. He shaved his head and wore Chinese clothing, though he admitted the illusion could not stand much scrutiny. Fortune preened over his transformation into a Chinese, and later, his Chinese servants had fun revealing the secret to others. Fortune said he "made a pretty good Chinaman,"[18] just as, earlier, Matteo Ricci had exclaimed: "I have become a Chinaman."[19]

The desirability of Western versus Chinese dress was a topic of debate among missionaries. Usually, those working in treaty ports or in Hong Kong retained their Western dress, while most of those working in the interior adopted Chinese dress for at least part of their day. Many took to wearing Chinese clothing, not only because it was so much easier and cheaper to acquire, but also to blend in. Some Chinese were more interested in the missionaries' clothes than in their words, so that Chinese clothing may have been less of a "distraction" from the missionaries' sermons. Sometimes, missionaries wanted to blend, "putty-like," into the "dismal sameness."

As we might expect from a pioneer culture, missionaries considered cities particularly resistant to the Gospel. The bodily density of the population in the cities seems to have played upon the imaginations of missionary writers. Picture the panorama of fertile chaos and sensual decay in the following description: "In every place we came to the buildings were in an extensive state of dilapidation, and a Chinese city looks to the eyes of a Western barbarian like an immense mass of ruins, covered with an unbounded population wallowing in filth and thoroughly enjoying it."[20]

We have already noted the fear that "a *million a month* are dying in China." The sheer number of Chinese has been a consistent motif in Western discourse, both in missionary writings and in the vision of an endless, untapped market evoked by *Oil for the Lamps of China* (the 1933 book by Alice Tisdale Hobars, and the widespread catchphrase). For missionaries, China was always a vast, untapped market. Perhaps, too, the multitude of the people overlapped with the multitude of the gods worshipped, as the sense of a vast population reinforced missionary horror of the amorphous polytheism of popular religion: "As you would expect, the fear of a *host of evil spirits* and the worship of a *crowd of idols* does not satisfy every Chinese girl."[21]

Religious practice was, according to the Rev. Dr. M. T. Yates, at the very root of the overcrowding. In 1877 he wrote that one effect of ancestral worship was "the aversion of the Chinese to colonize when they emigrate. They fear the consequences of neglecting the tombs of their ancestors. Consequently the country is kept overcrowded. The result, is squalidness, vice, thefts, piracy and insurrection. Hence they devour each other while chained to the tombs of their ancestors."[22]

As a justification or glorification of their own acquisitive migrations, empire builders often assert that the refusal to emigrate leads to unhealthy overpopulation. On the other hand, behind some of this image of dense population was a fear of Chinese immigration. We should recall that the 1882 Chinese Exclusion Act, the first explicitly racially-based anti-immigration law in America, was directed against "persons of Chinese or Mongoloid races."[23] There was also a series of riots against Chinese "coolies" in America — in Denver in 1880; Rock Springs, Wyoming, in

1885; Snake River, Oregon, in 1887, and many others locations. Some missionaries, such as S. Wells Williams, tried to defend the Chinese against such laws. Some argued that the Chinese would be easier to convert to Christianity once they were in America and/or speaking English. But John MacGowan wrote in 1907: "What the West has to fear is not the warlike spirit of the Chinese, which has never been a very important factor in their past history, but their numbers. They are a people that multiply rapidly" (and hence tend to migrate). Furthermore, MacGowan wrote: "These, as far as the native populations have been concerned, have rarely been desirable immigrants, but this is especially the case with the great nations of the West. The Chinese are a strong race, and can live in comfort, and even luxury, on incomes that would mean starvation to American or Australian workmen. The battle of the future with the Yellow race will not be fought on any battlefield, but in the labour markets of the nations that they would invade."[24]

The metaphors of mindlessness that I previously discussed permeate much of the missionary reportage, but there was also praise for Chinese minds, for their industrious ingenuity, moments of great zeal, and the high status which they placed on education. Thomas M'Clatchie remarked: "The Chinese are, without doubt, a reading and a thinking people."[25] Usually, though, there are more or less nuanced qualifiers in the words of praise; good attributes are mentioned only to make a strong contrast. For example: "The present [1848] state of China is an awful illustration of that general truth, that the highest state of intellectual refinement is compatible with the lowest condition of spiritual ignorance and moral degradation."[26] Chinese spirituality may have been low, but its "intellectual refinement" was high. Eugene Stock wrote: "The Chinaman, with all his shrewdness and ability, is as much a slave to his superstitions as the most degraded negro."[27] The Imperial system of education and the widespread respect for education received mixed reviews. Some regarded Chinese education as admirable, but for others it stood for useless erudition. Criticizing what he saw as the softening of English education and trends toward book-learning, the moralist Samuel Smiles predicted: "We may, before long, be almost as highly educated as the Chinese, and with quite as impotent a result."[28] As we will see in chapter 5, Chinese literature as a whole was sometimes dismissed as a white elephant. (The white elephant was another Victorian symbol of Asia: a burdensome and useless subject of great honor, in this case from a Siamese practice.) On the other hand, at least the educational system meant that a good number of Chinese could read religious tracts and the Bible.

Just as the Chinese acquisition of knowledge was impressive but also a curse, so their native intelligence was first acknowledged and then immediately suspect. Was that intelligence — or cunning? Evariste Huc remarked on "the pallid, cunning-looking faces of the civilized Chinese."[29] In some of the accounts of Chinese business practices, especially in the diaspora, one can see suggestive parallels between two sets of stereotypes: the clever Chinese and the clever Jew. Did this praise for Chinese cleverness (often expressed in negative terms) have anti-Semitism as a precedent? The Chinese have been called the "Jews of the East," a phrase which usually implies a diasporic community of adept merchants, but in Protestant missionary writing also implied ritualism and a parallel to the Jews' rejection of Jesus as the messiah. S. Wells Williams wrote of "the literati who are just as inimical to us as the Scribes and Pharisees were against new truths brought in to supplant what their position depended on."[30]

Given the American popular sentiment against "coolie" labor, John MacGowan's positive assessment of Chinese fortitude and hard work was hardly unqualified praise. Some assessments of Chinese physical vigor were straightforward: "Liveliness is a prominent characteristic of the Chinese,"[31] and, "Energy of mind and body is a national characteristic."[32] These positive assessments of Chinese physical vigor were in the minority, but they increased as more converts were made, as more YMCAs and Christian schools were established, and as more Chinese assumed leadership positions in the Church. There are also many words of praise for Chinese practical ingenuity and thrift. Many publications printed pictures such as a peddler's wheelbarrow, illustrations of farming techniques, or of two Chinese methods for carrying tea-boxes. Chinese handicrafts in the Great Missionary Exhibition of 1909 were praised as "charming" by the *Church Missionary Gleaner* and by the ladies from Nottingham who sold them. But for at least some Americans, the commendable industriousness of the Chinese was rendered threatening by the sheer numbers of the Chinese population.

After the fall of the Qing dynasty, even some religious rituals won praise, if only for the expenses incurred, which implied the idolaters' great dedication to their gods. In contemplating Chinese religious zeal, British Protestants may have seen "an example of earnestness set us by the heathen Chinese, as we call them." So Thomas Blakiston wrote in 1862, further adding: "We may be inclined to laugh at and condemn this idolatrous worship, but after all there is something *real* about this style of worship. Where in Protestant countries do we find people going to such an expense as is entailed by the number of candles, incense-sticks, and paper consumed every evening?"[33]

It might have been idolatry, but at least the Chinese spent a lot of time, energy, and money on it, which was better than indifference. After the influx of certain Western ideas (Marxism, Bertrand Russell), and during the modernist anti-superstition movements, some writers became almost nostalgic about good old wholehearted idolatry: at least it was some kind of sincere striving after God, however misplaced. In 1929 Bishop Sing Tsae-seng lamented that in the old days, "at least the people did reverence and fear the idols; now they reverence neither idols nor the true God, and fear nothing and no one, and there is worse chaos than before, and there is no peace anywhere."[34]

Missionaries, focusing on the bodiful other, could not see, did not recognize, or did not entirely credit the cerebral or spiritual in Chinese culture. The best way to "see" these invisible qualities was through language, by investigating the highest cultural products — philosophy, literature, and scripture. Ironically, the logocentric classicism of such investigations tended to create a sense of the ideal past and a degenerated present. But language itself was also a barrier, more so during the earliest (and most formative) period of a missionary's stay in China. In the next chapter we will see how, in some cases, the Chinese language was seen as an obstacle — due to the supposed inherent defects of the language. China Coast Pidgin was also degraded as defective, even though such Chinese speech-acts were the most directly intelligible to the newly arrived Briton.

CHAPTER 5

The Lexicon of Babel

The Great Wall of Language

Along with Greek (as in "It's all Greek to me"), the Chinese language was seen and heard as particularly strange and became a quintessential unknown language. China typified Otherness with respect to its language. China appeared in Victorian writing as a trope of inversion, as in this exclamation of 1913:

What a funny country it is! The people seem to do everything upside down. When they write they begin at the wrong end of the paper, and when they read a book they begin at the end and read backwards. When they want to say "How do you do?" they shake their own hands instead of yours. They keep their hats on in company, instead of taking them off, and they mount a horse from its right instead of its left side. They begin dinner with dessert and end with soup. They drink their wine hot instead of cold, and when the schoolboys are saying their lessons, they turn their backs to the schoolmaster instead of their faces. In fact we really feel we have come to Topsy-Turvy Land.[1]

Amid these bodily inversions of ritual behavior, clothing, horse-riding, eating, and classroom arrangement, the language itself was back-to-front. Popularly, the Chinese language came to signify a quintessential "topsy-turvy" Otherness from Western languages. It was (apparently) non-phonetic in nature, it moved from right to left in columns, and from "the end . . . backwards" in books.

The Chinese language as a system of communication, both as written and spoken, was considered defective, cumbersome, and an obstacle to the good. In this chapter I examine aspects of the missionaries' learning process, their views of the Chinese language, problems with translation into Chinese, and (for many visitors) the one alternative in practice: Pidgin English.

The Chinese language was also notoriously intractable for the processes of translation. More than one commentator felt that the language was incapable of communicating Western science: "Translations into Chinese of scientific works . . . are, for the present, either impossibilities or monstrosities. The Chinese language being yet in a state of vagueness, makes it impossible to enter into scientific details with sufficient exactness to convey definite notions. A term-question-dragon is lurking."[2] According to S. Wells Williams, the language was itself a curse upon the Chinese: "The Chinese are greatly to be pitied, among other misfortunes, in having such a miserable language through which to obtain ideas and knowledge of foreign countries."[3] The Chinese language was thought of as a barrier to Western knowledge, a barrier but also regrettably the only choice of mediation. Others felt that teaching converts English (not Hebrew or Greek, of course) was a better way to convince them of the Bible's truth than attempting further translations. In this view, translations were so inevitably bound to produce bad Chinese — or to be fundamentally unfaithful to the original — that the enterprise of translation should be rejected. Such a rejection was never a majority view, however. Most missionaries enthusiastically supported translation work.

Nonetheless, the view of Chinese as a barrier was common. During an 1897 bicycle ride through China, British journalist John Foster Fraser and his companions experienced great frustration in their amateur attempts to speak Chinese. Fraser was strictly a tourist in China, and a hostile one at that, but he wrote: "The Chinese spoken by the Chinese was different from the Chinese spoken by three enlightened Britishers, and it was provoking to find how few Chinamen knew their own language."[4]

Fraser excused Chinese illiteracy as a quite reasonable response to an intractable language: "The worst wish you can wish a Chinaman is that he be obliged to learn his own language. In fact, nobody, since the time of Hwangti, the gentleman who invented Chinese writing, five thousand years ago, has known it properly."[5] Some kind of "illiteracy" was inevitable, given the nature of the language as conceived by Fraser, in which only its founding "inventor" knew it wholly. Of course, there are vastly more characters than even an educated person can learn; but this is true of any written language and has nothing to do with "knowing" a language properly. Other observers made similar remarks, and John Francis

Davis had long before taken the time to point out the fallacy: "To assert that there are so many thousand characters in the language, is very much the same thing as to say that there are so many thousand words in Johnson's Dictionary; nor is a knowledge of the *whole* at all more necessary for every practical purpose, than it is to get all Johnson's Dictionary by heart, in order to read and converse in English."[6] Despite such sober opinions, the end result, according to many works on China, was that the Chinese didn't even know their own language — they had concocted a language so excessively complex that it stumped not only foreigners but the Chinese themselves.

In this case, Fraser's ethnocentric chauvinism was delivered with wry irony and a wink to his own culture. But many nineteenth-century visitors to China were less ironic. Though we should take Fraser's remark as humor, it needs to be seen within a larger pattern of attributing *meaninglessness* to Chinese voices — not only in terms of the difficulty of deciphering their language, but also in their inability even to know their own language, which thus became mere noise. We have already seen how a dualistic mind/body logic represented the Chinese as voiceless or with impaired or underdeveloped speech (asleep, drugged, comatose, mentally deficient, childish, or dead); nonetheless, it was obvious that the Chinese *did* speak and furthermore that they had produced written works for three millennia or more. The presence of a vast and ancient literature in continuous use for so long made it impossible for Westerners to dismiss the Chinese so easily, as they had dismissed so many other nonliterate (noninscribing) cultures elsewhere in the colonial world.

Surely, language would seem to be *nothing but* meaning, the primary domain of rationality, and therefore carrying more weight among missionaries who were so firmly logocentric in their assumptions about "religion" and "culture." But some nineteenth-century reportage on China and Chinese religion presented at least some of the Chinese language as noise. This attribution of meaninglessness to the Chinese language closely paralleled representations of Chinese religion, ritual, theater, and music as empty and meaningless. Such representations may be seen in the context of a distinctively Protestant view of ritual, but they also signify a deeper and more fundamental dynamic of intercultural contact.

In contrast to many Westerners in China, one of the distinguishing marks of missionaries as a group was their facility with local dialects. What was the missionary experience of learning Chinese? The first thing most missionaries had to do upon arrival in China was learn spoken and written Chinese. Until they acquired some fluency, their practical frustrations (buying food, dealing with public problems) were compounded by the frustration of their evangelical project. William Aitchison noted the great masses of population in China and his galling inability to speak Chinese: "It is painful to mingle daily in these crowds of perishing men, and yet be speechless."[7] Many missionaries complained of the initial struggle with the language: the tones, the strain upon one's memory involved in reading, and the pronunciation of certain sounds not found in European languages. The preface to "The Rev. 'O Kwong-Yiao's Report on Z-Ky'i" begins with a joke about pronouncing Chinese place-names: in pronouncing a certain place-name, a missionary who knew Chinese "uttered a sound very much like a sneeze."[8]

The months and years of this learning process culminated in "solo" preaching directly to Chinese, and in subsequent worship, administration, and work as an interpreter. Some missionaries went on to translate Chinese texts: poems, Imperial edicts, Buddhist tracts, public placards, and historical inscriptions. Some of the great founding Western Sinologists were missionaries, and many more were the children of missionaries in China. Yet their earliest experiences of Chinese must surely have been difficult and frustrating, even for all the university graduates among them. A large number of the CMS missionaries were graduates of Oxford, Cambridge, Dublin, or Trinity College. Undoubtedly, they would have learned some French, German, Latin, and New Testament or Classical Greek. Certainly, they would all have had experience and probably some success in acquiring fluency in at least one foreign language. As different as those Western languages are from each other, in the nineteenth century the acquisition of Chinese must have felt like a quantum leap into a radically different world, from which perspective French and English seemed merely like two dialects of the same language. Most would probably have agreed with the Jesuit missionary Nicholas Trigault, who wrote: "I would venture to say that no other language is as difficult for a foreigner to learn as the Chinese."[9]

Not all of the Old China Hands agreed with these evaluations. John Francis Davis commented: "The rumoured difficulties attendant on the acquisition of Chinese, from the great number and variety of the characters, are the mere exaggerations of ignorance, and so far mischievous as they are calculated to deter many from the pursuit, whose business takes them to the country, and would no doubt be greatly promoted by some practical acquaintance with its language."[10] The notion that Chinese was hopelessly difficult to even attempt was for Davis a rumor, exaggeration, and mischief. He did not say it was easy, but he recognized that the reputation of Chinese as superlatively difficult was a detrimental stereotype and a self-fulfilling prophecy.

Still, at least initially, even basic language training must have been overwhelming. Chauncey Goodrich complained of a "hopeless variety" of culture and dialects: "In respect to the single subject of dialect, how suggestive is it of the tower of Babel!"[11] A telling analogy. In Genesis, God saw the great tower built by the monolingual people and, apparently concerned that "this is only the beginning of what they will do; and nothing that they propose to do will now be impossible for them" (Gen. 11:6), went to "confuse their language, that they may not understand one another's speech" (Gen. 11:7). Although in this case linguistic confusion was an act of God, the event came to be associated with the hubris of mere mortals, and the tower with the resulting chaos of unintelligible speech. Incomprehensibility in human communication was taken as divine punishment for sinful pride. In a number of other pronouncements, Chinese was characterized not just as the language of Babel, but as actually satanic. Another missionary, a Mr. Inslee, "maintained that the study of the written language was a snare of the devil to keep missionaries from learning the spoken dialect."[12] Samuel Woodbridge commented on the problems of locating a church on a hilltop, "above the pestilent miasms and the stench of a Chinese city with all its disease-spreading flies, mosquitoes, centipedes, and other unspeakable crawlers. There was an occasional breeze to fan the fevers away and cool the tired heads oftimes confused with *bewildering Chinese characters and outlandish idiom, invented by the devil,* it was thought, to keep the Gospel out of China."[13] Against a backdrop of pestilence, fever, bad smells, and "unspeakable" insects, the language appeared as a perverse and punishing obstacle to righteous service.

Directing porters, buying potatoes, and, in fact, most mundane transactions required only enough mastery to do the immediate job. However, because the semantic precision of their message was so important to the missionaries, the "topsy-turvy," "vague," or "diabolic" nature of Chinese made them fear that translation would produce "monsters" from the very words of the Gospels . The need to pin down the meanings of words, to render Chinese as free from ambiguity as possible, was most keenly felt in the act of communication at the very core of the whole mission: preaching the Gospel. A sense of the history of Christendom, with its many factions and schisms, underscored the importance of the creed — the definitive formulation of doctrinal truth — and the dangers of stray words, latent heresies veiled by polysemy, and unforeseen vernacular connotations.

Hence, translation was a major problem for evangelists. Chinese seemed to lack obvious translations of certain words — "God," for example. A report in the *Church Missionary Gleaner* remarked: "There is no word in their language which expresses the same with our word 'God.'"[14] Notwithstanding this view of Chinese as a language without "God," W. H. Medhurst and James Legge proposed the terms "Shangdi" or "Di" as the most appropriate translations for "God," and most English missionaries went along with that. American missionaries tended to agree with E. C. Bridgeman and W. J. Boone in using the term "Shen." Naturally, all the Protestants avoided the standard Catholic translation, "Tianzhu."

Such issues had plagued the Jesuits centuries earlier, and, for that matter, the Buddhists, even earlier. Faced with Sanskrit words for concepts quite new to Chinese philosophy at the time, Buddhists in many cases had given up on translation and had settled for the transliteration of such difficult terms as "nirvana" (in modern Mandarin, *niepan*), Buddha (Fotuo, or Fota), and "prajna-paramita" (*boluo boluomituo*). Some proper nouns were transliterated — "Amitabha" into "Amituo," for example — but others were translated — "Avalokitesvara" into "Guanshiyin," for example. (Further confounding the modern reader, the Protestant missionaries usually worked with Southern or coastal dialects, so that modern Mandarin often renders these terms quite remote from their English sounds: Christ becomes "Jidu," Luke "Lujia," and Israel "Yiselie.")

The absence of clear equivalents for key religious terms was more than just a practical consideration, since language was widely thought to be an expression of racial or cultural consciousness, "the revelation of the national mind."[15] The lack of a word in a language implied the lack of any such thought, and the impossibility of such a thought in the minds of those who had been shaped by that language: "Chinese language can awaken only Chinese thoughts in Chinese minds not yet acquainted with foreign objects."[16]

Chinese literature was also regarded as a distasteful mess or a barren wasteland. Anglican missionary Maud Bettersby commented upon the antiquity of classical Chinese discourse, even noting some ethical proverbs that were similar to certain verses in the Old Testament: "But how dead and barren all this literature is! How unsatisfying to any awakened soul!"[17] The sheer volume of literary production could not prove its meaningfulness. Archibald Colquhoun remarked on "the stupendous mass of Chinese literature (which, as a monument of human toil has been, not inaptly, compared to their Great Wall, the one carrying no real useful knowledge and the other no protection)."[18] All the books of China, "carrying no real useful knowledge," were merely white elephants.

Eventually, Chinese literature came to be more highly regarded, as missionaries and the children of missionaries set about the tasks of translation. Writing before 1840, John Francis Davis felt that Chinese literature had been judged harshly, but he also had critical words about the naiveté of some translators, whom he identified as missionaries:

> Of some of the missionary translations, especially those of our own country, it may be observed, that if there is much that is obscure or worthless in the original works, this has been rendered still worse by the wretched attempt to render word for word, thus exhibiting the whole in a jargon which has not inaptly been distinguished as "missionary English." This of course must be anything but a *faithful* picture of the originals, which, with all their defects in point of matter, are well known to be, in respect to manner and style, the models of the language in which they were composed. [19]

Unfortunately, overly literalistic translation has been pervasive, leading to the impression that the Chinese speak a baby-talk even in their own native tongue. Thus, E. C. Bridgman translated the Chinese questions of his Chinese visitors: "'What for you come to China' — 'how old you have' — 'you have father-mother' and so on."[20] The lack of a Chinese equivalent for the definite and indefinite articles ("the" and "a"), for example, is often represented by their absence in English translations, despite the fact that by so doing, a perfectly refined Chinese sentence becomes an incorrect English one. In popular American media, this clipped speech was associated with characters such as A-Sin and Charlie Chan.

As mentioned earlier, scientific terminology was also considered a problem, and perhaps an insurmountable one. An 1886 issue of the *Journal of the China Branch of the Royal Asiatic Society* debated "The Advisability, or the Reverse, of Endearvouring to Convey Western Knowledge to the Chinese Through the Medium of their Own Language." The contributors had mixed opinions. Although few held the extreme opinion that Chinese could not ever express the new, Western ideas, it is interesting that the issue was debated at all. The most frequent complaints among the contributors were the perceived inherent vagueness of Chinese and the laborious or obfuscating methods of acquiring new vocabulary. Translations of Western scientific works were considered to have been monstrosities.

The strong emphasis on translating the Bible into the vernacular was a great part of Protestant identity and was often contrasted to the monopoly of Latin during the "Dark Ages." Nonetheless, translating hymns and Biblical verses into Chinese presented aesthetic problems. Robert Henry Cobbold wrote: "Chinese turned into English sounds generally very poor stuff to us, and so does English turned into Chinese sound very poor to them. Our beautiful communion service seems to lose *so* much of its beauty when we read it in the strange tongue of this people. But after all it is not the words nor the form, but the *heart* that is required."[21]

This last line succinctly recapitulates one of the basic messages of the Reformation (as Protestants recalled it), that the "heart" could be turned to God through the understandable vernacular Bible and liturgy, thereby necessitating a rejection of the (mere) "words" of Latin, and of the (mere) "form" of ritual and of the ritualistic uses of language. Cobbold ignored his feeling that the "strange tongue" turned their beautiful Protestant liturgy into "poor stuff" and stayed true to his Protestant emphasis on the vernacular.

The rate of illiteracy in late Qing China was still high, certainly among the social classes most missionaries evangelized. Missionaries often encountered Chinese who could not read, but who still desired the texts being handed out, either to sell them (to re-use the paper) or for talismanic use. The Protestant emphasis on "getting the word out" inevitably led to giving such texts to illiterates, but the missionaries' sense of the overwhelming population yet "untouched," together with their faith in the miraculous power of the Word, justified a degree of wastefulness in their pamphleteering. There were jokes about Protestant missionaries "evangelizing" China merely by prudently dumping crates of Bibles on beaches and then sailing away. Robert Morrison, banned from setting foot in China, threw chests of Bibles into the sea so that they would wash ashore. The Catholic Evariste Huc wrote: "The Methodist ministers, who lie in ambush in all the five ports open to Europeans, having remarked that the prodigious quantity of Bibles furtively scattered along the shores of the Empire have not proved remarkably efficacious in working the conversion of the Chinese, have at last given up this harmless and useless system of Propogandism."[22] Perhaps the Methodists' Bibles were talismans, too.

Pidgin, Baby Talk, and Foreigner Talk

If Chinese was so difficult to learn, many Westerners in China had another medium of communication: English — of a kind, but this alternative was limited, disreputable, and marginalized. Throughout the world, whenever trade has established certain conditions of interaction among multiple languages, there have been small groups of people, in ports and along caravan routes, who have acquired enough knowledge of another language to muddle through basic transactions. Such improvisations seem to be neither one language nor the other; they are ephemeral and unworthy of recording, or are only recorded as a curiosity or amusement, perceived as defective speech, irrespective of whatever truth might be communicated. Chinese Pidgin English (CPE), also known as China Coast Pidgin, is one of the earliest documented pidgins. It developed in the eighteenth century around Canton and spread along the coast during the nineteenth century. The use of this pidgin rapidly increased after Hong Kong was established and the treaty ports were opened in 1842, and also in the context of Chinese immigration to California and Australia. In fact, the very term "pidgin" probably derives from the Chinese Pidgin English term for "business." Some influences can be traced from an earlier Portuguese pidgin based in Macau, but then all pidgins draw eclectically from many sources. CPE had a limited lexicon of perhaps around 750 words, including the well-known *chop-chop* (quickly), *chin-chin* (to pay respects), and the use of *pisi* (piece) as a count-word replacing the Chinese *ge, kuai,* and so on. One of the earliest recorded examples of the use of CPE is, as it happens, on the subject of religious difference: "He no cari Chinaman's Joss, hap oter Joss" (He does not worship a Chinese god, he has another god).[23] "Joss" derived from the Portuguese *deus,* hence josshouse (temple), joss-stick (incense stick), and joss-pidgin (deus-business, or religion).

Various sea-shanties, plays, travelogues, and other texts represented pidgins to the West, but Charles G. Leland probably did the most to establish China Coast Pidgin in the Victorian imagination. His *Pidgin-English Sing-Song: Or, Songs and Stories in the China-English Dialect* (1876), popularized and reinforced Western perceptions of this pidgin and was accepted as authoritative by linguists until the 1980s.[24] It should be said, however, that Leland never went to China, and he wrote his book, which assembled twenty-two poems and twelve short prose pieces, prefaced by an introduction, based upon secondhand sources..

One of the poems Leland reproduced, "Mary Coe," described a Joss-pidgin-man (cleric) named Coe whose wife Mary, from Boston, spends her time talking with the cook and servants, in the process picking up pidgin to the point of not being able to speak English any more. A visitor comes and asks,

> He say, "Dear child, may I inquire
> Which form of faith you most admire?"
> .   .   .   .
> [Mary replies:] "My like Chinee Joss-pidgin best;
> My love Kwan-Yin wit'h chilo neat,
> An' Joss-stick smellum muchee sweet."[25]

(Paraphrase: "I like Chinese religion best/I love Guanyin with the beautiful child,/And the incense sticks smell very sweet.") Note that the fiction of accuracy here is undermined by the fact that the visitor's question is in correct Victorian English, despite the fact that the entire poem supposedly represents a Chinese voice speaking CPE. Though humorous, the poem shows a colonizers' fears of "going native" — in this case, a Western woman dissolves into the semi-gibberish of a heathen cult. Many of the poems conclude with a "Moral-pidgin." In this case:

> If Boston girley be let go,
> She sartin sure to b'lieve in Fo [Buddha];
> An' he nex' piecee in he plan,
> Is to lun lound an' act like man.[26]

(Paraphrase: "If Western women are not controlled, they will believe in Buddha; and then women will behave like men.") Leland describes the "low" origins of pidgin as the expedient vocabulary of servants incapable of pronouncing English properly, who thus speak according to Chinese grammar, and notably, Mary spent all her time with servants.

Of all the Western languages, English was supposed to be particularly difficult for Chinese to speak. However, Leland argues that "as Chinese learn a Latin tongue more easily than pure English, it is probable that had it not been for the Pidgin jargon, a corrupt Portuguese would have formed the popular medium of communication between foreigners and natives in China."[27] Why did Leland think the Chinese could pick up a "Latin" tongue more easily than "pure English"? Perhaps this assumption reveals an implicit association of Portuguese Catholics and Chinese? Just as missionaries felt that the Chinese could accept Catholicism more easily because of its similarity to their own native religion, perhaps the implication here is that "Latin" languages are somehow closer to Chinese. But it is difficult to conclude anything decisive from this remark.

Preparing the reader for the inevitable struggle of making sense out of these samples of Chinese speech, Leland drew two telling analogies, explaining that there were some foreign words in the verses, but that "what remains can present no difficulty to anyone who can understand negro minstrelsy or baby talk."[28] Pidgin has often been mixed up with baby talk, and with what is known in linguistics as foreigner talk. "Foreigner talk" refers to the speech of foreigners who simplify their own language and import fragments of the local language in an attempt to be understood; it often involves loud repetition and the loss of prepositions, tenses, and plurals. In the early stages of intercultural communication, before pidgins had "solidified" into set patterns, foreigner talk and pidgins were relatively indistinguishable.[29] Though it is easy to confuse the two, foreigner talk is distinct from pidgin in a variety of ways: pidgin is a relatively consistent language, spoken as a non-native language, whereas foreigner talk is an improvised and ad hoc simplification of a native language. Foreigner talk is closer to baby talk than to pidgin. Pidgins, creoles, baby talk, and foreigner talk are quite distinct as spoken but nonetheless tend to be perceived as similar by those adult native speakers who are not fluent in pidgin.

In fact, foreigner talk is grammatically inconsistent. Foreigners trying to get their meaning across to Chinese who (the foreigner hopes) understand a little English will tend to imitate baby talk, drawing on their own (largely imagined) childhood speech and/or experience talking with babies (sometimes known as goo-goo-talk, confusing the speech *of* infants with speech *to* infants). Goo-goo-talk is not only for babies; it is also for lovers. Charles Ferguson notes that a child grows up and out of baby talk, but that the adult "retains some competence in baby talk for use in talking with young children and in such displaced functions as talking to a pet or with a lover."[30] There is a strange associative commonality in speech to foreigners, infants, animals, and lovers.

According to a Victorian specialist on Chinese dialects, E. H. Parker, foreigners in China could not speak Chinese as well as they thought they could and tended to be dismissive of efforts to learn it properly. If they can speak a bit of *guanhua* (standard or official Chinese), they "at once assume that they can speak the language perfectly correctly, and that all painstaking and accurate study is a mistake, or at least a waste of time. The fact that, even amongst Chinese scholars [i.e., Western scholars of Chinese] of reputation, men can be found who declare the tones to be a myth, the aspirates to be useless; and so on, is sufficient of itself to prove that the general knowledge of colloquial Chinese is as yet very superficial."[31]

Hence, in addition to "Chinese Pidgin English," we might speak of "English Pidgin Chinese," the "rude," "distorted," and "horrible" sounds of Westerners speaking Chinese. But "English Pidgin Chinese" did not really exist: it is unlikely that two Europeans (a German and an Italian, say) would speak their simplified Chinese to each other, though they might speak French or English. Though many foreigners speaking foreigner talk thought they were speaking pidgin, CPE as a language was spoken primarily among Chinese of different dialects. Hence, "instances occasionally occur in which Chinese from different districts, speaking very different dialects, have recourse to 'Pidgin' as a medium of conversation."[32] Such instances may have been more frequent than Leland knew.

More specifically, according to the linguist David Decamp,

> the occasion which necessitates the use of the interlingual pidgin is the bringing together of different Chinese speakers under the domination of English speakers. . . . The pidgin will contain a great deal of English vocabulary. Rarely does the Englishman or American take the time and effort to learn pidgin as he would have to learn any foreign language. Though he may claim to speak pidgin, it is more likely only a baby-talk English larded with bits of Chinese and of real pidgin. The speakers of genuine pidgin English, the Chinese, treat this improvised interlingua with contempt. If the Englishman or American overhears his servants speaking pidgin English to each other, he will probably not recognize it and assume that they are speaking Chinese.[33]

Among native English speakers, too, contempt for pidgin has always been widespread. There is a long history, expressed in pejorative attitudes toward "barbarous," "debased" speech, or "the barbarous lingo," of viewing pidgins and creoles as barriers to communication.[34] Pidgin was considered a second-best expedient spoken by a populace unwilling or unable to learn the "pure" correct English. Though he argued that Pidgin-English was basically Chinese, in the same book Leland also defined it as "English as imperfectly spoken by Chinese,"[35] and he emphasized the difficulty the Chinese had in pronouncing English. Modern scholars of pidgins have noted the pejorative terms for pidgins, as corrupt or "broken English," and attribute this contempt in part to the heritage of the Western European study of Latin and the position of Latin as a model for all language-learning, which is to say, true languages are rule-based. Only recently, since the 1950s, have there been studies of "language that appears to lack order: the speech of very young children, foreigners, aphasics, and linguistically heterogeneous communities."[36] Academic linguists have given serious treatment to pidgins, but popularly they remain the stuff of ridicule and stereotype, cause for laughter but with a darker aspect, since what is perceived as "vile gibberish" may be associated with (popularly imagined) backward, uncivilized, or even subhuman peoples.

In a moment of whimsy, Thomas Blakiston had the porpoises near Hong Kong speak "Canton English."[37]

Some Western versions of CPE were reproduced and brought to popular attention, for example, in Bret Harte and Mark Twain's *A Sin,* or in the stories of Charlie Chan, Fu Manchu, and in other Western fantasies of China. In Earl Derr Biggers' books, Charlie Chan's grammar is good, if not impeccable, but in the films, Chan's grammar suffered: "Mind like parachute — only function when open!" (*Charlie Chan at the Circus,* 1936). Setting aside the grammar, some of Chan's fortune-cookie pronouncements, known in fan circles as Chanisms, are so outlandish that they suggest a kind of (imagined) "pidgin rationality": "Can cut off monkey's tail, but he is still monkey" (*The Black Camel,* 1931).

Because CPE derived its vocabulary from English, it was often taken as bad English. We would not call CPE good English, but neither was it bad English. The ambiguities of CPE meant that many Westerners had the subjective experience of hearing degenerate, primitive, or childish speech from the mouths of some adult Chinese. A good deal of Western experience with Chinese communication involved hearing "defective" language, whether because Chinese was itself thought to be impenetrable, or because CPE was taken as defective speech.

Cat Music

Just as some Chinese speech was imagined as a sing-song of debased English and Chinese writing was seen as a hopeless tangle, so, too, Chinese music was often regarded as debased, defective, or mere noise. Western classical music was seen as a mark of high civilization in Europe, but by contrast, David Abeel remarked: "There is very little musical talent or taste in the nation," and "The musicians are not unfrequently lads, who appear in a great measure to consult their own childish whims, in the manner and pauses of their performances. In the music which is generally heard at their processions, a person is strongly inclined to doubt, whether any thing beyond mere noise is intended."[38]

Rather than seek any deeper explanation, Abeel perceived Chinese music as lacking intention, structure, talent, and meaning. A similar note runs through many remarks on religious music. In 1948 Sae Gaussen described how, as icons are paraded through the streets, "every house has lanterns hung out and lets off crackers and fireworks to honour the hideous things as they pass, while many musical (?) instruments accompany them."[39] Note the parenthetical question mark, indicating a doubt about the sound's status as music. Harry Franck reported on a procession going to dedicate a temple: "At length the auditory tortures of Chinese 'music' were wafted more and more painfully to our ears as our animals brought us nearer the focal uproar."[40] Note the inverted commas.

We have just seen Chinese music described as childish. Other Victorian commentators described Chinese music as animalistic. A Chinese band, for example, produced "an infernal din of the most excruciating sounds that it had ever been my misfortune to hear. I found myself able at last to appreciate the feelings of the Western visitor who complained that her backyard in Shanghai was infested with both cats and Chinese musicians."[41] Bruno Hagspeil also makes a reference to "cat music."[42]

Robert Fortune, visiting a Chinese opera, reacted with the characteristic distaste most Westerners felt for Chinese theater and music. But for a moment, when the language paused, Fortune perked up: "The feats of tumbling which were now and then performed were extremely dexterous and clever, and attracted our notice more than anything else, probably because they were best understood."[43] Whereas the language and music were distracting noises to Fortune, he felt that the bodily displays (stylized battle scenes, probably) were worthy of his attention because he could "understand" them. This is a good example of the immediate perceivability of the body over language, though we do not need to accept that Fortune truly "understood" what he saw any more than he understood what he heard. But when the dexterous tumbling ended and words returned to the stage, Fortune probably wanted to "tune out." A good deal of foreigners' experience with Chinese theater probably included long stretches of boredom (because it was so hard to follow the dialogue) punctuated by brief periods of focus on the actors' bodies.

The missionaries themselves, and the long, involved process of their communication with the churches and living rooms of England, created gibberish out of Chinese, in a very literal sense. Readers in England saw samples of the Chinese script in various engraved illustrations, and these characters no doubt looked to them like a set of well-ordered chicken scratches. The Chinese script, already symbolic of the topsy-turvy — "When they write they begin at the wrong end of the paper" — was further convoluted by the mechanisms of representation. An 1856 illustration, "Interior of the Episcopal Church, at Ningpo," shows a British-looking church interior with a white priest ministering the Eucharist and nine Chinese kneeling in a semicircle (Fig. 5). On each side are Chinese signs, rendered into garbled unreadability by the artist. The accompanying arti-

FIGURE 5. "Interior of the Episcopal Church, at Ningpo." *Church Missionary Gleaner*, June 1856, opposite 73.

cle translates the inscriptions, but obviously not from the engraving itself.[44] Numerous transformative processes mediated the real object (in China) and the object that the British reader's eye. An image of, say, inscriptions on the wall of a Chinese Christian church appearing in a London publication inevitably suffered from errors and ignorance in the process of communication and reproduction. In books and journals about China, there are many engravings where Chinese characters end up upside-down, or garbled and unreadable, or reproduced as pseudo-Chinese to the West. English artists with no knowledge of writing Chinese must surely have had to improvise "Chinese" script, so that Chinese appeared as a happy jumble of odd angles with the characteristic (stereotypical) wedge-shaped stroke. Presumably, there were missionaries and others who recognized that the language had been rendered illegible. In fact, missionaries on furlough or in retirement often served as advisors to publications and exhibitions. Probably, many more errors would have remained uncorrected if they had not been present.

To almost all readers in England, the fact that Chinese was garbled or upside-down made no difference at all. To those completely untrained in Chinese, even accurately reproduced characters seemed to be chaotic.

The fact of linguistic difference required that missionaries engage in a particularly difficult course of language training before they could do the job they came to do. To this basic and generic obstacle was added a variety of cultural messages about the language itself, which predisposed many to think of Chinese as superlatively difficult or perversely obscure. Naturally, as missionaries, they interpreted the confusion of languages in Biblical terms, especially referencing the story of the Tower of Babel, in which linguistic difference was a punishment. Furthermore, their religious sensibilities made them see their problems in learning Chinese as a demonic opposition to their very mission in life. Perhaps externalizing their existential frustrations, some of them described Chinese as itself defective in a variety of ways. It was not phonetic. Reading and writing relied too heavily on a kind of pictorial memory. It could not be used to express certain important information (such as Western science). Its use to express Christian teachings was also precarious due to problems of translation and aesthetics. The only alternative to English-speakers' learning Chinese was for the Chinese to learn English. Church schools taught English, and Chinese fluency in English certainly increased, especially after 1911. But a far more common medium was Pidgin English, which was an expedient medium between different dialects of Chinese within the overall context of dealing with Europeans. Whatever its merits in practice, its widespread use had the effect that Western visitors heard a lot of Chinese people speaking what they took to be defective language. A basic study of Chinese dialects was required to perceive CPE as a language, and lacking such training, visitors communicated not by learning Pidgin but by borrowing from other analogous experiences of defective language: talking to babies, animals, and foreigners.

Looking for an explanation of meaninglessness in the perceptions rather than in the perceived, we may ask how Westerners rendered Chinese speech and writing "meaningless." It may be that there is something built into the processes of learning another language (in situ, and without the kinds of textbooks available today) that predisposes a learner to externalize frustrations. Though we are aware of the long process of childhood learning, by adulthood, speaking one's native language is largely effortless, internal, and natural, in contrast to the artificiality and externality of the other language. In the case of the China mission, part of this had to do with the nature of the language as particularly remote from English: it had tones, and the script was almost entirely outside of European experience, analogized only to Egyptian or Mayan hieroglyphics. But the accusation of meaninglessness was also due to the particular use of utterances, such as mantras, which were semantically blank to most Chinese. As long as speech is imagined as only semantic communication, mantras are indeed nonsense; one could hardly expect Victorian missionaries to have immersed themselves in the linguistic theories behind mantras. Partly also the subnormality of speech by the Chinese was perceived in their "business" (pidgin) English, which was always merely a functional expedient. It was through representations of pidgin English that many Westerners were able to conceive of the inner workings of the Chinese mind. China Coast Pidgin, a basically Chinese dialect easily misperceived as bad English, gave Westerners the common experience of hearing "bad English" constantly. Likewise, a kind of pidgin rationality, involving the use of elements of Western reasoning while using the conceptual grammar structure of Chinese, gave the appearance of simply bad Western reasoning. Did the experience of pidgin English predispose Westerners to think of Chinese as not only speaking a pidgin but also *thinking* a pidgin? Though pidgin had a logic and grammar of its own, it was heard as "bad English." Victorian visitors in China — and even more so, their reading audience back home — would have been more conscious of the bad English they heard than the bad Chinese they spoke. Uncomfortable failures of communication were not displayed in missionary publications.

And finally, the meaninglessness of Chinese speech to British visitors is simply one example of the greater or lesser unintelligibility of all foreign speech. The difficulty of learning any foreign language — but especially one as remote from English as Chinese — meant that a large part of the heard language was meaningless to the foreigner (less so as time went on, though first impressions were important). If one does not want to listen, it is much easier to tune out speech in a second, learned language than in one's native language. This sense of a whole world of speech now making only noise moved easily from a subjective experience to an objective description. Hence, one may trace a Western history of focusing on, even enjoying, the exotic obscurity of Chinese, even in acts of communication.

CHAPTER 6

Babel Embodied

Whereas in the previous chapter, I examined cases where Chinese language and speech were considered technically defective, this chapter deals with views of the Chinese language as morally deficient (speech without truth) or spiritually impotent. In the latter case, the primary example is mantras. The repetition of these apparently meaningless sounds reminded missionaries of their heritage of polemics against Catholicism, Anglo-Catholicism, and the trend of Ritualism. Speech, they felt, could become empty ritual.

Language without Truth

Ignorance of a foreign culture can lead us to suspect it as an illusion, mere appearance, a façade. Foreign systems of meaning make distinctions which we do not see, or they refuse to distinguish between things we consider different. Foreigners see things we don't see, and apparently can't see things which are obvious to us. The framework which allows us to divide the world into categories — to make sense — is itself largely invisible, and the apparent naturalness of our common sense of the world "as it is" gives foreign perceptions a touch of the unreal. The foreign world invites us to fantasize because we may not fully understand why our categories do not fit and the "normally" impossible seems now possible, elsewhere.

Sometimes we *enjoy* that sense of foreign unreality. Unreality is a pleasure in the space of play. But some interpret appearance as deception, as intentional illusion or lies. The Chinese, in particular, were thought to practice deception, to tell polite lies disguised by rituals of acceptance and courtesy. Evariste Huc voiced a common Western perception of the Chinese in very blunt terms: "This speech was completely Chinese — that is to say, a lie from one end to the other."[1] Robert Fortune wrote, "Of course I knew enough of the Chinese by this time to doubt every word they told me, unless I had good reasons for believing them to be speaking the truth."[2] Many Westerners perceived Chinese deception to be culture-wide, institutional, and systematic, a falseness that permeated the fine grain of the culture: "In every institution, in the daily affairs of life, in business, in common conversation, is there not a vein of deception running through the whole?"[3] The implicit or explicit racial contrast was to Europeans and/or Americans, and this basic contrast was extended homologously to other oppositions. Among British Protestants, for example, the contrast of deception and truth implicated "the Chinese" and "the British," heathens and Christians, Catholics and Protestants, and differing stages in the progress of civilization. MacGowan located that contrast with geographic accuracy: "The moment you pass through the Suez canal and have come upon the confines of the Orient, you realize that truth as it is looked upon in the West does not exist in all the vast and glowing regions beyond."[4]

"A myriad means 365, a Celestial is a liar, and the Central Flowery Land a myth," wrote Thomas Blakiston.[5] What did Westerners think the Chinese lied about? The most serious specific accusations of deception related to diplomacy, trade, and other interactions with government offices, but deception was thought to permeate the whole culture. "You are in a new land," wrote John MacGowan, "and the atmosphere of straight-forward honest expression of thought has vanished, and now it seems that, except in the most trivial affairs of life, where concealment is unnecessary, you are in a world where every one has a mask on, and the great aim is to conceal the face that lies behind."[6] Missionaries hoped that the introduction of Christianity would improve the Chinese atmosphere, which seemed especially dense in the realm of religion.

Though Chinese literature was described as lacking imagination, and Chinese culture was commonly viewed as stagnant, mechanical, and repetitive, the Chinese creative faculty was considered most apparent in the arts of deception. As Edwin Dingle reluctantly but confidently asserted in his 1911 travelogue:

In respect of lying, it seems to be absolutely universal. . . . It seems to be in the very natures of the people, and although it is hard to write, my experience convinces me that my statement is not exaggeration. I have found the Chinaman . . . the greatest liar on earth. I question whether the great preponderance of the Chinese people speak six consecutive sentences without misrepresentation or exaggeration, tantamount to lying. Regretting that I have to write it, I give it as my opinion that the Chinaman is a liar by nature. And when he is confronted with the charge of lying, the culprit seems seldom to feel any sense of guilt.[7]

Under a variety of circumstances, words don't mean anything: when they are unintelligible babble — or when they are seen as unreliable, unsubstantiated, or fictive, as when we lie. The Chinese were thus thought by some to have a congenital tendency to lie. Again, Chinese speech was belittled, drained of meaning on moral grounds, though a lie is not strictly speaking meaningless. Useless, false, corrupted, and childish speech share attributes such as incompleteness or lack of value, but nonetheless has meaning. Neither the frustration of learning Chinese, nor the acknowledgment of its vast lexicon, nor the supposed tendency to lie, amount to the attribution of literal meaninglessness. We may see the attribution of meaninglessness as an underlying attitude, evident in metaphor, casual remarks, and jokes. Poorly spoken foreign language and hybrids such as China Coast Pidgin inevitably lead to a certain amount of speech being incomprehensible. The implication that Chinese speech was in some ways meaningless took place within the larger context of constant, if flawed, communication. Yet the missionaries identified a particular case of specifically meaningless speech, which they repeatedly investigated, described, and condemned.

Ritual Noise

One category of speech-act — the use of mantras and the practice of repetitious chanting in general — distinctly offended many writers and was denied full conscious meaning. Thomas M'Clatchie, a Church of England missionary, visiting a Buddhist temple, reported in 1845: "In front of the altar was placed a table, on which lay their books used in worship, and not one syllable of which is understood, even by the Priests themselves."[8] This remark may simply indicate priestly illiteracy, but more likely it indicates the use of unintelligible language in scripture and liturgy. Missionaries were correct in saying Buddhist liturgy included words in languages unknown to the Asian practitioners. Such remarks refer to the use of Sanskrit or pseudo-Sanskrit words in Buddhist worship, primarily in the form of mantra and *dharani*. Many Buddhist scriptures and liturgies contain extended utterances with no discernable semantic meaning for the vast majority of their reciters. For example, the chanting of a liturgical edition of scripture might begin with the following mantra, to "purify the mouth": *An xiu li xiu li mo he xiu li xiu xiu li sa po he.* Scholars are sometimes able to "reconstruct" the Sanskrit, or "translate" it into English, but not always. In some cases, mantra can be translated into a vernacular, but to do so misses the point. Within a traditional episteme of correspondence, the production of the mantra's *sound* is the point. It literally resonates with the object or deity named, so that the actual sound rather than the semantic meaning is what is essential. In China, thinking about Buddhist mantra was related to the idea of *ganying,* variously translated as "sympathetic resonance," "action and response," or "stimulus and response." In its basic formulation, the stimulus of the sound of the mantra results in a response from the Buddha or other being whose essence is distilled into the mantra. It was thought that mantras, or even scriptural recitation, stimulated the natural surroundings — as when barren trees suddenly bloomed. It was not that trees understood normal language — it was that they responded to the sacred sound itself.

Some missionaries were aware that the act of chanting mantras was believed to have power in itself. William Milne wrote: "I once asked a priest, 'What advantage can you expect to derive from merely repeating a number of words, with the sense of which you are entirely unacquainted?' His answer was, 'True, I do not know the sense — it is profound and mysterious; yet the benefit of often repeating the sounds is incalculable; it is infinite!'"[9] The priest gave Milne a reasonable answer in the context of Chinese Buddhist philosophy, which is permeated with a sense of powerful mystery and the limitations of conscious knowledge. True reality is beyond language or conventional understanding. Language was always *upaya* (an expedient means), and the priest's comprehension of an utterance of the Buddha depended on the degree of clarity or obscurity in his own perceptions. As the practitioner progressed in Buddhist cultivation, previously incomprehensible words of the Dharma would become radiant with insight. An unenlightened practitioner might not expect to "understand" the words, but he would take their great power on faith. The efficacy of the sounds and the attitude of faith in them were attested to in many scriptures.

The revelation of truth in scripture was thus a benevolent manifestation from on high, but even the most lucid sermons of the Buddha relied upon the listener's receptivity. Hence, there were limits to the ability to explain or translate mantras. William Milne commented: "As a sect, however, they profess to cherish the most profound veneration for the language of Fân. They ascribe miraculous effects to the use of the written character and of the oral language, and consider both to be of celestial origin."[10]

A few missionaries discussed mantras with Buddhists, but one would not expect most British Protestant missionaries to have appreciated the complex theories behind the use of mantras, especially since they were steeped in a thorough critique of the use of "meaningless" liturgical language in Europe. Throughout Protestant Europe, the use of Latin had been rejected in favor of the vernacular, both during the Reformation and during the Victorian movement against Ritualism. This attitude toward religious language helps explain the missionaries' tone of exasperated contempt for the use of mantras.

Though Buddhist rituals usually included mantras, in most cases the mantras were mixed with Chinese passages. The chanting of the Heart Sutra, for example, involved 242 characters of Chinese (interspersed with some common Sanskrit-derived terminology) and ended with the eighteen characters of the *dharani*. However, the specific case of the use of mantras was taken as axiomatic of Buddhist liturgy in general. The missionary George Smith, having witnessed a Buddhist ceremony, remarked on "their unmeaning sounds."[11] Robert Fortune noted "an unmeaning phrase used by the Buddhist priests at the commencement of their worship, 'Nae mo o me to fa.'"[12] How do we interpret the word "unmeaning" here? The phrase of devotion to Amitabha, which in pinyin is rendered *namo Amituo fo,* is hardly meaningless to the Buddhist devotee. It is possible Fortune did not know what it meant, but more likely he did not care to find out, or the sheer repetition of the phrase made him feel it was spoken without intention. Fortune had inherited a whole attitude toward ritual which made it very easy for him to dismiss Chinese devotional practice as meaningless. Chinese religion seemed to make a cult of obscurity.

In addition to the use of an unintelligible language, mantras and Buddhist liturgy in general were also objectionable because of the fact of repetition. John Francis Davis wrote, "To the repetition of the bare sounds, without regard to the meaning, they attach the highest importance; hence they occasionally go over the same words hundreds and thousands of times."[13] Repetition is rendered absurd if the semantic meaning of the words is imagined as the only worthwhile function of speech, and where meaning is conceived strictly as semantic communication. There are a variety of reasons for repeating utterances: the listener does not hear them properly, or he/she obstinately refuses to acknowledge the utterance, or does not know the language of the speaker well. Flaws in the media of communication sometimes require repetition. Repeated utterances are also probably associated with mental retardation or insanity. Missionaries also associated endless repetition with Catholic practices of liturgical repetition, such as in the Hail Mary. In the 1860s many British Protestants objected not only to the fact of repetition but also to the chanting style in Anglo-Catholic Ritualist worship. Many British Protestants found "intoning" or "intonation" (also known as monotoning) to be aesthetically unpleasant, comparing it to dogs howling, but more importantly, they felt it was harder to understand than a plain reading voice. Missionaries in China, familiar with the conflicts in England over liturgy, would have found the almost-monotoned quality of Buddhist liturgy especially evocative of "Romanist" tendencies in the Anglican church.

One of the similarities between Chinese religiosity and Roman Catholicism lay especially in the preference for prayers spoken in languages that were unintelligible to the speaker — in "meaningless" prayer. Indeed, this phenomenon allowed William Milne and others to group together Catholics worshippers with many other species of the bizarre and the damned:

There is something to be said in favour of those Christians who believe in the magic power of foreign words, and who think a prayer either more acceptable to the Deity, or more suited to common edification, because the people do not generally understand it. They are not singular in this belief. Some of the Jews had the same opinion; the followers of Budha, and the Mohammedans, all cherish the same sentiment. From the seat of his holiness at Rome, and eastward through all Asia to the cave of the Jammaboos of Japan, this sentiment is espoused. The bloody Druids of ancient Europe, the naked gymnosophists of India, the Mohammedan Hatib, the Hoshang (Budhist priests) of China, the Catholic clergy, and the bonzes of Japan — all entertain the notion that the mysteries of religion will be the more revered the less they are understood, and the devotions of the people (performed by proxy) the more welcome in heaven for their being dressed in the garb of a foreign tongue. Thus the synagogue, the mosque, the pagan temple, and the Catholic church all seem to agree in ascribing marvellous efficacy to the sounds of an unknown language; and as they have Jews, Mohammedans, and pagans on their side, those Christians who plead for the use of an unknown tongue in the services of religion, have certainly a host, as to number, in support of their opinion. That Scripture, reason, and common sense should happen to be on the other side, is indeed a misfortune to them, but there is no help for it.[14]

Milne's comments show some irony or even sarcasm for those (Protestant) Christians who have a High Church nostalgia for Latin, noting that they join a large crowd: Jews, Buddhists, Muslims, pagan druids, Hindu yogins, and Catholics. This great diversity of non-Protestants (along with a few Protestants who should know better) are formed as a group specifically by their attitude to sacred language, by their practice of dressing up their devotion in foreign garb. Milne accentuates the macabre, making the yogins naked, the druids bloody, and the Jammaboos (*yamabushi*) live in caves. Geographically, Asia runs eastward from the seat of the Pope.

Mistakenly calling the unknown language Pali, Charles Gützlaff wrote that the monks were "content with repeating the prayers delivered to them in the Pâli, to them an unintelligible language; and they pay their adoration to an indefinite number of images, according to the traditions of their religion."[15] Gützlaff made explicit the parallel of speaking meaningless language and obeisance to icons. Furthermore, he argued, the inherent nature of the Chinese language was in part to blame for the speaking of pious gibberish: "In China, where the peculiarity of the language precludes its being written with alphabetic accuracy, the Pâli degenerates into a complete jargon."[16] That is, as Chinese is not a phonetic script, therefore transliteration inevitably further distorts the accuracy of the sounds, producing "jargon." (Even a completely accurate, phonetic method of transliteration would not have given mantras semantic meaning in China, though it may have brought them closer to their Indian originals.)

William Milne wrote, "There are, it is true, glossaries attached to some of their religious books, which are designed to explain these technical shibboleth; but the definition is sometimes given in other technical terms equally unintelligible, and from their general ignorance of letters, very few of the priests are capable of consulting such helps."[17] By using the term "shibboleth," Milne not only meant the distinctive vocabulary by which one might identify the speaker (as Buddhist, say), but he undoubtedly also intended the negative sense of shibboleth as "obscurantist jargon." "Shibboleth" was an Old Testament reference, a word whose function is to be misperceived by most who hear it. In one case, a specifically Judaic metaphor was used: at a large gathering, some Buddhist priests "spent about an hour in droning their cabalistic words, aided and timed by the beat of metal vessels."[18] What was meant by "cabalistic"? By the mid-seventeenth century, the English sense of the word had shifted from specifically Jewish connotations to more general meanings: esoteric, unintelligible (to most people), oral rather than written, and non-Christian.

Even Christian gibberish appalled the missionary May Griggs. She described visiting a church which no foreigner had visited for nearly thirty years, during which time the religious practice had changed: the church had "gone over to the Tongues Movement." Mainstream Anglicans were generally suspicious of and hostile to the Pentecostal movement and its practice of glossolalia. Griggs thought it was "pathetic to see how the Christians had been led astray. They professed to be full of the Holy Spirit, to be speaking with tongues, while uttering awful sounds and talking gibberish understood by none."[19]

Babel Embodied

Morally bankrupt, spiritually impotent, meaningless speech was also embodied. Ritual was consistently described as useless, degraded, empty, and ridiculous. It had no power to effect salvation. China was perceived as uniquely engulfed in ritual. Basic to the narrative of mission presented to readers in England was a view of China as a place where much of the culture was a matter of appearance, and all appearances were deceiving. Chinese ritual was presented as a kind of absurd theater, in which "a nation of actors" engaged in stylized fictions full of sound and fury but signifying nothing. Visiting a Daoist temple, George Smith saw a man whose wife was gravely ill making offerings, "while a priest went through a variety of evolutions, tossings, and tumblings on the floor, to procure a good omen." The priest "vigorously danced" and made "half an hour's frantic noise, and persevering somersets on the ground" before his "flagelations" came to an end.[20] This nearly epileptic episode (perhaps of spirit possession) was contrasted in the *Church Missionary Gleaner* with a decorous scene of a Protestant Bible class: frenzied dancing contrasted with reading books.

China was at times transformed into a huge kinetic entertainment, as in Evariste Huc's discussion of the Chinese character:

We said just now that they were a nation of cooks, and we might also assert, with truth, that they are a nation of actors. These men have minds and bodies endowed with so much suppleness and elasticity, that they can transform themselves at will, and express by turns the most opposite passions. There is, in fact, a good deal of the monkey in their nature, and, when one has lived some time among them, one can not but wonder how people in Europe could ever take it into their heads that China was a kind of vast academy, peopled with sages and philosophers. Their gravity and their wisdom, exclusive of some official proceedings, are scarcely found out of their classical books. The Celestial Empire has much more resemblance to an immense fair, where, amidst a perpetual flux and reflux of buyers and sellers, of brokers, loungers, and thieves, you see in all quarters stages and mountebanks, jokers and comedians, laboring uninterruptedly to amuse the public.[21]

China was one big act, one great fictional performance, due to the supposed "elasticity" of the Chinese, contrasted perhaps with the rigidity or solidity of Western Christians. Though as a Catholic, Huc did not associate this sense of theatrical illusion with Catholicism, many Protestant writers did.

We should not be surprised to see Protestant missionaries make Chinese religion into theater. This was not a compliment. In Reformation polemics, representations *as such* were suspect. Iconoclastic sentiments went beyond icons to problematize the entire visual field. Hence, we find a whole series of corresponding distastes in Reformation polemics: against theater, masks, ritual display, pictures, and visual illusions of any kind. Calvin had objected to the theater because it blurred reality and unreality, good acting more so than bad acting. The Mass in particular was seen as a grand sham, whereas an austere, minimalist aesthetic in worship was seen as a sign of purity. Ostentation and ceremony were thought to signal insincerity. By the time large numbers of Protestants were writing about East Asia, China had been constructed in the Western imagination as a land of limitless ceremonial ostentation, and therefore insincerity and hollow illusion, "a world where every one has a mask on," as MacGowan put it.

In Islington at the Great Missionary Exhibition, Christians had masked themselves and created stage sets to reveal the falsity (and spiritual need) of China to English audiences. Perhaps they knew that no one would ever be fooled by their illusions of China, and that no one would imagine that Fred Bloggs with the Cockney accent was really a Chinese under that costume. In general, Protestant views of ritual as a mask produced an impulse to *unmask*. Unmasking appearances to see truth required the rejection of ritual. As Jonathan Z. Smith has pointed out, because ritual is not directly translatable into words, and because Victorian Truth was so much a matter of the Word, ritual action could make no direct claim to the efficacy of Truth.[22] Indeed, one of the fundamental principles in Protestant theology is the inefficacy of human action, even that of the Mass. Protestant iconoclasm thus extended to performed icons and spoken words; ritual was "empty," a mere echo of the true Word.

Outside of the missionary context, we see the same attitude even in texts which seem to laud non-Christian religions. Ritual has been romanticized as the residue of an original, spontaneous, mystical "seizure" (*Ergriffenheit*) — now lost to us. An influential example of this approach in Religious Studies is Adolf Jensen's *Myth and Cult among Primitive Peoples* (1963), which contrasts *Ergriffenheit* — the "engulfment of man by his environment . . . the bright flash of insight, the creative moment per se . . . an uncontrollable psychic event, without rationalism or deliberate intent"[23] — with the *Urdummheit* ("primal stupidity") of subsequent "mere petrifactions, . . . misinterpreted vestiges, drained of their former significance,"[24] rationalized (if at all) by "pseudopurposes"[25] in accordance with a "law of semantic depletion."[26] Ritual is thus the "impoverishment" of meaning.[27] The great single moment of reality is diluted by its repetition and formalism. We can find an almost exact copy of this view in certain Jesuit and Protestant narratives of China's religious history, which was seen as degenerating from ethical monotheism to superstitious polytheism.

In nineteenth-century Anglophone scholarship on religion and China, the Chinese were regarded as particularly prone to the endless accretions of "mere ritual," or "mummery," as, for example, in Samuel Johnson's characterization of 1878: "The Chinese creative faculty remains within the plane of certain organic habits, failing to rise from the formalism of rules to the freedom of the idea."[28] The elaboration of ritual by the Chinese was an example of how "grotesque transformations may befall the higher elements of character when absorbed by an intense interest in concrete details."[29] Again and again, missionaries reported such "grotesque transformations" among Chinese Buddhist clerics.

Some missionaries expressed admiration for the literary products of Chinese culture, taking years to translate Chinese classics, publishing journals in Chinese, and laying the foundations of the Western study of Chinese. Nonetheless, one can also find many variations of the view of the Chinese language as lacking in meaning. The logocentrism of the Protestant missionaries notwithstanding, they were inclined to attribute to Chinese speech qualities of incoherence, babble, gibberish, mumbo-jumbo, untruth, uselessness, and obscurity. Missionaries were very quick to draw analogies to Roman Catholicism (as they understood it), specifically in the use of unintelligible or much-repeated language. As missionaries learned more of the native religions, the mantra and *dharani* (religious utterances more or less without semantic meaning) came to typify Chinese religion as a whole.

It is not surprising that an unknown language should come to stand for an unknowable language. Unintelligible speech is as much a part of our cultural framework as intelligible speech. Unintelligible speech is not, however, one thing. Seeking a lexicon to express the various nuances and subspecies of a language deficient in meaning, we range freely over a set of metaphors: baby talk and talk to babies, animal noise and speech to animals, foreign speech (and one's experience of being a foreigner), pidgins (imagined as degenerate), involuntary noises (such as a sneeze), scribbles and random markings, the untutored "mis-use" of musical instruments, the tower of Babel, demonic speech, and the ineffectual magic of other religions (liturgical Latin, mantras, alchemy, cabbalah). These perceptions, which cumulatively depict the speaking Other as more bodily than mental, blend into an image of language more or less lacking in truth, sincerity, or rationality. China had distinct characteristics not present in many other cultures encountered by Victorians — the exemplary history of literacy, for example — but in many ways these metaphors suggest the basic unintelligibility experienced by all foreigners fresh off the boat.

In the following chapters, I will focus on one particular body/mind issue that has already come up in various contexts: obeisance. Of all ritual actions, obeisance was the most potent and provocative, the most central to Protestant identity. In representations of the act of bowing, we find a potent set of homologies. For the missionaries and for many others, obeisance was associated with feebleness, Satan, irrationality, sleep, children, and women; with Baal, and with the Pope.

CHAPTER 7

The Idolatrous Body

Westerners made various diagnoses of China's problems, but for missionaries the crux of culture was religion, and in their view China could not truly progress without a complete spiritual reformation — specifically, a rejection of indigenous idolatry and acceptance of the Christian gospel. Despite their bias — and yet, precisely because of it — missionaries were tireless ethnographers of body-ful Chinese religion. In characterizing Chinese religion, they tended to focus particularly on ritual behavior. When they considered the words spoken during Buddhist rituals, they took Sanskrit mantra and *dharani* as axiomatic of Buddhist spirituality in general: "the repetition of the bare sounds, without regard to the meaning." The endless repetition of words with no discernable semantic meaning — at least, none the chanter understood — brought to mind analogies to Roman Catholicism, which was also viewed as prone to unintelligible, "meaningless" prayer.

This attitude toward Chinese religious speech as meaningless noise was parallel to the comparable view of religious actions. The incoherent chaos of Babel had been embodied as a characteristic of all human nature after the Fall, but the Chinese were seen as particularly prone to "mere ritual" or ritual noise. In the context of distinctively Protestant views of ritual and Western ideas about the relations of mind and body, rejecting the body's ritual tore off a mask and helped to reveal the truth of the rational mind (and from there, of the soul).

The rejection of icons during and after the Protestant Reformation is well known, but this iconoclasm of material objects went along with an iconoclasm of the body: religious ritual was significantly modified to exclude obeisance to "idols." But with very few exceptions, even the most radical anti-Catholic iconoclasts bowed in church, even if the torso remained erect. While they attacked the obeisance of Catholics, Chinese, or other "idolaters," British Protestants bowed during certain rituals (such as funerals or communion), and to their King and Queen. In church, they said that their obeisance was not directed at a material object such as a wooden cross but rather at what the object symbolized, namely, God. For many, this doctrinal caveat for their actions was deemed sufficient to justify the more erect forms of obeisance (lowering heads, kneeling with torso erect). Those who bowed much more deeply appeared to many Victorian Protestants not as more pious but as inordinately focused on the material object, especially when these objects of obeisance were cleaned carefully, given offerings of food, spoken to, kissed, and treated as great treasures.

Long before Protestant missionaries arrived in China, obeisance had been extensively debated in Europe, particularly in anti-Catholic polemics. I bring together China, obeisance, and Protestant/Catholic distinctions not arbitrarily. When Protestant polemicists spoke of China, they often spoke of Protestant/Catholic differences; when they spoke of Protestant/Catholic differences, China sometimes came up for discussion. In making these connections, the specific link was very frequently a similarity in obeisance practice, as well as the great multitude of objects of obeisance, the presence of monastic institutions, and the devotional practices of women.

Let us recall that, roughly speaking, the first major "wave" of reportage on Cathay appeared via the Jesuit writers, who praised China for its rational humanism and entertained a generally tolerant attitude toward Confucian obeisance. Protestant polemics against the Roman confession (and simultaneously against Chinese civilization) reveal distinctive attitudes toward ritual, obeisance, and the body. This chapter outlines Protestant ideas of idolatry as both heathen and Catholic. Missionaries consistently applied anti-Catholic categories to Chinese religion. In so far as Chinese religion was one species of heathenism, they also saw Chinese idolatry in Roman Catholicism.

Postural Theologies

It is worth exploring in some detail the legacy of arguments over the meaning of bowing. First, let me cite an example of the older Protestant discourse on obeisance. In 1683, a certain minister of the Church of England, John Evans, asked "whether Kneeling at the Sacrament be contrary to any express Command of Christ, . . . whether Kneeling be not a Deviation from that example which our Lord set us at the first Institution, . . . whether Kneeling be not Unsutable and Repugnant to the Nature of the Lord's Supper, . . . [and] whether it be unlawful for us to receive Kneeling because this Gesture was first introduced by Idolators, and is still notoriously abused by the Papists to Idolatrous ends and purposes."[1]

An example of the kind of argument which Evans opposed is a pamphlet by Henry Burton which argued: "Idolatry is utterly to be abhorred. But, Adoration or Bowing at the name Jesus is Idolatry. Therefore such adoration is altogether to be abhorred."[2] Burton asserted that it was no less idolatrous to worship a sound in one's ear than to worship an image on a wall. He blamed the introduction of the kneeling posture on the Medieval papacy (and/or on the Anti-Christ), an attribution that was, in turn, derided by Evans. But in both cases there was the (asserted or denied) connection between kneeling and the doctrine of transubstantiation, which Evans referred to as the doctrine of the "Breaden God." Indeed, the practice of iconoclasm by the Reformers was frequently linked to desecration of the host. One late-seventeenth-century "Fanatick Chaplain" wrote: "To worship the Bread is Idolatry; But to kneel at the Sacrament is to worship the Bread."[3] Though such a radical rejection of devotional practice was undoubtedly a minority view, posture was a problem.

In the mid- and late seventeenth century, the concern with this bodily posture was thus basically threefold. There were questions concerning (a) its *scriptural basis,* which involved a characteristically Protestant appeal to the priority of textual authority over institutional authority; (b) its possible insult to *human dignity,* which involved therefore an implicit definition of the properly dignified self with its properly dignified posture (erect); and (c) its *historical associations* with "idolatry" and the Roman Catholic Church, which involved therefore certain defining conflicts of religious, national, and institutional identity. Posture must be scriptural. By examining such moments of transition, when a particular posture is being questioned, debated, and problematized, we may be able to assemble a history of posture.

The critique of kneeling can also be placed within the framework of Protestant iconoclasm. In Lee Palmer Wandel's words, the destruction of all manner of clerical objects (including candlesticks, lamps, and altars) "made traditional worship impossible: They altered how others would worship, how they would approach God. . . . For the iconoclasts, how one worshipped could not be separated from what one worshiped."[4] The destruction of objects of obeisance — the "tinsel of idolatry"[5] — effectively lessened the role of obeisance itself. Acts of obeisance per se were taken as sufficient signs of idolatry: "Now I want to prove that Christians must confess that they venerate their idols. The grounds [for the proof]: because they bow and scrape before them (for the sake of dead holy men) I can definitely conclude that they venerate images."[6]

This kind of postural theology was immediately contested, since it seemed to disallow any physical expression of spiritual, emotional, and mental devotion to God. Obeisance was implicated in questions of the relation of God and creation, of God and humanity, and of cleric and laity.

In a 1679 moderate Protestant text, the radically iconoclastic "Fanatick Chaplain" pointed out the resemblance of Roman and Church of England obeisance. The Protestant Divine admitted the similarity but qualified it: "We kneel, and the Papists kneel: but we declare when we kneel, we intend no adoration to the Elements: but the Papists cannot deny that they do give proper adoration to that which is before them; which we say is bread."[7] The crucial difference between idolatry and orthodoxy was thus a declaration, a doctrinal assertion, that this act worships God and not a material object. The implication is that the Divine considers the extreme iconoclastic/anti-idolatry position to be excessively fixated on mere bodily form (bowing *itself* constitutes idolatry), whereas the Divine's position is that a doctrinal assertion that the act is *not* idolatry is sufficient.

The Fanatick Chaplain refused to distinguish between different acts of obeisance — "It is all one to me"[8] — and denied any significance to mental states: a bow is a bow is a bow. The Divine, in response, asked, "Do you think that bowing down is meant of the Mind or of the Body?"[9] (The Chaplain did not comprehend and had no answer.) Given the mind/body opposition here, to be mind-less is to be "body-full," and the Divine intended that since obeisance "is meant of the Mind," the body is simply untouched by idolatry. The Protestant Divine can bow, as long as the bow is accompanied by a mental (spoken) element defining the intention, labeling the posture.

Though John Evans and other Protestants judged kneeling acceptable, his questions suggest a fundamental ambivalence toward ritual, and bowing, in particular, in the Protestant world. One of the "founding fathers" of Protestantism, Martin Luther, for example, admitted the necessity, and also the falsity, of ritual: "The five senses and the whole body have their gestures and their rituals, under which the body must live as though under some sort of mask."[10] Ritual was basically theatrical. Victorian evangelicals shared a similar distaste for the theater, not only because theaters were seen as sites of temptation and sin, but also because the actor was *acting* and thus inherently false. Many evangelicals also condemned excessive concern with the artifice of etiquette and fashion, in contrast to the positive values of sincerity and simplicity.

Victorian Protestants inherited and cultivated distrust, or at least ambivalence, toward ritual in general, and toward obeisance in particular. The physical act of obeisance was in some cases sufficient to warrant the accusation of idolatry. For most people, certain restrained forms of obeisance (torso erect) were acceptable, especially if combined with spoken, mental, or implied statements as to their meaning (worship of the signified, not the sign). The preferred mode of religiosity involved a more erect posture, which is among the more familiar characteristics of Low Church Protestantism: emphasis on direct access to the Bible, partial rejection of priestly authority, and visual simplicity in worship. The primary figure against which this model of religious life was posed was the Catholic religious body (especially clerical or female). The *Church Missionary Gleaner* published "A Letter from Rome" in 1892 which claimed that "the Christianity of Rome is no longer the religion of Christ. If any one doubts that Romanism is anti-Christian, let him come here and see . . . the bronze statue of the apostle; let him watch the poor Italian woman come up reverently and kiss the statue's bronze toe. . . . Then let him read the Second Commandment!"[11] In the hostile stereotype, this Catholic was quintessentially prostrated before the priest, the Pope, images of Jesus, Mary, and the saints, or the Golden Calf. Through this postural stereotype, Protestants were able to freely associate Catholics with other non-Protestants, including the Chinese.

Exemplary Ritualists: The Catholic/Chinese

The projection of Catholic–Protestant polemical distinctions onto China has its roots in the way that Jesuits presented the Chinese to the European and Enlightenment gaze: as civilized, rational, and in some cases, monotheistic. In part, Catholic writers created this image in order to use the Chinese literatus as the impartial judge in disputes over credibility and authority, disputes in which rationality was privileged. For example, in a 1659 text by the Jesuit professor Vitus Erbermann (1597–1675), called "Dialogues among a Lutheran theologian, a Jesuit, and a Chinese Philosopher," the latter "represents the embodiment of right reason,"[12] who thus "angrily refutes the accusation of idolatry leveled at him by the Lutheran theologian, and professes the following creed: the Chinese, he proclaims, in accordance with the light of nature, acknowledge one God, creator of all things, the best, the wisest, and the most powerful."[13] (If the Chinese judge seems to side with Catholics, it is because the Jesuits created him.) The Chinese, Erbermann claims, also believe in the immortality of the soul and union with God after death. There were efforts to find in the Chinese Classics a primordial monotheism and the prefiguring of the Gospel.

Protestant accounts of China, however, meticulously countered each of these claims. They expounded at length on the ignorance, lack of rationality, mechanical ritualism, and clerical parasitism of Chinese religious life. In this view, if the average Chinese consciously "believed" anything at all, it was a belief in his petty and absurd idols and not in any Creator or in an afterlife. "The heathen in his blindness/Bows down to wood and stone."[14]

Protestant writers repeatedly asserted the resemblance of Chinese religious practice to the "the holy mummeries of the Romish Church."[15] This kind of assertion served to attack the credentials of the Chinese gentleman as a rational and impartial judge and asserted the spiritual bankruptcy of the Catholic Church. One of the most effective ways of showing the inferiority and error of Chinese (and therefore Catholic) religiosity was to damn it as idolatry, especially by focusing on the practice of deep obeisance.

Jesuit missionaries, Enlightenment philosophers, and the fad of Chinoiserie had created a certain "Enlightened" image of China which later Protestants opposed. When in the early Qing, Jesuit reportage dominated Western representations of China, the strength of that remote civilization contrasted with the chaos of Europe; China was "in some measure at the zenith of her prosperity."[16] Missionaries praised China and did not choose to dwell on its bad aspects. Evariste Huc lamented in the 1850s that "modern missionaries have perhaps fallen into the contrary extreme,"[17] making only negative judgments, often based on brief stays and no language competency, and "slandering the Chinese, for no other reason than that the missionaries formerly overpraised them."[18]

In this 1893 comment from two Anglican missionaries preaching "In Chinese Villages," we see a number of intimate intersections of diverse issues: a contestation of previous historical narratives, a fixing of gender distinctions, a branding of the real practice of Confucianism as Catholic idolatry and of Catholicism as heathen idolatry.

In England we heard so much of the power of Confucianism, that we were hardly prepared to see the Chinese so "wholly given to idolatry." It is a well-known fact that the very followers of Confucius (who in his writings teaches there is but one God) also seek long life, fame, riches, and honour at the hands of deaf and dumb idols, in common with the illiterate class. In the above-mentioned temple, some of the idols were of colossal size, others were remarkable for their costly robes of embroidered silk and satin, strangely resembling those of the Romish priests. Nor is this the only point of affinity between Roman Catholicism and heathenism: at this same temple may be seen crowds of women, who come periodically to burn incense, count their beads, and mutter prayers before the idols.[19]

The religious history of China was conceived by the Jesuits as having begun with a primordial monotheism, available to the ancient Chinese through the workings of natural theology, and having then fallen into degeneracy due in large part to the introduction of Buddhism. Protestant narratives of Chinese history often agreed. William Burder in 1870 described Confucianism as an ancient Chinese "primitive creed" (the simple worship of a moral supreme being) which had degenerated into "a multitude of superstitions," so that "the people forgot the simple worship of the Shang-tee [Shangdi] and embraced every new invention of idolatry with the utmost avidity."[20] Charles Gützlaff noted the similarity of the ancient worship of Shangdi to the practices of Noah. But, Gützlaff argued, so much time had passed, it was impossible to be sure how pure the ancient religion was; the sources were mixed: "Idolatry gained ascendency at a very early period." Hence, "We believe that the records which come down to us were greatly and purposely mutilated by the transcribers, and even modelled according to the prevailing customs of later ages."[21]

The purity of origins (as with Moses, Jesus, Buddha, or the ancient Chinese sense of Shangdi) had degenerated into ritualism and corruption, but (in the case of Jesus) it could be recovered in a progressive rejection of "idolatry." In this way, a historical narrative was transposed from Europe to China. However, the large-scale Protestant narratives of China and the West differed in at least one regard: China was receiving the true Gospel only in the nineteenth century. "Western Europe awoke at the Reformation, but Eastern Asia slept on till our own day. Now, however, even the 'antiquated' empire of China is rapidly awakening."[22]

The basic narrative of primordial purity followed by degeneration was not only applied to Confucianism, but also to Buddhism, which spread to China "by bending and crouching and accommodating itself," according to a popular novel of 1901.[23] The form of Buddhism that had entered China, Mahayana, was itself thought of as having degenerated from the original teachings of the Buddha. The *Gleaner* informs its readers in 1899: "Once it was not so much a religion as a gloomy pantheistic philosophy; but it has long since become an elaborate system of idolatry, strangely resembling Roman Catholicism in its ordinances and methods. The original pantheism would now be entirely forgotten had it not been revived by English and American admirers."[24]

Once again, it was left to Westerners to revive the original moment of Buddhist inspiration. A reader asked the editors of *India's Women and China's Daughters*: "If there is no prayer in Buddhism, how is it that prayer wheels and other mechanical implements for prayer are used in some Buddhist countries?" The answer was that the Buddha's original teaching left "no room for prayer," but that Mahayana Buddhism, as it was practiced in China, had gone awry: "Northern Buddhism is distinctly Theistic and intensely ritualistic and has a vast machinery for continual prayer."[25] Similar narratives were applied to Daoism, which supposedly began with a simple and yet mystical love of nature (expressed in the *Daodejing*), but then became encrusted with the magical detritus of superstitious imagination.

Following a related set of metaphors, the Chinese themselves appeared as puppets, robots, machines, statues, or automata. Religious actions served to typify "the great propensity of the Chinese to do everything mechanically."[26] Examples were cited of Chinese apparently not knowing the reason for ritual: when asked why, they said, "We do not know. We do as we do because our fathers and forefathers have done so too."[27] Rather than acting upon rational motives or even on faith, the Chinese were described as mechanistically following outward custom: "The merest shell of conformity is all that is demanded."[28] The accusation of mindless obedience to outdated authority was widespread in Protestant polemics.

At the same time that Protestant polemicists spoke of Catholic–Protestant differences and of China, they usually agreed on the spiritual mindlessness of the Chinese, claiming that most Chinese, even the priests, could not offer any rational account of their ritual action. They remarked on what they saw as the stupidity of Buddhist monks, in particular. They took the inability to give an account which conformed to their expectations of rational explanation — in other words, an account which made sense to them — as a sure sign of the inferiority of the other religion (as they perceived "religion"). In contrast, Jesuits, in particular, had made some exceptions for Confucianism as valid wisdom, or as a religion of sorts, revelatory of God's grand design, albeit fatally flawed through its absence of Christ.

The explicit association with Roman Catholicism pervaded Protestant representations of China. The *Church Missionary Gleaner* described the interior of a Buddhist hall, including a seated "great lama": "His costume closely resembles that of a Romish bishop."[29] The whole devotional ritual "recalled vividly to my recollection the ceremonies of Roman Catholics."[30] In fact, even the Jesuits, who did the most to construct China as a wise civilization, conceded the similarity: the Jesuit Johann Greuber described obeisance to Buddhist Lamas in China:

When strangers come to him, they fall upon their faces, they creep to him upon their knees, and kiss his feet, as the Papists do the toes of their Pope, with a wonderful respect.

From hence we may discover the Devils subtilty, in appropriating this ceremony and testimony of respect due to none on Earth, but to the Pope of Rome, to the barbarous Superstitions of this Idolatrous Nation. He hath had the malice to transfer and usurp all the other mysteries of our Faith to his own Worship.[31]

Here is a Jesuit noting the demonic inspiration of Chinese/Lamaist obeisance and at the same time its resemblance to Catholic obeisance, but drawing an entirely different conclusion — not that Catholics are idolaters but that the obeisance of idolaters derives from Catholic obeisance, through the Devil's ironic malice. By contrast, Protestants pictured a pure Mosaic faith and/or a pure early Christianity, which was later — even as soon as St. Paul — corrupted by exposure to idolatry; so the resemblance implied for Protestants that idolatrous obeisance entered a pure Christianity from the outside. Here, instead, the Jesuit shows the pure Church, complete with obeisance from the start, and he shows the Church as the origin of even that false obeisance now seen among idolaters. For Greuber, the diffusion of obeisance moved outward from purity to pollution, from reality to delusion. For Protestants, idolatry seeped inward.

Various theories could be used to explain the observed similarity of Chinese Buddhist and Catholic practices, such as the idea that the Nestorians had given the Chinese a fragment of Christianity, or that Saint Thomas had proselytized not only India but also China, or that Satan had played a devious trick. John Francis Davis brushed all this aside: "To those who admit that most of the Romish ceremonies and rites are borrowed directly from paganism, there is less difficulty in accounting for the resemblance."[32] To others, who borrowed from whom did not make much difference. One of a series of *Church Missionary Gleaner* articles, entitled "How the Heathen Pray," included a quote from an unnamed friend in Ningbo:

These converts, with their shaven, idle, begging monks, and the nunneries for women, their fasts and enforced celibacy, the incense, rosaries, images of the virgin with a child in her arms and a cross on her bosom, reminded me so strongly of what I had seen in Italy and other parts of Christendom, that it appeared to me the Romans must have borrowed of the heathen, or they of them; and which has the first claim to be the father of such superstitions I must leave them to settle.[33]

The question of the ultimate origin of idolatry was not clearly resolved.

From One Form of Idolatry to Another

Protestant missionary reports on Catholic missions in the *Church Missionary Gleaner* are mostly negative, in part because of the Protestant perception of the Catholic church as "a fallen and corrupt Church,"[34] "a mere travesty of Christianity,"[35] and in part because the competitive spaces of the Catholic and the Protestant missions overlapped and blurred. Some Protestant missionaries were frustrated to find Chinese who had already been converted by Catholic missionaries, making it even harder to convert them than if they had never heard of Jesus at all. "The heathen, when perverted to Romanism, are much more inaccessible and indisposed to listen than they were before."[36] The Chinese, especially government officials, were often characterized by Victorians as "inaccessible" and "indisposed to listen," and here we see that officious remoteness multiplied "much more" by Catholic missions, as if Catholicism added a further layer of obstinate refusal to the already unfertile ground of heathen China. Some missionaries saw signs posted in Catholic villages warning the converts against reading Protestant tracts.

Walter Medhurst spoke to the people in a village he visited with George Smith, and

finding that they were principally professors of the Roman-Catholic Religion, dwelt on the more prominent truths of the Incarnation and Atonement of Christ, to which they assented; but, on his subsequently enlarging on the necessity of trusting in Christ alone as the Saviour, and the sinfulness of raising other Saviours and Mediators — such as the Virgin Mary, who was only a sinful mortal like ourselves — they appeared to be somewhat staggered, and looked in his face as if incredulous and distrustful of his remarks.[37]

The missionaries were then told of four European Padres who came by periodically, from a nearby Roman Catholic church. The two Protestants then walked to that village and preached a sermon while standing in front of the village tutelary idol (but not, apparently, in front of the Catholic church). When Medhurst told the villagers that the idolatry was absurd, the crowd just laughed. These people, at least, were not "somewhat staggered" by the missionaries' denunciations.

Some missionaries resented what they saw as the Catholic church's tendency to rely on political and military influence. The tendency of France, in particular, to intervene politically and militarily on behalf of its Catholic missions drew the ire of the American S. Wells Williams: "What a pest France is in the world! She never learns to treat others justly, nor is she content to mind her own affairs, while the mass of people are almost as ignorant as heathen, and quite as superstitious. She has made more wars, more trouble, more tyranny, more persecution, than any other Christian (so-called) nation. They are a strange mixture; I'm glad I wasn't born one — or a Chinaman either."[38]

Protestant missionaries operated within a framework which clearly distinguished Protestant from Catholic (and from Orthodox, where relevant), especially in their dealings with officials and potential converts. However, when considering their relations with other Protestant churches, they were often disinclined to be sectarian in this foreign land. There were certainly conflicts among the sects and organizations of Protestantism in China. The signs of these conflicts are much clearer in the archives of personal correspondence than in published sources, which tended to erase the sometimes bitter disputes, the personal antagonisms, the complaints, and the worries about small sums of money.

Missionaries and other visitors usually conceded a grudging respect for the hard work and commitment of Catholic priests in China, but their success was attributed to a perceived similarity of Catholicism and popular Chinese religion: "No wonder that the Jesuits have made so many Converts in China, where there is such a striking similarity between their mummeries and those of the Priests of Buddhu."[39] The Jesuit Johann Greuber had noted the same similarity in 1676. The points of similarity included the use of icons (especially the Virgin Mary), monastic institutions, and practices of obeisance. To the Protestant eye, these created the infrastructure of idolatry, whether in China or the Vatican: celibate monks, nuns, and priests maintaining spaces for bowing to icons and other ritualized objects. The similarities were framed as a shared superstitious idolatry. An 1852 *Gleaner* article asserted that "the Romanists, taking advantage of the close similarity which exists between their system and that of Buddhism, are endeavouring to transfer the natives *from one form of idolatry to another.*"[40] Hence,

when Christianity was corrupted, this evil [worship of the dead] was introduced with many others. Thus we find large bodies of nominal Christians — such as Romanists and others — as well as the heathen Chinese, worshipping the spirits of dead men and women. It is not more sinful and absurd for a Chinese to make prayers to the spirit of his ancestor, than for a Romanist to pray to his patron saint; nor is the invoking of Confucius a grosser error than the invocation of the Virgin Mary. Yet even in this, their strongest superstition, the Chinese are earthly-minded.[41]

The equivalence of Chinese ancestor cults and Catholic cults of the saints is quite blunt here — in both cases, it is treated as the worship of the dead.

The same human weakness and error operated on heathens bowing to their ancestors and on Catholics bowing to saints or the Virgin.

Catholicism was in some ways more threatening to the Protestant missionaries than heathenism. The proximity of Catholicism and Protestantism was problematic for Protestant missionaries, who were annoyed that Chinese Catholics could come so close to their truth and still not get it right. Indeed, they may not be able to see the truth precisely because they came so close. But even for some missionaries Catholicism seemed to retain a disturbing allure because of its deeply Christian content, however flawed. Visiting Paris, S. Wells Williams wrote of the overwhelming sensory excesses of French Roman Catholic churches. "One who has lived in China, where the idolatry is effete, unartistic, ungraceful, feels that it has no power over the soul; for who cares for Kwanyin, Ma-tsu-pu, or Kin-hwa, or who sympathizes with their worshippers? But when the associations of a pure faith are combined with statues and paintings of consummate art, spiritual things become to us degraded to the level of worldly things, carnal and sensuous."[42]

To paraphrase: ugly idolatry was no problem but Catholic idolatry had some beauty, and this mixture of Christianity and art made spirituality into a matter of the senses and of the flesh. Images of heathen gods had little influence on Williams, but he seemed to find Catholic iconography much more unnerving, because it depicted Christ and because it conformed more closely to Western conceptions of beauty. Marjorie Morgan has noted a common Victorian desire to keep evil repulsive and the good completely pure. Vice should not be beautiful. She explains: "Implicit in this whole concept of sincerity, however, was the reciprocal hope that those of evil disposition would exhibit a *totally* disagreeable presentation. Such an unambiguous distinction was imperative, according to moralists, primarily in order to preserve the inherently repulsive nature of vice. When displayed in all its grossness, they argued, vice was relatively innocuous because easy to detect and shun."[43] Hence, many missionaries found themselves admiring heathen temples for their beautiful designs and locations and then reminding themselves of the Satanic aspect of both the site itself and even its very beauty.

While Victorian Protestant missionaries constructed their imagination of China according to historical conditions and within their particular agendas, I take their views of Chinese religion as evidence of a fundamental dynamic of intercultural contact. In most cases of intercultural exchange, recently arrived foreigners only stroll around the edges of a culture's systems of religious meaning, even as they walk right into temples and see the most obvious bodies. They tend to think of the natives primarily in terms of their bodies, and they freely assign meaning — or meaningless-ness — to the body of the semantically unintelligible Other. In the case of China, there were strong associations of bowing bodies. Chinese ritual bodies were made legible as performers of a sham, as prisoners of cour-tesy, and quintessentially, as bending or groveling.

This chapter has explored the Protestants' negative associations of bowing as idolatry, as it was practiced, so they thought, by Catholics and by heathens. Catholic/Chinese obeisance tended to be imagined as much deeper (more horizontal) and more frequent than Protestant obeisance, which was quite limited and rarely if ever involved full prostrations. For Protestants, the arguments against Catholic obeisances had been made in the very founding moments of their sectarian identity. Objections to deep bowing were linked to arguments against other aspects of Catholicism that the Reformers objected to, or that were commonly railed against in Victorian England: the Virgin Mary, the Eucharist, the Pope, Jesuits, and Anglo-Catholicism. In theological terms — which for Victorian evangel-icals, also meant historical terms — the act of bowing to icons had been a fundamental weakness in human nature since Adam. They found scrip-tural support in the second of the Ten Commandments and in the Old Testament's many rants against local cults.

The idolatry of Roman Catholicism was thought to have come into the pure early Christian church from the heathenism of the old Roman and Greek cults, or even from Asian religion. Acts of idolatry typified the cor-rupted, degenerate condition of the church, which necessitated the Reformation. Even Chinese Buddhist obeisance was treated as evidence of Buddhism's degeneration. In the next chapter, I explore the specific case of Chinese obeisance, especially by Buddhist monks, female devotees, and filial descendents. In addition to the overlaid views of deep obeisance as Catholic and heathen, a series of other associations will become clearer. These associations may help to explain the powerfully visceral revulsion Britons felt when faced with Chinese obeisance. Bowing evoked distinc-tions of gender, class, ethnicity, colonial status, and level of civilization, and it was implicated in fundamental models of human dignity and embodiment.

CHAPTER 8

Obeisance and Dis-obeisance

Catholics and Chinese were imagined to bow more often and more deeply than Protestants, and the depth of their obeisance was taken to signify not great piety but misguided devotion — idolatry. When the differences between Catholic and heathen were momentarily ignored in the assertion of their similarity, their contrast to Protestantism was never clearer. Facing their deity, Protestants bowed only slightly, by comparison, conceiving this restrained bodily posture as evidence of correct piety rather than indifference. In this chapter, I explore the rigid refusal to bow in China. While in the self-flattering stereotype, the Briton does not prostrate himself even to the Emperor, on occasion, the Chinese bowed even to ordinary Britons. According to popular imagery, the Chinese were so especially prone to obeisance that English dictionaries absorbed a Chinese word, kowtow, usually redefined as abject groveling. The visceral reactions against deep bowing were informed not just by religious identity but also by class and gender. Civilizations were judged by the depths of their obeisance. There grew up a lore about not bowing, which focused on the idealized, erect body of the British Protestant, "with knee to man unbent." The stoical Briton with his "stiff upper lip" let no emotion show. Attempts to communicate these bodily values in religious ritual led to the transformation of converts who also refused to bow, not even to their own ancestors, let alone to the "grinning faces" of the "ugly little idols." First, let us examine the horror of the icon.

Wooden Bodies

A good deal of missionary preaching was directed against the images in Buddhist and Daoist temples, but missionaries were not always negative about images. Sometimes they wrote complimentary descriptions of the beauty of the images, temples, and even of some of the rituals — in purely aesthetic terms. More often, their descriptions were mixed: "The place is a labyrinth of carved rocks, a happy valley of laughing Buddhas, and Queens of Heaven, and squating Buddhas, and hideous hook-nosed gods of India."[1] In this quote the Buddhas are laughing, but more often they are leering or grinning. There are innumerable references to the idols as "hideous." The idols are always *squatting,* never sitting. Most often, the images were "ugly little idols," "senseless blocks":

There on the steps before they enter, they see the big image of the god, ugly, and worn by wind and weather. . . . The temple is dark and very dirty. Cobwebs hang from the walls. The place is never washed, and but rarely swept. . . . The group of idols stands before them. The images with fierce or grinning faces, streaked with red paint and blackened by smoke from candles and incense sticks, look at the worshippers with staring immovable eyes. Sometimes long rows of these images glare and stare in hideous fashion. The girls offer their rice, burn their incense, prostrate themselves before the idols, and pass out again [i.e., exit].[2]

Whereas sometimes the icons are trivialized as "little" and powerless, in the above 1921 anecdote "the girls" bow down to something demonic: big, hideous, fierce, leering, dark, and dirty. Icons were sometimes regarded as strictly "wood and stone" and therefore fragile, but at other times they were clearly regarded as demonic and therefore powerful. We have seen the malevolent power of the heathen idol in the story told by Mary Darley, related in Chapter 1. Now, imagine a mass of such idols, on the move:

The first day the procession quite surrounded our house, going up a garden at the side and round by the back; we were praying in the school. I did not like the idols surrounding us in that way, I had never seen the same thing before. The next day I saw that the idols were losing their power here. The people spent one day in the temple. They painted the idol's eyes, and said that they were to have good sight to protect them. Then the nose was painted and told to have breath; and then the mouth, and it was told to speak. There is a hole in the back, into which they put something, inviting the spirit to enter, and then shut up the hole. While the priest is doing all this, numbers of people, especially women, are reading prayers. But the Gospel is making its way, and the people here are beginning to know that these proceedings are worthless, thank God![3]

Fear of the demonic mingles with ethnographic description, which moves to a cry of the futility of their behavior and of the dawn of their awakening to its worthlessness. Clearly, many missionaries knew at least some basic aspects of image consecration, which usually involved placement of animating talismans inside the image. In 1905 Mary Darley wrote a more gruesome version: "We heard of a horrible discovery in the north of the Prefecture. A huge procession following a brand new brass idol; bloodstained, it attracted notice, and suspicion was aroused. Inside the idol a hollow place was found full of eyes and mutilated parts of the human body!"[4]

Missionaries might have expected reactions of pious indignation as they poked at, insulted, and destroyed images, but they did not expect laughter or indifference. While they could see that there were regular devotees at the temples, it was also clear that many Chinese felt little need to bow to such images on any regular basis. Western observers often noted this take-it-or-leave-it attitude in Chinese religion. However, as the Jesuits had found hundreds of years before, the one act of obeisance that virtually all Chinese practiced was obeisance to their ancestors. The proper degree of toleration of the ancestral cult was the hottest topic of the General Conference of the Protestant Missionaries of China held at Shanghai in 1890, and this debate was left for last probably for that reason. While most participants condemned obeisance to the dead, the most provoking paper was "The Worship of Ancestors—A Plea for Toleration," written by William Alexander Parsons Martin and read in his absence. Martin was an American Presbyterian missionary and educator who had been appointed the first president of the imperially supported Tungwen College in Peking. In his paper, he argued for toleration and for only indirect attacks. He praised the moral effects of the ancestor cult, and in contrast found the strict Protestant refusal to pray for the dead very "dreary."[5] But most contentiously he denied that obeisance to ancestors constituted idolatry: "The posture is always that of kneeling, alternating with prostrations . . . but it does not in itself form an act of idolatry, because the same posture is employed to show respect to the living. Children fall on knees and face before their parents; subjects before their sovereign; officials of every rank before those above them; and common people before their magistrates. Beggars in the street assume that attitude in asking alms."[6]

In other words, the physical act of obeisance did not automatically constitute idolatry because it was identical to many acts of clearly secular or civil courtesy, in which the object of obeisance is not assumed to be divine. A British subject kneeling to Queen Victoria is not thereby an idolater. Martin thus replicated some of the arguments of certain Jesuits, who had tried to persuade the Vatican and others that obeisance to Confucius and the ancestors was not a *religious* action *in itself.* Martin concluded that the three aspects of the ancestral cult — posture, invocation, and offering — were not necessarily idolatrous. "Considered as a mode of salutation, it merits our contempt as a fit expression of the abject condition of most oriental nations, but it is not sinful. . . . Whether the invocation is an act of idolatry depends on the attributes ascribed to the deceased."[7] While it was widely felt that Chinese non-Christian idolatry was at the root of their "abjection," Martin thought that a prostrated body expressed that abjection but not necessarily idolatry. Martin also explicitly connected the uncompromising views of other missionaries to the Reformation: "The violence that attended their rupture with the other church, unavoidably carried Protestants to an opposite extreme, leading them to abandon many graceful observances, in themselves as innocent as the painted windows which Puritan soldiers took such pleasure in smashing."[8]

A paper by H. Blodget, which followed, took care to distinguish between idolatrous and non-idolatrous expressions of natural grief for deceased parents. After describing the ritual of installing the spirit in the tablet, he concluded that the ritual was not merely "graceful" or "innocent" but unambiguously idolatrous. In reference to the history of debates between some Jesuits and the Vatican, Blodget sided with the Pope. The conference proceedings include responses to the papers, and most of the speakers disagreed with Martin, denouncing the practice and rejecting his compromise position. High Church liberalism would not yet have its day. Martin had argued that the idolatrous elements of ancestral practice could be removed and that the remaining practices would then be fine; others argued that it was all idolatry or tainted by idolatry. Y. K. Yen, the only Chinese speaker, argued that one could not remove the idolatrous element. Henry V. Noyes argued that the ancestral cult was indeed idolatrous, "for the same Chinese word is used to designate this worship and the worship of idols; the same forms of worship are observed; the prostrations, the burning of incense and candles and the offerings of food."[9] Hudson Taylor suggested that all who "wish to raise an indignant protest" against Martin's view should *stand up.* "Almost the whole audience did so."[10]

Bending Bodies

By highlighting Chinese obeisance and judging it as idolatry, Protestant writers could both debunk Jesuit images of China, invoke anti-Catholic sentiments in depictions of Chinese religion, and implicate Catholicism with idolatrous heathenism. Reports in the *Gleaner* frequently presented acts of obeisance as comical or absurd. In "Praying for Rain in China," Arthur Evans Moule reported seeing a procession in which the principal object was not an idol but a toad. The toad was being taken to the *yamen* office, where the magistrate was "obliged to come out with his secretaries and attendants, clad in mourning, to bow down to this toad in the broiling sun."[11] Also, "Here was 'a devotee beating his head with fearful violence upon a doorstep'; there 'a Buddhist priest walking on his knees.'"[12] Such devotional behavior was seen as the "debasing domination of grovelling superstition."[13]

British Protestants, however, didn't do that sort of thing. On occasion, they physically pulled Chinese up who had bowed to them as they had bowed to Buddhist monks, rulers, and ancestors: "Some Christian Chinese discovered themselves to us at Wan, and, taking Mr. Schereschewsky for a padre, they prostrated themselves before him, but he raised them up and quickly gave them to understand that such was not the fashion in our religion."[14]

The *Gleaner* and other sources reproduced many pictures of bowing and bending Chinese bodies, often contrasted with erect Protestants. For example, Figure 6 shows Thomas M'Clatchie standing benignly over a native convert who is bowing repeatedly and exclaiming, "Ah, Jesus! Jesus! thus I worship Jesus!" M'Clatchie is clearly pleased at the convert's earnestness but gestures toward the man, telling him to stand up, in words and with his hands: "I raised him up, and placed him on a chair."[15]

Perhaps the most preposterous representation of Chinese obeisance to an Englishman was in the popular 1901 novel, *A Flower of Asia: An Indian Story*. Though set in India, it featured a representative Buddhist priest, called "John Chinaman," with a pigtail. One night, the priest stumbles out of an opium den and mistakes our hero, one Dr. O'Dowd, for an idol: "His unfocused eyes saw in the Doctor a statue of Buddha, and he salaamed profoundly before him."[16] Of course, O'Dowd would have nothing of it: "'Up with you, for a fool,' said O'Dowd. 'What do you mistake me for? I'm none of your idols, but a plain Christian man.'"[17] As O'Dowd retreated, the priest pursues him, on his knees, touching his head to the ground. His devotion reached the stage of actually grasping O'Dowd's legs, crying "Buddha! Buddha!" This idolization incensed the Briton: "Do you mistake me for a heathen Chinee? . . . Take off your hands, or I'll — I'll go for your pigtail. . . . Hands off, you grimy thing!"[18] The episode ended as an Indian policeman dragged the Chinese man away, speculating that his true intention had been perhaps to pick the Doctor's pocket or even to murder him. But O'Dowd explained: "'He

FIGURE 6. Thomas M'Clatchie and Chinese convert. *Church Missionary Gleaner,* January 1851, 113.

mistook me for an idol of his,' said the Doctor; 'and came licking the ground at my feet. When I spurned his vile flattery, he tried to seize me in his arms.'"[19]

Contrast the image of a bending, non-Christian Chinese with that of the erect body of a converted Chinese, for example, in the engraving: "China — Ordination of a Native," which is a portrait of "the Rev. Dzaw Tsang-lae" (see Fig. 7). Here, we see a full-length, frontal depiction of a stately Chinese man with Bible in hand, his finger gesturing as if he were teaching. (The engraving is unusual, in that most portraits of Chinese converts show them seated.) To be a fully confirmed Christian is to stand up. Likewise, the 1866 report, "Good News from Fuh-chau," told the story of a Chinese convert whose daughter was pledged to marry a heathen. According to the story, much abuse was directed at the Christian bride during the wedding ceremonies: "She was dragged from her father's house amidst torrents of abuse, and taken to a heathen home, where she was commanded to fall down and worship the domestic and ancestral idols. Did she at once renounce her faith in Christ? Ah! no. She at once

FIGURE 7. "Portrait of the Rev. Dzaw Tsang-lae."
Church Missionary Gleaner, November 1863, 133.

refused to bow the knee to the idols, and said she had learned to worship
the one living and true God. But this did not satisfy her cruel husband,
who stood by ready to enforce his wicked commands with threats and
blows."[20]

The wickedness of those who would use violence and physical strength
to force converts to bow was a theme in missionary reportage. John Wolfe
reported on a widow and her twelve-year-old son who had converted.
After conversion, the woman had met with local opposition and persecution, and "they compelled the poor boy to bow down to the idols, and
burn incense to the gods, — the poor little fellow crying, and protesting
the whole time that he did not believe in them; — that he only believed
in Jesus."[21] The episode warranted an illustration in the *Quarterly Token*

FIGURE 8. Illustration from "Persecution in China,"
A Quarterly Token for Juvenile Subscribers, April 1868, 8.

for Juvenile Subscribers, a CMS publication for young fundraisers (see Fig. 8). The publication approved of the child's pious tantrum.

Chinese in the more erect forms of obeisance were approvingly represented in pictures of Christian worship. "Interior of the Episcopal Church, at Ningpo" shows a British-looking church interior where a white priest is ministering the Eucharist to nine Chinese kneeling below him in a semicircle (see Fig. 5). Even then, there could be doubts: "Of course it is a very easy thing for bad men to kneel, or to avow themselves determined to become Christians. It is not easy for a sincere man."[22] Nonetheless, kneeling with the head bowed was an accepted practice in receiving the Eucharist. This kneeling posture implied modesty and humility appropriate for one's condition as a creature contemplating the Creator; whereas the reverse — standing up, making eye contact — evoked resolve, willpower, and decision. The crucial decision, the initial gesture toward becoming a Christian, was in many cases a ritual of standing up. It was common practice during services that the preacher would ask Christians and non-Christians alike to kneel, and those who wished to turn to God were then invited to rise and make eye contact with the preacher. At a Sunday service in 1925, "I asked any who were willing to decide for Christ to stand up, and immediately several rose to their feet."[23]

Stiff Upper Lip

It would be a mistake to attribute disdain for obeisance to Protestantism alone. The conflict has much broader and more elusive cultural implications, in terms of class, gender, and ethnicity. Part of Northern European identity is a contrast to gesticulating Southerners, especially "Latin" and/or Catholic cultures. A common British stereotype portrays Italians, for example, as wildly demonstrative, arms flailing around as they speak, kissing each other, emotional and sensual. The British often perceived these attributes in contrast to a kind of fetishized self-image: stoical, pointedly undemonstrative — a whole *habitus* evoked by the phrase "stiff upper lip."

The origin of this interesting phrase is obscure, though it first appeared in use in the 1830s and may have been coined in North America. The Canadian humorist Thomas Chandler Haliburton (1796–1865) has his fictional alter ego Sam Slick say: "Providence requires three things of us before it will help us — a stout heart, a strong arm, and a stiff upper lip."[24] The American Phoebe Cary (1824–1871) advised a child:

> For I see your proud struggle
> To keep back the tears.
> That is right. When you cannot
> Give trouble the slip,
> Then bear it, still keeping
> "A stiff upper lip."[25]

Notwithstanding a possible North American origin of the phrase itself, it came to be associated with Victorian English, and especially, colonial ideals.

If the British upper lip was stiff, it presumably disallowed smiles or other facial displays of emotion. The child struggles to keep back tears. The British have often been considered notoriously and even proudly inexpressive, compared to those people from countries that have stronger Catholic traditions. The economist Adam Smith once remarked that the British preferred "a calm, composed, unpassionate serenity noways ruffled by passion. Foreigners observe that there is no nation in the world which use so little gesticulation in their conversation as the English." And polite Britons were said to speak of life's most urgent matters, "without altering a muscle."[26] Steadiness was contrasted with "passions, fashion and public opinion."

Though the inspiration of the Holy Spirit may have animated them with pious fervor, Victorian evangelicals and middle-class moralists praised the virtue of "steadiness," that is, of being uninfluenced by others, "independent of capricious influences." According to Marjorie Morgan, "Moralists considered those who were dependent puppets of popular prejudice to be incapable of achieving moral integrity in themselves or in their relations with others."[27] The popular writer Samuel Smiles, who was all for physical vigor and frankness, admitted British "rigidity," but preferred to speak in terms of a characteristic "shyness." The Englishman, he wrote with some affection, "is stiff, awkward, ungraceful, undemonstrative, and apparently unsympathetic."[28]

The mythology of the stiff upper lip was spread less in missionary publications and more in popular fiction, such as in the more than seventy boys' adventure books written by George A. Henty. Typical Henty heroes barely show any emotional response to danger, death, praise, or pretty girls. In *With the Allies to Pekin* the hero, Rex Bateman, kills over a dozen Chinese men (and two Russians) in a cheerfully businesslike manner. He registers only slight changes in his emotional expression when bombarded with praise from senior officers, his father, or his pretty cousins. Henty liked to compare the British "stiff upper lip" to demonstrative French and Italian men, and to women in general. In *One of the 28th,* a French man says, "We are not like you cold English! A Frenchman laughs and sings when he is pleased and cries when he is sorry. Why shouldn't he?"[29]

"Oh, I can't tell you why," Ralph replied, "only we don't do it. I don't say I shouldn't holloa out if I were hurt very much, though I should try my best not to; but I feel I shouldn't cry like a great baby. Why, what would be the good of that?"[30]

Moving to a different genre, the sense that superior civilizations are less physically emotive, and bow less, was expressed by the founding figure of sociology, and British Protestant, Herbert Spencer, who argued at length that obeisance, and prostration in particular, were more widespread and emphatic in primitive, militaristic, and preindustrial cultures — "wherever despotism is unmitigated and subordination slavish."[31] Spencer noted, "It is observable that between the more militant nations of Europe and the less militant, kindred differences [in obeisance practice] are traceable. On the Continent obeisances are fuller, and more studiously attended to, than they are here."[32] As with obeisance, so, too, the expressive activity of the entire body was seen as notably muted in England. Spencer's theories of obeisance will be discussed later in this chapter.

There are also class dimensions to gestural expression: in broad terms, in England, it was (and still is) part of class consciousness that working-class speakers tend to gesticulate more. During his extended diplomatic negotiations over the kowtow, Lord Macartney made an explicit association of China and the working class: "[The] mass of the people in China are gross idolators. . . . The vulgar, as everywhere, are in general excessively superstitious."[33] In Gilbert and Sullivan's *Iolanthe* (first produced 1882), the chorus announces the arrival of the Lord Chancellor: "Bow, bow, ye lower middle classes! Bow, bow, ye tradesmen, ye masses." Bowing was, on the one hand, aristocratic and courtly, but on the other hand it was associated with a working-class habitus (especially that of servants and peasants). Bowing was not middle-class. Erect and forward-looking was the posture of progress, as Disraeli said: "The youth . . . who does not look up will look down; and the spirit that does not soar is destined perhaps to grovel."[34]

Pierre Bourdieu has suggested that the ritual opposition between straight and bent is, at its most fundamental level, sexually determined.[35] James Hevia sees the kowtow debates in terms of a fear of cultural "feminization."[36] In reference to seeking votes, Samuel Smiles opposed bowing to masculinity: "It is so much easier for some men to stoop, to bow, and to flatter, than to be manly, resolute, and magnanimous."[37] The ideal model of middle-class womanhood was not supposed to be physically demonstrative, but women were nonetheless regarded as more emotional than rational, more tied to the body, more bent, closer to the earth, more prone to faint, and more inclined to bending down.

Refusing to Kowtow

Any examination of the discourses against Chinese obeisance among Victorians inevitably takes one back to the eighteenth- and nineteenth-century diplomatic missions from the throne of England to the throne of China. These include the Macartney embassy of 1793 and the Amherst mission of 1816, in which the performance of the kowtow (*koutou,* or *ketou*) became a matter of significant contention in China and in Europe. Even Napoleon Bonaparte offered an opinion on the issue.[38] Until we take bowing (and the production of the display of bowing) seriously, there will be a kind of surreal oddity to the intensity of the arguments about the placement of chairs, audience sites, and the kowtow. It seems peculiar, even comical, now, that with so much at stake, great nations would bicker about knees. Yet in the hard-won Boxer Protocol of 1901 the

Western powers succeeded in removing the kowtow and other Chinese practices from Imperial audiences and in instituting European protocol instead. Arguments about bodies were always mingled with negotiations over trade, reparations, and access.

Subjects of the British and Chinese thrones had been meeting face to face for some time, of course, but such encounters could be kept "off the record" as long as the Emperor himself was not approached, or as long as the Westerners were not taken formally to represent their monarch. The latent issue came to a head when the most strictly ritualized English and Chinese obeisance practices met, face to face, for the first time in 1792. King George of England had sent a high-ranking ambassador, George Macartney, to present a letter and gifts to the Emperor of China, Qianlong. The Chinese worked hard to make this visit fit into the category of a tribute payment from a vassal state, and the mission was not particularly successful for the British. In its later representations, the episode came to be known primarily as a conflict over obeisance: the Chinese had insisted on a full prostration of "striking the head" (*ketou*, or *koutou*) nine times on the ground before Qianlong, and Macartney had refused to bend down any lower than he would to King George (one knee to the ground, head bowed). In two excellent studies of the mission, by Alain Peyrefitte and James Hevia, the negotiations leading to the formal audience and the actual moment of the physical encounter make up the theoretical and historiographical crux, a kind of Durkheimian *fait typique* toward which the suspense builds. Lord Macartney became the first foreign representative to not perform the full prostration before the Chinese emperor. Most of the historical evidence indicates that on this occasion the *koutou* was not performed, even though Chinese officials repeatedly insisted and later claimed that Macartney had indeed struck his head to the ground. In the negotiation of an exception to the normative mode of encounter with the Son of Heaven, Macartney's knees and hands assumed political and historical significance because the course of diplomatic relations between England and China depended on his posture at that critical moment.

Representations of body practices — in this case, the kowtow — populate the cultural imagination of the Other. Real or imagined demands for prostration before the Chinese ruler appear repeatedly in the Western imagination. Take, for example, Sir Francis Hastings Doyle's poem "The Private of the Buffs" (1866).[39] Doyle was inspired to write the work by an incident which took place during the approach of Lord Elgin's army on Beijing in 1860. Doyle is supposedly quoting a China correspondent of the London *Times* (although I have not been able to find any such report in the *Times*): "Some Seiks, and a private of the Buffs . . . fell into the hands of the Chinese. On the next morning, they were brought before the authorities, and commanded to perform the *kotou*. The Seiks obeyed; but Moyse, the English soldier, declared that he would not prostrate himself before any Chinaman alive, was immediately knocked upon the head, and his body thrown on a dunghill." This report followed others that also described other captured Britons as being "treated in a most cruel manner, forced to kneel before every Mandarin, however petty, their faces rubbed in the dust" (*Times,* December 10, 1860). Doyle used the story to imagine a moment when the difference in habitus could no longer be ignored — the moment when an ordinary English soldier comes face to face with the Chinese "authorities" (if not the Emperor himself):

> *To-day,* beneath the foeman's frown,
>   He stands in Elgin's place,
> Ambassador from Britain's crown,
>   And type of all her race.
>
> Poor, reckless, rude, low-born, untaught,
>   bewildered, and alone,
> A heart, with English instinct fraught,
>   He yet can call his own.
> Ay, tear his body limb from limb,
>   Bring cord, or axe, or flame:
> He only knows, that not through *him*
>   Shall England come to shame.
>   . . . .
> Let dusky Indians whine and kneel;
>   An English lad must die.
> And thus, with eyes that would not shrink,
>   With knee to man unbent,
> Unfaltering on its dreadful brink,
>   To his red grave he went.

Representing Queen Victoria and the English "race," a simple commoner with free "English instinct" in his heart stands unafraid of pain or death, and concerned only with national honor. A proud white lad is martyred for maintaining eye contact and an erect posture.

So why did the English refuse to perform the *koutou*? And why were representations of that moment of refusal circulated in England? James Hevia writes that such an act would have violated the "dignity," first, of the English monarch, and second, of the English gentleman. But why was

it considered undignified in the first place? Hevia provides a few suggestions: for Macartney and his peers, it "seems to have conjured up all sorts
of distasteful images in the imagination of the bourgeois gentlemen, not
the least being the conflation of ground/low with dirt and the 'vulgar'
orders."[40] Hevia describes the kowtow in the English imagination as "the
sign par excellence of Asia's slavish and feminized masses."[41] Near the end
of his book, Hevia takes the discussion of these "conjured up" associations further:

Kneeling had long been associated in Great Britain with subjugation, but such
associations took on added urgency in the nineteenth century as a result of the
transformations of physical space in the emerging bourgeois world. The opposition between kneeling and standing upright resonates with others such as
high/clean and low/dirty, distinctions which figured not social class and the geography of the nineteenth-century city, but . . . the feminization of servitude in the
figure of the kneeling chambermaid. The Victorian gentleman and maker of
empire was just the opposite — stalwartly upright, only touching the ground with
more than one knee when wounded or dead at the hands of savage barbarians.[42]

In these remarks, we see the meaning of obeisance as determined in part
by a gendered "order of difference," which conflates domestic servitude,
the feminine, and the bent physical posture. Macartney did not want to
be *put in the position of* a chambermaid. The Protestant Englishman's
revulsion of the kowtow takes on richer historical nuances when we jux-
tapose the "feminization" of China with Andreas Karlstadt's view of "the
worshippers of images as whores and adulterous women," and of idolatrous churches "as whorehouses."[43] The Fanatick Chaplain and the
Protestant Divine agree that Rome is idolatrous, but the Fanatick
Chaplain calls the Church of England "the younger sister to the Whore
of Babylon."[44]

"Subjugation," was sexual, class-based, occupational, diplomatic, and
political. But for Protestants, prostration was also "Catholic." As
Macartney wrote: "The paraphernalia of religion displayed here — the
altars, images, tabernacles, censors, lamps, candles, and candlesticks —
with the sanctimonious deportment of the priests and the solemnity used
in the celebration of their mysteries, have no small resemblance to the
holy mummeries of the Romish Church as practiced in those countries
where it is rich and powerful."[45]

The "Romish" appearance of Chinese religious practices was noted
with regularity, even predictability, throughout Protestant accounts of
China. S. Wells Williams emphasized the religious nature of the kowtow:

What, then, becomes of the quibble of the Jesuits, who declared that it was merely a form . . . ? There is, really, not the least difference between the reverence paid by their subjects to the Pope and the Emperor; both demand it, on the ground that they are the viceregents of heaven, and sitting in the seat of God, and claim the honor due to gods. Knowing what these Chinese functionaries said to-day, no Christian man should ever again discuss the question of performing the *kotow*. It would be an idolatrous act.[46]

It is thus wrong to make "even a curtsey," because the meaning of it is that the Emperor is the Son of Heaven, and "this assumption is like that of the Pope to be the Vicar of Christ."[47]

Precisely because the physical act of obeisance was the same (or similar) in approaching the Imperial throne and in prostrating to the Buddha or the ancestors, many missionaries viewed the kowtow problem as fundamentally a religious issue, and that is why it became so important. We have seen how Martin, for example, argued that obeisance to ancestral plaques was not idolatry because it looked just like bowing to the Emperor; more commonly, missionaries concluded that the kowtow to the Emperor was idolatrous because it looked like obeisance to idols.

Obeisance as a Measure of Civilization

Inherent to the Protestant Reformation was a broad, diffuse effort to straighten the body, keep it vertical, to avoid postures involving the torso becoming markedly horizontal. The erect posture was in contrast to Catholics, idolators, heathens, and pagans, and in contrast to the Chinese. "Chinese" and "Catholic" became fused in the definition (by exclusion) of Protestant Churches. Thus, Macartney's refusal to bow was not only a matter of politics but also of religion.

Chinese and Catholic religiosity were linked in Protestant polemics, in part because of the apparent prominence given to obeisance, but these two terms, Chinese and Catholic, were not the only links in the chain of idolatry: the accusation of "popery" was widely applied, beyond Catholics and even to other Protestants. An example of the multiple associations made possible by the general accusation of excessive obeisance is to be found in the chapter "Obeisances," in the Herbert Spencer work *Principles of Sociology*. Though Spencer was not a missionary, his discussion is revealing, and, I believe, typical in the way that degrees of obeisance were interpreted. A thoroughgoing Social Darwinist, Spencer considered that

the behavior of social animals and humans was parallel or on a contin-
uum. Hence, his chapter on obeisance begins with the example of a small
dog cringing and offering its belly to a large dog. The primal origin of
obeisance is the contrast, after physical combat, of the victor standing
erect over the fallen and disordered body of the defeated: "From the
beaten dog which, crawling on its belly licks its master's hand, we trace
up the general truth that ceremonial forms are naturally initiated by the
relation of conqueror and conquered, and the consequent truth that they
develop along with the militant type of society."[48]

Spencer saw continua running from the results of actual physical
combat and entirely symbolic enactment, and from the most extreme
enactments (prostration, self-mortification, removal of clothing) to faint
remnants of these gestures, as in the nod of the head or the touch of the
cap. This "abridgement"[49] corresponded precisely to the evolution from
the past to the present, from primitive to modern, from Catholic to
Protestant, and from the "other" to "us" (meaning the British). In
Spencer's terms, the gradation of obeisance also corresponded to the
difference between "militant" societies that were based on physical coer-
cion, fear, deception, and distrust, and "industrial" societies that were
based on cooperation, honesty, and trust. The origin of obeisance is the
single pugilistic "primal moment," real or threatened. Prostration onto the
face, for example, occurs only in the most militaristic, despotic, and slavish societies. Attention to obeisance survives in modern Europe where
"militancy" survives: among the upper classes, the army and navy, and, in
general, on the Continent rather than in Protestant England.[50]

Neither the prostrations and repeated knockings of the head upon the ground by
the Chinese worshipper, nor the kindred attitude of the Mahommedan at prayers,
occurs where freer forms of social institutions, proper to the industrial type, have
much qualified the militant type. Even going on the knees as a form of religious
homage, has, among ourselves, fallen greatly into disuse; and the most unmilitant
of our sects, the Quakers, make no religious obeisances whatever.[51]

Obeisance practice thus functioned as an empirical measure of the
inherently non-coercive and honest nature of "industrial" social structures, and as an index of the dignity and integrity of British social institutions. On one end of the yardstick obeisance was full prostration, self-
mortification, ritual nudity, despotism, militarism, deception, slavishness,
China, Siam, Japan, primitives, Catholics, idolators, and dogs. At the
other end was Herbert Spencer's ideal world: faint echoes of obeisance
(growing fainter every day), freedom, industry, free-market capitalism,

honesty, dignity, Britain, Protestantism (and perhaps even God). In the nineteenth century, British colonialism was at its peak, yet Spencer's archetypal scenario — the victor towering above his beaten victim — was projected in its purer forms on the very cultures Britain was dominating or threatening. Whatever we might say about these associations as a theodicy of nineteenth-century European colonial privilege, Spencer uses obeisance as an index of these national, religious, sectarian, historiographic, racial, and political polarities.

The qualities of masculinity and virility were performed in physical postures of erectness and eye-to-eye contact. In contrast to the losers who cringed, the quitters who slumped, and the flatterers who stooped, the Victorian vision of proper human dignity was a stylized, erect rigidity and stoical lack of expression. The vertical logic underlying obeisance and dis-obeisance is a perfect example of George Lakoff and Mark Johnson's "metaphors we live by."[52] Note the vertical metaphors in the following comments on the aggressive and manly spirit needed for missionary work: "Yes, — a healthy, courageous, manly Christianity, gently yet firmly manifesting its conscious elevation and superiority to the heathenism it meets."[53] Whatever their more abstract meanings, terms such as "elevation" and "superiority" mean, simply, above-ness. Or, "And it is very unlikely to be improved by going down to the level of the heathen, in their modes of living."[54] Obeisance is the performance of vertical distinctions.

Other Questions

Before MaCartney, before the Portuguese arrived, there was already a long history of debate over obeisance in Asia, on the question: Should Buddhist monks and nuns be commanded to bow to their parents and to the emperor? Confucian imperial ritual required that all subjects bow to their ruler, but Chinese Buddhist monks claimed the right to abstain from bowing to *any* laity. The monks' refusal to bow was not in any way a rejection of the bow itself as a strategy of embodying social distinctions, as a system of expressing and creating hierarchy, or as an essential element in the broader monastic technology of the self.[55] Furthermore, Asian Christian converts sometimes refused to bow. An interesting case of not-bowing was the famous act of the Japanese Protestant Uchimura Kanzo, who in 1891 bowed, but not deeply enough, to the imperial signature on the 1890 Imperial Rescript on Education.

Although the Chinese word "kowtow" in English usage links the act of obeisance, China, and abjection, a larger framework of study reveals contiguous attitudes toward obeisance in other fields. Some of the implications of anti-Catholic attitudes to obeisance may perhaps be detected, for example, in representations of bowing Muslims in the popular media. The Japanese are also strongly associated with bowing. (Is it only that obeisance is more photogenic than people just standing around?) A salute to a flag is also a kind of obeisance. It achieves its vertical distinction higher in the atmosphere — up at the top of a flagpole — rather than primarily in the lowering of the prostrated body. This "idolatry" is also periodically contested in public performances, such as placing the flag under one's feet.

In researching obeisance in the literature of Religious Studies, I found a peculiar dirth of analysis of this widespread religious practice. Certainly, some of the roots of Religious Studies are in missiology and in the field experiences of missionaries. In a controversial article, Gregory Schopen argued that the bias in the study of Indian Buddhism toward written sources may stem from a logocentrism dominant in the Protestant traditions of most Western Indologists and Buddhologists. The bias often hinges on the logocentric assumption that the essence of real religion is textual, and that popular practices are irrelevant, trivialized, or condemned.[56] Some of my research confirms that view, but surveying the "Protestant presuppositions" in the whole of "Religious Studies" is too huge and too hazy a project to generate more than anecdotal evidence or diffused impressions. Still, by some measures, the academic study of obeisance reproduced standard Protestant rhetoric. Staying within the time period of this book, A. E. Crawley's article, "Kneeling," in James Hastings' *Encyclopaedia of Religion and Ethics* of 1914, takes great care to distinguish between bowing, kneeling, and prostration, arguing that any confusion of the three would be erroneous. The distinction between kneeling and prostration was precisely sectarian in nature: "Among organized religions Christianity alone has given special significance to the posture of kneeling. During half its history the posture signified penitence; during the rest it signified prayer. At the change (marked by the Reformation) it was, by a curious association of ideas, identified with adoration or idolatry."[57]

Crawley characterizes prostrations as "Oriental," as well as characteristic of Islam. He identifies the normal prayer posture of Jews and the early Christian church as standing, yet also mentions Paul's pious wish that "at the name of Jesus, every knee should bow" (Phil. 2:10), but the torso remains erect. He concludes by reproducing the standard Protestant historiography: "The pioneers of the faith probably emphasized the penitent and suppliant posture . . . on all possible occasions; but, when the faith attained a secure position, the posture was relegated to its traditional use. The case would thus be a microcosm of the change of attitude shown by Christianity itself as a whole."[58] In other words, kneeling as the quintessential Protestant posture is evident from the original Apostolic usage (initially penitent, but signifying prayer as faith became "secure"), from Luther's writings, and from the history of Christianity, which progresses from Catholic penitence to Protestant prayer. Postures involving greater lowering of the body are alternately Catholic, Oriental, Islamic, or idolatrous.

The causal sequence mentioned in Chapter 3, of exercise — appetite — digestion — limbs — brain — soul, linked body movement to spiritual condition. There were some energetic body movements that were *not* good for the soul (such as obeisance to idols), but this set of associations indicated a strong sense of the body not only as sign of the spirit but also as generating the fundamental character of individuals and of whole cultures. For Victorians, a bowing body led to a bowed mind and a bowed soul. But would not a bowed soul be a good thing? Missionaries focused on templegoers, and hence, especially on women, as more susceptible to conversion efforts because although they were thought to be misguided in the *object* of their devotion, their physical movements expressed (or trained into them) a sense of spiritual humility and desire for transcendence. In a positive sense, even heathen prostration was at least a sign of a humble seeking after transcendence. Missionaries operated with a sense of natural theology, even if their recognition of the heathen's glimpse of truth was ad hoc or implicit. Sometimes English visitors lamented that Christian England's participation in religion was not as enthusiastic as that of the Chinese Buddhists. Thomas Blakiston commented: "We may be inclined to laugh at and condemn this idolatrous worship, but after all there is something *real* about this style of worship. Where in Protestant countries do we find people going to such an expense as is entailed by the number of candles, incense-sticks, and paper consumed every evening?"[59] He did not ask where in Protestant countries might be found people bowing so deeply, however; in this case at least, his measurement of Chinese religious earnestness was entirely economic.

CHAPTER 9

How the Heathen See the Light

John MacGowan was a prolific Sinologist and a senior evangelist for the London Missionary Society when he contributed a chapter to a small 1905 volume called *Some Typical Christians of South China*. He chose to tell the story of a Chinese Christian called Goon ("Silver"), whom MacGowan claimed to know intimately: "I had the honour of working together with him in the service of Christ" (8).[1] MacGowan wrote nothing of Goon's family background, except that "He came from a very poor family and was absolutely uneducated." He explored in some detail the inner workings of Goon's theology and his personal transformation. In this chapter, I examine this conversion narrative to understand what the missionaries thought they were trying to do, how they thought the Chinese might be saved for Christ. The story brings together many of the themes of the previous chapters.

Theology of a Noble Heathen

MacGowan lauded Goon for his piety, which was "most simple and earnest-minded." Furthermore, "There was a magnetism about this illiterate man that brought all classes under his spell, and that roused them to enthusiasm for spreading the Gospel. One could not remain an indifferent spectator when Goon was near by. His genuineness and sincerity were so thorough that they touched all to whom he appealed."

Though the idea of "magnetism" or "animal magnetism" as a kind of aura was a popular field of psychology during the nineteenth century, by 1900 the theory had waned considerably or had blended into psychiatry or Spiritualism. MacGowan's use of the term was probably popular rather than technical, in the same sense that we use the term today. Nonetheless, it is significant. The story of Goon centers on an unsophisticated illiterate who has never heard the Gospel and who yet has magnetism, charisma, or as MacGowan put it, a "prophetic sense."

One striking feature about Goon was that he was an intensely religious man long before he had ever heard of the Gospel of Jesus Christ. The unseen was to him a reality, which in some mysterious way touched and dominated the poor struggling life that he lived day by day. It is most touching to think of the men like him scattered throughout the great Empire of China, who are groping through darkness for the light, and to whom God has given a kind of prophetic sense, that there exists beyond their ken something infinitely more spiritual than that which all the idols or the teachings of heathen priests can give them. (8–9)

What kind of prophetic sense was this? Goon had an "Old Testament" prophetic sense — which in Protestant doctrine was incomplete, lacking Christ, but still of great merit in itself. God had spoken to the prophets. But what glimpse of God was available to an uneducated Chinese? There were differing opinions on the possibility of a natural theology among the Chinese. Three centuries before, Jesuits had found in the Chinese Classics evidence of an indigenous Chinese knowledge of God in the remote past. Matteo Ricci and others came to see in the Classics God at work in the heathen cultures. That primordial monotheism had subsequently degenerated into the superstitious polytheism of the *vulgus*, but Ricci felt that the literati class had at least resisted the lure of idolatry. Their remaining acts of obeisance — to Confucius, to the emperor, to senior family members, and to ancestors — could be reconciled to Christianity by defining these acts as secular gestures of respect rather than worship. Though natural revelation remained part of Catholic thinking, in the eighteenth century the Vatican rejected the accommodationist view of Chinese ritual and declared the ancestral cult incompatible with Christianity.

Many of the same theological and ritual questions were again debated among Protestants in the nineteenth century, such as during the 1890 General Conference of the Protestant Missionaries of China, described in the previous chapter. Some felt that since the Bible was the unique revelation of God, the Chinese could have had no true knowledge of God. Elijah Coleman Bridgeman (1801–1861) took this view, as did American fundamentalists in general. For MacGowan to attribute to Goon "a kind of prophetic sense," pre-Christian and yet God-given, clearly marked his position on this contentious issue. Perhaps MacGowan was also trying to "save" Goon from idolatry, minimizing or erasing his obeisance to icons, though later in the story we see Goon's household icon. More explicitly, MacGowan wrote: "The conception which the heathen have of this great unseen force is as near that of God as it is possible for people without a divine revelation ever to arrive at, and Mr. Goon had this conception in an intensified form, which modified and dominated his whole life" (10).

In the absence of Biblical revelation, Goon's intensified conception of the supreme yet unseen moral force could not be true in any of its specifics, but unlike idolaters he stopped short of attributing particular form or narrative to Heaven. He did not give Heaven a human form, or try to depict that form, or direct his worship at any depiction of God. Necessarily, then, his conception of Heaven was quite abstract and hazy. In fact, according to MacGowan, he could not explain Heaven at all: "The great force filling Goon's spiritual horizon was heaven. If you had asked him to define what he meant by 'Heaven,' he would have been at a loss to do so" (9).

It may be that Goon was unable to articulate the meaning of "Heaven." We might ask why a poor, illiterate Chinese man would not be able to explain the precise meaning of Heaven. When an educated and forthright Westerner asked him to define in words his highest sense of divinity, it is hardly surprising that he was unable to articulate a satisfactory answer. But perhaps it was not only a lack of practice in articulating theological abstractions. As we have seen in Chapter 5, some Westerners thought of Chinese as a language without "God," without truth or certain other Christian virtues. Thus, as Goon approached an understanding of true divinity, even through a "natural theology," one would expect his Chinese speech to dwindle into silence. "God" in Chinese was long-forgotten and available only in glimmers through textual study of the Classics — available, in other words, to Western scholars but not to Chinese literati (who refused to see the Christian God there), nor to Goon (who could not read). In Chapter 6 we also saw the notion of Chinese speech as inherently deceptive, the practice of "meaningless" speech, and the attachment to a purely liturgical language. However, there was already a long tradition in Chinese religion of ineffability as a characteristic of divinity or reality, such that forthright definitions would seem presumptuous. The ultimate powers in the universe are *xuan* ("dark," "obscure," "mysterious"). Or "inconceivable" (*buke siyi*), as in Buddhist liturgies and other texts. The *Daodejing*'s attitude toward language was well-known: "The nameless was the beginning of heaven and earth," "The way is forever nameless."[2]

Confucius was also known to prescribe the limits of language: "You do not understand even life. How can you understand death?"; "The topics the Master did not speak of were prodigies, force, disorder and gods."[3] Would an "absolutely uneducated" man like Goon have known of this kind of view of language? I think so, if he had spent time in Buddhist or Daoist services, and if he was as contemplative as MacGowan suggested. Though Goon was uneducated, we must not underestimate the sophistication of popular temple discourse.

Though a view of Heaven as beyond language may explain Goon's apparent reticence, his silence also fits into a larger pattern in Protestant reportage. We have seen how missionaries perceived Chinese religion as action without full consciousness. They thought Chinese could not answer the question of why they did these rituals. The apparent inability of the Chinese to give any account of their religious world was more likely an absence of any account that missionaries could recognize as rational. We will never know what Goon actually said if asked about Heaven, but the image of a religious practitioner unable to explain his own religious practice was consistent with Protestant representations of heathen religion. We can now see why Goon's explanations (whatever they were) would have seemed like nothing at all to MacGowan.

Nonetheless, pushing the question of what "Heaven" meant to Goon, MacGowan answered for him, starting with a simple observation of natural phenomena: "No doubt the visible sky with its sun, moon and stars, and all the wonders which the great light flashed into the universe, were mighty factors in his thoughts about it" (9). Indeed, in ordinary speech, "heaven" (*tian*) is used for "sky," and by extension "day." Heaven, like the sky, was always upward and filled with light:

> But they [these ideas] by no means exhausted all the conceptions that he had concerning Heaven. He believed, in a dim and misty way, that behind all he saw, there was a mysterious Power always working for righteousness. Life and death, he believed, were absolutely at its disposal. . . . The ills of life were all under its control, and the wrongs of men with all the injustice and cruelty in the world, though tolerated for the present, would one day meet with a stern reckoning, when this same unseen mysterious Power would rise up and manifest itself by executing vengeance on all evil-doers, and by making full amends to those who had suffered for righteousness sake. Still, his ideas about Heaven were hazy and indefinite. It never crystallized into a personality. (9)

In the trajectory of MacGowan's narrative, Goon's spirituality had already moved beyond polytheism toward a moral monotheism, in anticipation of his conversion to Christianity. The move from the observation of natural phenomena to a single and supreme moral judge replicated many evolutionary theories of the development of religion at that time. Friedrich Max Müller, for example, imagined the evolution of religion, from the beginning of language, to the translation of natural phenomena into myths, to a moral monotheism, and finally to rationalistic philosophy. MacGowan shared the teleological assumption that religious sensibilities would naturally "crystallize" toward a moral monotheism. As noted in Chapter 7, Chinese history therefore represented a regression, the retreat from an ancient glimpse of monotheism into polytheistic idolatry derived from Indian Buddhism. Elsewhere, MacGowan wrote: "In the very earliest days of Chinese history, ages before idolatry was introduced into China from India (A.D. 61), there is no doubt but that the people worshipped the true God. In the course of time the word for God became mixed up with certain heroes that were deified by successive emperors, and so the monotheistic craving of the nation took refuge in the word Heaven."[4]

Though Goon acted on this noble craving, his hazy conception lacked compassion and divine self-sacrifice: "There was no great heart within it that bled for the creatures it had brought into existence. . . . Heaven was to him merely a stern force that never could be bribed like the idols into injustice" (9–10). Consistent with the perception of Chinese religion as a materialistic manipulation, described in Chapter 4, MacGowan and most missionary writers expressed a view of popular religion as bribery. They often perceived Chinese religion as essentially materialistic or self-interested, as a system of more or less amoral bargaining rather than piety. MacGowan even denied it the category "religion": "There is absolutely no religion in it, for the occasional worship of the idols, when some favour is requested from them or some sorrow to be averted, has no moral effect upon a single member of the home. The idols are supposed to be mysterious forces that have great power in the supernatural world, who have to be bribed and coaxed not to send down evil upon men."[5]

In this view, Chinese obeisance was not an act of worship but of subjection and negotiation, like visiting a corrupt local official or gangster. While some forms of ritualized posture in prayer were acceptable to missionaries, deep obeisance was simply abject, for all the reasons described in the previous chapters. Here, the specifically manipulative aspect — toadying to superiors for one's own petty gain — was condemned. In accordance with his pre-Christian prophetic sense, Goon prayed to

Heaven, but "He had never been conscious that any of these [prayers] had ever been in any special manner answered. His great concern was that he would stand right with Heaven, and that he should never incur its anger and so come within the lash of its vengeance." Although Goon asked for favor, he was not daunted by Heaven's apparent lack of response. Unlike the worship of idols, the worship of Heaven involved the confession of sins, and commanded a greater ritual dignity: "It is believed among the Chinese that heaven may not be worshipped at the random times at which the idols may be approached. It is too mighty and majestic a power to be treated in anything but the most profound and reverential manner" (10).[6]

In contrast, popular temple worship must have seemed chaotic to British Protestants, who were accustomed to group worship in church at set times with all participants synchronized in the liturgical structure, either singing in unison or all listening to the same sermon. True, many evangelical Protestants prayed at "random" moments throughout the day, occasionally doing so alone in a chapel but more often in their homes or workplaces, before meals, or during their travels. However, the image of a church-like site where very little of the communal prayer was synchronized or coordinated must have struck the newly- arrived missionaries as anarchic. Missionaries often visited temples to observe or to preach. As noted in Chapter 6, they saw Babel embodied there, a crazy carnival of spirit possessions and fraudulent Daoists cavorting through their rituals. Public temples, like other public spaces, were not always clean and served as gathering places for all sorts of people, in a way that churches rarely were. Any popular urban temple in Taiwan today is a place for retired people and transients to pass the time, socializing and resting outside the home. Puzzled by this multifunctional space, Robert Fortune wrote that "things were going on amongst the worshippers which as foreigners and Christians we cannot understand. Many, who had either been engaged in these ceremonies or intended to take their part in them, were sitting, looking on, and laughing, chatting, or smoking, as if they had been looking on one of their plays."[7] In general, the most orderly and solemn religious rituals were practiced in relative privacy by lay societies, monks and nuns, and by the emperor.

Though there were calendars of festivals and fast days emphasizing the first and fifteenth days of the lunar month, there was little approaching the Victorian idea of the Sabbath. While Goon's worship of Heaven was not on any Sabbath, it was at least precisely ordered in time: "It is considered that the most appropriate time is just at early dawn, whilst the light is struggling with the darkness, and before the solemn hush that rests upon the world is broken in upon by the noise and passion of mankind" (10).

Obviously, the moment of dawn had rich analogical resonance; it is hardly possible to speak of spiritual awakening without reference to light. The dominant motif of light overcoming darkness in this story is consistent not only with the common metaphor of light in general, but also with the theme of China "in midnight darkness," and of the Chinese as blind or asleep. Even Goon saw Heaven in a "dim and misty," "hazy and indefinite" way. Goon emerged from slumber still in darkness, looking for the first light of dawn. Here was the ritual position of a "heathen . . . without a divine revelation":

> It was Goon's custom, therefore, to rise every morning while it was still dark, and, standing in the open in front of his door, wait with his incense sticks in his hands, ready to catch sight of the first streak of light that gave the faintest tinge of colour to the Eastern sky. He would then, in the very sight of Heaven, with nothing to interpose between him and it, let the fragrance from his lighted incense gradually ascend, whilst with clasped and uplifted hands he poured forth his desires to the great Unseen. (10–11)

He directed his attention not to any particular object, but simply to an area of the sky, to nothing more formed than a faint radiance. Though he had the ritual offering of incense sticks, his clasped hands were uplifted toward the sky above the eastern horizon. He did not bow down to this light. He stood. As we read this chapter by the missionary MacGowan, his ritual posture "with knee to man unbent" seems to prefigure the Protestant rejection of deep obeisance. His receptivity to Christian truth was signaled by his posture, by his refusal to bow deeply while at the same time gesturing to something higher. His posture — erect, hands uplifted, focusing on no object but "the great Unseen" — contrasted sharply with the image of Chinese religion in the vast majority of Western representations, that is, with people prostrated before icons.

In directing his attention at a virtually formless "object," he enacted an iconoclastic aesthetic. His worship was aniconic — his gaze had a direction, but it was not directed at any particular object. As MacGowan told the story, Goon's proto-Protestant spirituality was resolutely against mediation. There was "nothing to interpose between him and it" (11). Goon's "prophetic" rejection of form clearly paralleled the Reformation iconoclasm in which (at its most thoroughgoing) all visual form was suspect and many particular forms were actively repudiated by iconoclasm or by the refusal to bow.

Light on the Horizon

Goon practiced this nearly objectless spirituality for many years, "with unswerving faith," before hearing of the Christian gospel. "But at last a day came when the homage of years was to be acknowledged, and the God whom, without knowing Him he had worshipped, was to appear to him as his loving Father and Saviour in Christ Jesus" (11).[8] In other words, the God whom Goon had worshipped for years prior to hearing the Gospel appeared to Goon and acknowledged his many years of worship. Again, MacGowan asserts the qualified validity of natural theology.

It was during one such moment of aniconic worship, there in the thin light of dawn, that Goon had his first indirect encounter with the Gospel, specifically, the gospel of idolatry — by which I mean the "Good News" that one's present system of worship is wrong. First, the scene is set:

He was standing in his usual place outside the open door, with the ascetic look that always rested on his face. The first of the sun's golden rays, unsullied by the touch of earth, had begun to flash through the village, and the leaves of the great banyan, that stood like a sentinel at its entrance, trembled under their touch. The scene was one of exquisite beauty, and harmonised well with the worshipping figure that stood unconscious of it all, as the sunbeams played around the place where he stood. (11)

Goon stood with his hands raised to the dawn sky. Then he heard the footsteps "of a passing stranger, who was hurrying on his way to some place beyond, with no sense that he was a messenger from Heaven, to speak the words of a great revelation to the worshipping figure that was reverently offering up his devotion to it" (12). Although Goon and the stranger did not perceive it as such, we (the readers) are clearly meant to imagine the passing stranger as a messenger of Heaven/God. He was "on his way to some place beyond," and once he said his piece he disappeared from the narrative.

The stranger told Goon: "The worship you are performing now is of no manner of use, and there is no sense in your going on with it" (12). Rather than being annoyed at this rather unconstructive advice, Goon apparently saw something in the man's face, lowering his hands from "the very act of adoration to Heaven" and asking with "wonder" what the stranger meant. The stranger continued with his own encounter story: "'The other day I entered into a church in Amoy, and I listened to the preacher, who was discoursing about his religion. He said that men ought to worship God, who is the Father of all mankind both Chinese and foreigners, for only He can protect men and deliver them when they pray to Him. Now, I should advise you to stop this worship and to do as the preacher directed, and address yourself to God'" (12).

With more sunlight "darting hither and thither, as though joy were filling their hearts," the stranger rushed away, leaving Goon "dazed and perplexed at the words of this stranger, who had flashed in upon his life" (12–13). We hear no fanfare of trumpets, but MacGowan has dazzled us with all the dancing sunlight. The stranger's brief remarks, "with thoughts that he had never heard suggested by any other human being," would hardly seem to have included any ideas so radically new to Goon, but "his life was to be completely changed" by them (13). "He was of too religious a nature to allow the matter simply to be dropped" (13). MacGowan praised Goon's curiosity, his desire to seek out the truth in contrast to the widespread perception of the Chinese as a people satisfied with their own truths, or content not even to think deeply at all.

Twilight of the Gods

"He was determined to investigate for himself" (13). The next morning, he breakfasted before dawn and left for the church "while the dim shadows of night still rested upon the earth" (and upon his mind) (13). It was a Sunday, and he met many Christians gathered there, "hearing from their own lips of the faith in which they believed" (13). His early encounters at the church seem to have been with Chinese converts, people he could relate to: "The men gathered about him and gave him the experiences of their own lives. They were farmers like himself" (14). The testimonial format to missionizing meant that different groups had very different narratives. The Protestant churches gradually nativized in the later nineteenth century and then increasingly in the twentieth. Missionary journals certainly mention and sometimes highlight native Chinese Christian leaders (such as in the book *Some Typical Christians of South China*, or as was done for the Rev. Dzaw Tsang-lae [see Fig. 7]), but the principle narrative in missionary publications was of the foreign missionary, of someone from "here," going "there," among the heathen. Many missionaries were apprehensive about native churches, referring to them as "baby Christians."[9] Victorian missionary publications emphasized how shallow and absurd heathen religion was, how joyous were the native converts and yet how few (it must have seemed) of the huge population were actually converting. By the time of *Some Typical Christians of South China,* missionary

publications often acknowledged that native ministry was more successful than foreign missions, but subscribers to the *Church Missionary
Gleaner* were still less aware of the native church than of the missions,
which were by definition foreign.

Goon was welcomed: "Though a perfect stranger to them, they
received him as though he had been one of their own relatives and was a
member of their own clan" (14). The analogy of kinship would have been
natural, due to the cultural emphasis on the household (*jia*) or clan-lin-
eage (*zong*). The Buddhist Sangha, for example, was a patriarchal,
pseudo-genetic lineage in its discourse and rituals. The term "religion"
entered Chinese as *zongjiao*, "the teaching of the clan-lineages." Kinship
was also the underlying metaphor in the rhetoric of friendship. Kinship
was a natural model for Christian community.

"He was greatly amazed at everything that he saw" (13). Goon stayed
for an afternoon meeting and a communal meal, and later returned for
several other Sunday services, "and gradually he became more and more
convinced that the Christian faith was the only thing that could really
comfort his heart. At last he made up his mind to cast in his lot with the
Christians, and to worship the one living and true God, and Jesus Christ
his only begotten Son" (14–15).

Though MacGowan's readers might have recognized the workings of
the Holy Spirit, Goon was convinced gradually, by rational discussion.
The moment of "conversion" had a very influential scriptural model for
evangelical Victorian missionaries: Paul's "Road to Damascus" experience, in Acts 9. Though the scriptural model in Acts draws attention to
this "blinding flash of light," other people, even in the same book, are persuaded in a variety of ways, and Chinese conversion accounts more typically describe gradual acceptance punctuated by a number of incremental commitments.[10]

"Goon was deeply impressed," MacGowan wrote, but "his mind was
in whirl. He could not see his way to at once give up his own ideas of religion, but certainly a glimpse had been given him into the new faith" (14).
Acceptance of Christianity meant the rejection of other religious practices,
but these two moments were not necessarily simultaneous. His mind had
accepted one, but he could not yet reject the other. Hence: "Before breaking with his old faith he determined to take one final step, in order that
he might be quite assured that what he was going to do would not be
something that he might regret by and by. He determined to ask the
advice of the old family idol, that he and his friends had worshipped for
so many years" (15).

We were earlier led to believe Goon had no truck with icons. Many Chinese performed only those rituals required by the social setting of the ancestral cult, but in this case we are told his friends also worshipped the idol, which would probably rule out an ancestral icon.

If Heaven was Goon's highest god, why not ask Heaven? Because, it is implied, Heaven and God are one and the same? We have already been told that Goon expected no response from Heaven, whereas icons were living presences known to interact and communicate with people on quite familiar terms. The god in Goon's house had a long-term relationship with his family. "It ought to know what was best for him to do, and surely its interest in the home, where it had been worshipped by more than one generation of people, would lead it to give a generous and impartial advice" (15).

Within late Qing culture, how could gods impart advice? Divination could take many forms: spirit-possession and spirit-communication, various techniques of casting the Yijing, dropping wooden blocks, or shaking a jar of numbered sticks until one fell out. In a larger sense, divination interrogated not a particular spirit but the more abstract concepts, such as Principle (*li*), destiny (*yuan*), or changes in *qi,* such as divination of the surface of the body (its shape, as well as moles, scars, and lines), interpretation of handwriting, dreams (oneiromancy), observation of birds' calls, and astrological phenomena. Fengshui also has some divinatory qualities. For MacGowan's British readers, communication with a spirit and various other forms of divination would have been associated with Spiritualism, popular in England since the 1850s.[11] For mission supporters in Britain, Goon's dialogue with the spirit in the idol would have been unorthodox but not incomprehensible.

According to MacGowan, Goon chose to throw "rods" to the ground:

Standing reverently in front of the god he said, "I am here now to tell you of an important decision I have recently come to. I have become a disciple of the Lord Jesus, and I am going to give up my worship of you. I think it is only right that I should let you know this. You have been kind to me in the past, and I would not have you think that I am ungrateful to you for the mercies you have bestowed upon me. What I want to ask you now is, do you think I am wise in giving you up and becoming a Christian?" He then threw up the divining rods into the air, and as they clattered to the ground he saw that the answer they gave was "Yes." (15)

The god had given its approval for Goon to cease all worship of itself. "His mind was at once relieved, for he saw that the god approved of the step he was going to take" (16). MacGowan was certainly capable of skepticism regarding divination. Elsewhere he had noted that some people continued to perform the divination "until they give the reply that they wish to have."[12] Of course, in this case, Goon (and MacGowan) got the right answer the first time, but just to be sure of it, Goon asked again:

"You have just told me that you think I ought to worship God rather than you. Now I am exceedingly anxious there should be no mistake in the matter. Are you quite certain that you fully understand what I have been saying to you? What I mean is, that from today I am going to give up my worship of you. I am never going to burn incense to you, or burn paper money to bribe you, or make any offering of food on your birthday. I am going to worship God only. Do you approve of this, and do you think I am doing right in coming to this determination?" (16)

Again the divination said "Yes."

"Once more standing erect before the god, Goon, bowing reverently before it, thanked it for the kindness of years and bade it a final farewell" (16). MacGowan commented: "This incident proves that at that time when he had fairly decided to break with idolatry, he was still in the twilight. He was not long, however, in emerging from that, and with the intensely religious character of his mind, he soon threw aside all doubt as to the power of the idols, and became a most earnest and zealous follower of Christ" (16).

How do we interpret this anecdote? Did MacGowan mean us to accept that there was real communication between Goon and his icon? MacGowan does not present the story as if the divination came out by random chance, but as a communication. Was it God communicating through the divination? or, was there a demon seated in the idol who nonetheless acknowledged the supremacy of God? The anecdote from Mary Darley about the Spirit Tu-Cu, quoted in Chapter 1, would perhaps support the latter view.

The icon was thought to be "interested" in the whole family; it had consciousness, and reciprocal relations had been established. With Goon's best interests at heart, the icon had said, Stop worshipping me. Was this an admission of defeat? There have been many cases in Chinese religious history where the indigenous deities are "converted" to Buddhism, as when monks "open the mountain" (*kaishan*). (Our religion is so much better than yours, even your gods believe it.) So, too, the indigenous spirit knows he is beaten and like the spirit Tu-Cu, acknowledges the superiority of Christian worship.

Working for Jesus

Within the chapter by MacGowan, this "twilight" episode is the pivot between (what Goon in retrospect judged to be) misguided and fruitless idolatry and what he accepted as a truer way of life. Goon's conversion process involved a significant change in his whole way of life, his mode of interacting with others: a transition between distinct devotional practices, models of community, and discursive practices. Even if Goon's conversion had been a flash of light, the church would not have accepted him so quickly: "After he had been tested for a considerable time he was received into the Church" (17). Churches in the mission fields developed systems of education, examination, and probation, along with a series of specific measurements of commitment which consisted of giving up all worship of the idols and (where applicable) polygamy, foot-binding, temple employment, and vegetarian vows.

In fact, Goon was more than received: "Before long he was employed as a colporteur by the British and Foreign Bible Society" (17). A colporteur was someone employed by a society to travel around distributing Bibles and tracts. The women who did this were called "Bible women." The missions employed a number of Chinese in various tasks: translators, Chinese language tutors, servants, coolies, porters, and various assistants in missionary schools and hospitals.

Frustrated missionaries sometimes felt that a small amount of money would encourage Chinese to convert. For example, when old women said they believed in Jesus but relied on income from chanting in temples, they could not be accepted into the church, and there was temptation to find work for these women in the mission enterprises. Obviously, the missions could employ only a limited number of converts, but more importantly, missionaries wanted to avoid the phenomenon of the "rice Christian" — the apparent convert who desires only the material benefits from association with the mission: food, employment, legal protection, and books (to sell). Again we see the worry that the Chinese are only materialistic and sensory. Nonetheless, a high proportion of Chinese in foreign employ were (or became) Christians. Missions employed converts in part to support their fellow Christians and in part to bring "inquirers" into the mission sphere of influence. Accepting Christianity involved complex changes in embodied knowledge (habitus), such as could best be absorbed by physical proximity in a household or mission compound.

Goon continued irregular farm work and work as a colporteur, but he also assumed a degree of church leadership: "Finally he became a settled preacher in one of the churches that he had been the means of establishing" (17). He was successful in his ministry, MacGowan wrote, and well-known in the area of his work. Despite his illiteracy, "he had an administrative turn of mind" and opened many new stations: "Quite a number of new little churches appeared in various directions over the extensive plain" (17).

He died in harness deeply regretted by all who knew him, and most of all by me, who knew him most intimately, and to whom all his schemes for the advancement of Christ's Kingdom, and all his labours for Christ, were known as they were to few others. (18)

John MacGowan's story of Goon alluded to many of the active concerns and problems of missionary culture. These concerns included doubts about the sincerity of converts and doubts about the spiritual and cultural depth of native Christianity. Most of MacGowan's story is about Goon's pre-Christian piety and his conversion experience, with just a page at the end mentioning his many years of preaching and leadership. Still, this appended wrap-up provides some evidence of the beginnings of a rather muted acknowledgment of the growing native church leadership. MacGowan emphasized how sincere, pious, and proto-Protestant Goon was even before his conversion, but Goon was, in his view, exceptional, and even Goon had to be "tested for a considerable time." Though writers like MacGowan freely pronounced on the fundamental nature of the Chinese (on "the Chinese mind"), the real cultural alienness of China (in other words, the missionaries' own alienation) perhaps made foreigners doubt their ability to evaluate native peoples' inner states. Occasionally, Revivalist individuals and institutions challenged the need for such probation and emphasized the immediate transformative power of baptism in the Holy Spirit. Larger institutions such as the London Missionary Society were nervous when a Charles Gützlaff or a Hudson Taylor proclaimed that great waves of Chinese were converting in huge numbers. Skeptics complained that such miraculous tides ebbed very quickly since these evangelists gave little attention to follow-up, education, counseling, or larger lifestyle issues. It is to one of those lifestyle issues that we now turn: the question of dinner.

CHAPTER 10

Blessed Are the Meat-Eaters

Exercise — appetite — digestion — limbs — brain — soul. Exercise makes you hungry, hunger makes you eat, food is digested, the brain is nourished through the blood, the mind is better able to understand the Gospel, and the soul is saved. Some aspects of Victorian missionary views of exercise, strength of limbs, and the brain have already been discussed in Chapter 3, but two terms in the causal sequence of salvation have yet to be examined: appetite and digestion. What was particularly different about the missionary diet? Even if they adapted local products to European styles of cooking, missionaries certainly ate food different from their own English diet. Outside of the limited expatriate society, their modes of eating were often different as well, characterized by the use of chopsticks versus knife and fork. In terms of food content, perhaps the food group most fraught with meaning was meat. This chapter is about the very fundamental bodily practice of eating where it was most problematic, in the eating of meat. In what I call a "baptism by meat," the consumption of meat became essential to salvation.

Buddhists in China have traditionally held that not eating meat is a religiously meritorious form of fasting. The association of Buddhism and a non-meat diet has been so strong that many Christian missionaries have felt the need to attack vegetarianism, not in any abstract or generic form but adapted specifically to counter Buddhist rationalizations. As part of their efforts to convert the Chinese "heathen" to Christianity, missionaries marshaled their own resources against vegetarianism. It is not that "the West" or "Christendom" was ever unanimous in endorsing meat-eating, nor that Chinese Buddhists were all strict vegetarians. It may be that if vegetarian diet had been religiously neutral (as it is for many today who avoid meat strictly for health reasons), missionaries would have had nothing much to say about it. However, missionaries in China who opposed vegetarianism did so with reference to a series of religious associations connected to discourses on idolatry, anti-Catholicism, and conversion. In addition to this religious aspect, there was a basic difference in diet: most of the Westerners in China during the last four centuries simply ate more meat per person than most Chinese, at least until recently. Anti-vegetarianism can in some cases also be seen as a criticism of the native Chinese diet, which was historically high in vegetable and carbohydrate content but low in protein.

Westerners in China have often remarked on how vigorous Chinese workers were, given the relative absence of meat (or, specifically, red meat) in their diet and the absence of livestock.[1] By contrast, the Western — and, notoriously, the English — appetite for meat was much greater and was conspicuous to the Chinese. The fifteenth-century Dominican friar Domingo Fernandez Navarrette was not being fanciful when he complimented the Chinese on the fact that their urine helped their crops grow, whereas Western urine killed plants.[2] Indeed, meat is very high in protein, which produces urine high in nitrogen, which makes for poor fertilization. In the 1930s Carl Crow listed percentages of diet by type for Chinese and British in Shandong, with "meat and fish" making up 2.3 percent for the Chinese diet and 13 percent for the British. Crow also gave statistics from Shandong Christian University, with "meat and fish" at 6 percent for the Chinese and 23 percent for the Americans.[3] That the Western diet contained more meat than the Chinese diet is a broad generalization, but I believe it is basically valid. Certainly, it has been part of Westerners' self-perception, as, for example, in Robert Louis Stevenson's poem "Foreign Children," in which its young English narrator remarks: "You have curious things to eat,/I am fed on proper meat."[4] This broad generalization does not, however, account for class or gender: in Europe or in China the rich ate more meat than the poor, and men ate more meat than women. A 1929 article in the *Journal of Oriental Medicine* by Biochemistry professor Hsien Wu noted the connection:

The difference between the Oriental and occidental diets is no doubt associated with the fact that the West is more prosperous and on the whole less populous. Although opinions may differ as to which is the cause and which is the effect, there is no doubt that poverty drives a man towards vegetarianism, and vegetarianism may in turn affect adversely his health and efficiency that prosperity becomes more difficult of attainment. . . . The question of vegetarianism is not one of purely academic interest but one which is of vital importance to some race of people.[5]

During the formative nineteenth century when the Manchu government resisted efforts to assimilate Western culture, missionaries were the
primary communicators of "the West," and they articulated this aspect of
diet in specifically religious terms. Emiko Ohnuki-Tierney's comment
about Tokugawa and Meiji period Japanese dietary culture is probably
also true of China: "From a Japanese perspective, meat was *the* distinguishing characteristic of the Western diet, and thus of 'barbarian' cultures."[6] However, more so than in Japan, the popular representation of
the *Christian* life in China inevitably took on the association of meat-
eating and anti-vegetarianism. Indeed, one phrase used by Chinese to
taunt converts was "eat the foreign religion" (*chi yangjiao,* or *chijiao*). Religion was edible. Foreign religion was described as sustenance, though not
primarily meat. In a culture where rice was the definitive food, the term
"rice Christian" was commonly used. Conversely, deriving income from
non-Christian temple activities was referred to as "eating the idol's rice."[7]

In this chapter I examine the confluence of anti-vegetarianism and
anti-Buddhism in Christian missionary discourse on Chinese religion,
focusing on three cases: the Italian Jesuit Matteo Ricci, nineteenth- and
twentieth-century British Protestant reportage, and recent attacks on vegetarian diet by the Chinese Protestant Timothy Kung (Gong Tianmin).
What were the arguments made to support eating meat and to attack the
vegetarian diet? What continuity or change appeared in these arguments
over the course of four centuries? What were the religious and cultural
consequences of Westerners' meat-eating and this "Christian" dietary
assertion? What might be learned from this issue about missionary encul-
turation? How did missionaries interpret the dietary practice of potential
converts? How did this dietary issue play into Western perceptions of the
Chinese and Chinese perceptions of Westerners and/or Christians? Over
the historical course of these cases, is there a discernable trend in the
nature and intensity of attacks on meat avoidance? Arguments against
meat tended to be articulated with reference to fundamental doctrines,
such as creation and the nature of souls, but as time went on the arguments ranged more widely, into perceptions of cultural difference, science
and medicine, and the entire history of "East–West" interaction.
Exploring the relations of a dietary practice and such civilizational narratives is another goal of this chapter.

Before Westerners commented on the issue, there were already diverse opinions and sectarian differences in China, though a full exploration of this discourse is outside the scope of this book. Buddhists had inveighed against meat for many centuries. Fasting, and the vegetarian feasts at the ends of fasts, became merit-making techniques strongly associated with Buddhists. Buddhists campaigned against the use of meat in popular festivals, and numerous emperors sponsored or commanded nationwide meat abstentions during the Medieval period. Naturally, anti-Buddhists included such dietary peculiarity among their points of attack. Also, the more specific avoidance of pork by Muslims was a well-established marker of identity that was similarly attacked in anti-Muslim polemics. Jokes and popular sayings tended to focus not on the avoidance of pork per se, but on the supposed hypocrisy of Muslims who would say they avoided pork but did in fact eat it surreptitiously.

Ricci and God's Gift to Man

The first wave of Catholic missions in China occurred during the late Ming and early Qing. Of the several hundred missionaries sent in this period, the best known is Matteo Ricci (1552–1610). After early experimentation with cultural assimilation in which the missionaries adopted quasi-Buddhist identities, the Jesuits quickly reinvented themselves as Confucian literati (*ru*). They absorbed and then energetically contributed to Confucian anti-Buddhist rhetoric. They thereby distanced themselves from the one religious group that was apparently similar to their own: like Buddhism, Christianity was introduced to China by robed, celibate men from "the West" carrying novel technologies and speaking of hell. The need to align Christianity with elite Confucianism and against Buddhism (especially popular Buddhism) forms the context for Ricci's criticisms of vegetarianism.

Ricci's tract, *The True Meaning of the Lord of Heaven,* began with proof for the existence of God the creator of the universe, carefully distinguishing this God from the Supreme Ultimate (*Taiji*) or Principle (*li*) in Neo-Confucian thought, but justifying the use of Tian (heaven) and Shangdi (Sovereign on high) as translated terms for God. Ricci then distinguished between human souls and those of plants and animals, arguing that "vegetative" and "sensitive" souls die with the body, whereas the human "spiritual" soul persists. He also rejected the notions that spirits and souls are *qi*, that "Heaven, earth, and all things form one body," or that God and the creation are one. Ricci wrote at length on the incorrect Buddhist ideas of souls, and his comments on killing animals followed from his rejection of the concepts of past lives and transmigration. After his critique of meat avoidance, he moved on to discuss the true motives for fasting and, more generally, for moral cultivation. He appended some explanation of the Jesuit practice of celibacy, conspicuously avoiding mention of Buddhist monastic celibacy. Finally, he summarized the life and significance of Jesus. The arguments against Buddhist meat avoidance were thus embedded in a larger critique of Buddhism, which was, in turn, part of an attempt to justify Christianity to (anti-Buddhist) Neo-Confucians.

Ricci summarized his arguments against transmigration in six points: (1) we cannot remember past lives, and those Buddhist and Daoist accounts of past lives are the result of Satan speaking through humans; (2) God created human and animal souls distinctly, and there is no evidence of any change in the intelligence of animals (which one would expect from a "human" soul inside an animal body); (3) plants have a vegetative or living soul (*shenghun*), animals have a sentient or perceiving soul (*juehun*), but only humans have the capacity for rational thought due to their intelligence soul (*linghun*); (4) the human bodily form is different from animals, so their souls must be different; and a particular kind of soul can only go into the appropriate body, just as a blade can only fit into the right scabbard; (5) rebirth as an animal is regarded as Heaven's punishment, but surely violent men would appreciate their rebirth as tigers, and robbers would not mind being reborn as foxes; evil people would not mind their animal forms, because even as humans they would have animal natures; and (6) people fear to kill animals because of the notion that the animal may have been their ancestor in a past life, yet they use animals in hard farm labor, which they would not force on their ancestors.

To say that there is no reason to avoid meat is not quite the same as saying one should eat meat. Ricci's attack on vegetarianism may also be seen in terms of the Jesuit emphasis on moderating traditional Christian asceticism — even to the point of laxity — in order to attract converts in the missions. The founder of the order St. Ignatius of Loyola considered it appropriate to mitigate the requirements for fasting in the interests of the higher virtues of obedience, service, and missionary success. With reference to 1 Timothy 4:8 ("While bodily training is of some value, godliness is of value in every way"), Ignatius suggested using "the testimonies of the Scriptures to exalt spiritual exercises above physical ones, 'which count for little.'"[8] By contrast, other monastic and mendicant orders usually required more stringent limitations on diet. The abstention from meat, in particular, was crucial in the discipline of one's physical desires. The Jesuits argued against these ancient traditions of fasting and abstinence from meat, just as they claimed exemption from the constraints of choral liturgy. In any case, dietary restrictions were imposed as a technique to curb physical desire, not as an end in itself: the animal did not matter.

Ricci's arguments against vegetarianism were based on a theology of creation in which God made animals for human use. Hence, "The Lord of Heaven created birds and beasts for us to use at will. What, then, can be wrong with slaughtering animals and using them to nourish man's life?"[9] Not to make use of animals was thus at least meaningless, and at worst a form of ingratitude. "If the Lord of Heaven does not permit men to kill animals for food, has he not endowed them with excellent flavors to no avail?"[10]

Ricci argued that humans have a rational soul, which is not true of animals or plants. This tenet could both justify meat-eating and refute the Buddhist idea of rebirth. Furthermore, the existence of a rational mind was the dividing line not only between humans and animals but also between classes of humans: those humans who do not exercise this rationality but follow their physical desires were perceived as animalistic: "The majority of such persons pay no heed to the way a man ought to behave to be a true man, and give free rein to their animal natures. The only difference between them and animals is that they have the appearance of man."[11]

Taking another tack, Ricci also argued that meat-eating actually benefits animal species, and that calling for an end to their slaughter would ultimately harm them. We need them for food, so we raise them. "In the West there is a place where people are afraid to eat pork, and the result is that there is not a pig in the country. If the whole world were like that pigs would cease to exist."[12] The choice of pigs here suggests a reference to pork-avoidance among Muslims, which would have been well-known in China, but Ricci is not explicit. A diet without pork would also have seemed a deprivation in China, where pork consumption far exceeded that of beef.

Though the (tangential) argument that meat-eating benefits animals strikes us as slightly absurd, on the whole, meat-eating was linked to more fundamental issues of cosmology and theology. Ricci was not merely arguing for the sake of argument (nor merely for the benefit of animals). His opponent was Buddhism and/or a diffuse set of more or less Buddhist teachings clustered around the vegetarian diet usually called *zhai jiao* (literally, "the teachings of dietary restriction") or associated with "vegetarian societies" (*caishe*). The critique of meat avoidance was part of a longer attack on the Buddhist concept of the transmigration of souls. Ricci recounted the idea that Buddhists refuse to eat meat because of the underlying assumption of rebirth: "The rules forbidding the taking of life are due to the fact that people are fearful lest the oxen and horses they slaughter are later incarnations of their parents, and they cannot bear to kill them."[13] Naturally, he expended some energy to refute the idea of rebirth, which need not concern us here.

Ricci also criticized what he saw as an inconsistency between the practice of vegetarianism and its Buddhist rationalization: "But when we turn to those who believe this false teaching, we find that they only refrain from killing living creatures when they fast and abstain on the first and fifteenth of the month. It is therefore patently an illogical doctrine."[14] Ricci felt that because Chinese did eat meat, except on the first and fifteenth of the lunar month, it was hypocrisy to claim that such restraint was consistent with the Buddhist interdiction against taking life.

These remarks hints at a fundamental difference between Western and Chinese conceptions of "vegetarianism." Before proceeding, however, the term question should be addressed. There is an imprecision bordering on erroneousness in the English translation, "vegetarian," of the Chinese terms *chisu*. In fact, *chisu* does not mean "to be a vegetarian," or "vegetarianism." The English terms suggest a total, exclusive commitment, an ideology. If I eat no meat today, but I ate meat yesterday and plan to eat meat tomorrow, no one would say I am a vegetarian. Perhaps the best one could say is that I am a failed, lapsed, or insincere vegetarian. An added complication is that the term *su* implies not only abstention from meat but also from the "five pungent herbs," which include garlic and onions. In this respect, one can be "vegetarian" and even vegan and still not be eating *su*. But if I did achieve these deliberate abstentions, I could say in Chinese that for my meals, today, I *chisu*. One can *chisu* for lunch and have steak for dinner. Hence, *chisu* is better translated as "to eat vegetarian food," not "to be a vegetarian." *Nihui chisu ma?* means "Can you eat vegetarian food?" not "Are you a vegetarian?" Naturally, though, there is some overlap between *su* as a marker of a particular meal and *su* as a religious or ideological term. Generally speaking, Chinese Buddhists feel that if it is good to avoid meat, it is better to avoid it at all times; but a reasonable starting point is to avoid meat on holy days.

Ricci does not cite scriptural passages to justify eating meat — his audience was Chinese and they would not have been familiar with the Bible, nor would they have necessarily regarded it as authoritative. Indeed, Ricci's *Tianzhushiyi* barely mentions Jesus until right at the end. Still, the basis of Ricci's arguments against vegetarianism was his theology of creation, in which God made animals for human use and without souls. This basic theology of creation was shared by the Protestants who began to missionize in China in the nineteenth century. When we turn to the records of the Protestant missionaries, we find a general continuity of Ricci's arguments, though very few Protestant missionaries specifically read Ricci's works. The major religious dimension added to Christian anti-vegetarianism by Protestants in China was their legacy of anti-Catholicism.

Victorian Missionaries and the Baptism by Meat

To move from the early to the late Qing is to change context is many ways. The opening of the treaty ports and the inland areas of China in the nineteenth century brought a large influx of Protestant missionaries. They wrote prolifically to their readers in Europe and America, in part as a means of maintaining financial support. Though in the sixteenth and seventeenth centuries Jesuits and other Catholic missionaries had evangelized the poor, the writings coming out of the Catholic presence in China tended to accentuate the literati. The dominance of the Jesuits in representing China to Europe, and this basic bias in their works, tended to give the impression that to deal with China was to deal with the literati. By contrast, the textual production of the nineteenth-century missionaries (Protestant and Catholic) directed attention to the peasants and working classes rather than the elite.

In the nineteenth century vegetarianism was more widely practiced in Europe. The *Oxford English Dictionary* contains no references to "vegetarian" prior to 1839; the term "vegetarianism" was popularized by such organizations as the Vegetarian Society, which was formed in Ramsgate in 1847. Vegetarianism, in the nineteenth century, came to be associated with atheism, freethinkers, movements against slavery and hunting, feminism, yoga, Hinduism, and appeals to innate human goodness. Before the term "vegetarian" came into use, non-meat-eaters were sometimes called "Brahmins." Meanwhile, in publications such as the *Church Missionary Gleaner, India's Women and China's Daughters,* and popular travel literature, there were numerous reports of vegetarianism and its religious implications. Occasional voices in missionary culture spoke out for meat-avoidance: one extreme of the temperance movement extended its prohibition of alcohol to meat (and even sex), and the missionary Karl Ludwig Reichelt adopted the vegetarian diet as part of his Christian-Buddhist synthesis. However, on the whole, missionaries were not part of the cultural demimonde who were interested in vegetarianism or in a sympathetic hearing for Asian religions. But they were generally well educated, often beginning their evangelical careers preaching in college. Even during extended stays in the field, missionaries kept in touch with cultural trends in England, and the system of funding for missions meant a constant flow of communication from missionaries to churches at home. They were an influential voice, but not the only source available to Western readers on Asian meat-avoidance.

One might expect that the Eucharist — eating the "body" of Christ — would have been a potent metaphor in discussions of eating flesh. Although the Protestant missionaries were obviously aware of this doctrinal association (the host is the flesh), their theology tended to minimize it or even reject it. By contrast, they imputed to Catholics a simplistic and superstitious notion of the host as the actual body of Christ. For the missionaries, theological debates about the host do not seem to have been relevant to their critique of meat-avoidance, since Protestants usually made a point of denying the real presence of Christ in the host.

Rather than attaching itself to disagreements about the Eucharist, Protestant missionary reasoning in favor of meat-eating shows a basic continuity with Ricci and other Christian writers. One R. Palmer of the Church Missionary Society met a seventy-seven-year-old man who seemed quite courteous and interested in the Gospel, but who had taken vegetarian vows. Palmer argued that "God had created all things that we might enjoy them . . . and appealing to the well-known fact that many of those who do live on vegetable diet are evil livers, I told him that God wanted pure and good hearts."[15] Purity and goodness of the heart was linked to meat-eating, in contrast to the poor morals of vegetarians. It was assumed that animals are supplied for human nourishment, and that there is no religious merit in avoiding meat.

The distinction between Buddhism and *zhai jiao* is reflected in the use of the phrase "sect of vegetarians." The Rev. J. R. Wolfe reported from Fuzhou: "Before her conversion to Christianity, she belonged to the sect of vegetarians in connexion with Buddhism. A great many women joined this sect, and are supposed to practice with greater priciseness the religion of Buddha than the ordinary adherents of that form of idolatry."[16] In most cases, the distinction between Buddhism and *zhai jiao* was not considered significant and the categories blur. Indeed, one may find meat-avoidance and other fasting practices in Chinese culture outside of Buddhism, though the connection to Buddhism was and still is very distinct. Certainly, everyone knew that Buddhist monks were not supposed to eat meat. The underlying connection to rebirth (or "metempsychosis") established a strong association with Buddhism that could not be overlooked. An 1802 English diatribe in favor of vegetarianism almost defined Buddhism as a diet: "The religion of Fo, or Fo-é, the most common sect in China, consists in not kiling [*sic*] any liveing [*sic*] creature."[17] In a 1914 note, Arthur Evans Moule explained that the vegetarian vow was connected to Buddhism, but that "it also constitutes a religion of its own, with a special name for the sect; and it has been said that such vegetarian sects and the numerous secret societies, such as the White Lotus sect, connected with them, are probably the only thoroughly Chinese religious bodies, with duly admitted and registered lay members."[18]

Missionary accounts always noted the solidarity of vegetarians as a group and considered it a special challenge to convert their leaders and/or Buddhist monks and nuns. A report from a missionary named Lloyd tells us, "The old man, Ing Sëüng, who, after forty years of vegetarianism, joined us at the beginning of the year, has proved himself very earnest in seeking the truth. Much consternation took place amongst the other vegetarians when the news of Ing Sëüng's conversion became known." Another hopeful was a man "who occupies a position somewhat similar to that of a priest amongst the vegetarians." [19] That man, too, began to join in the services, much to the consternation of his vegetarian followers. There are similar accounts elsewhere.

In 1902 Hon T'ai Ma, the matriarch of a large household near Pakhoi, decided to give space in one of the household's buildings for use as a chapel. While arranging this move, Mrs. Edward Horder learned that Hon had previously sponsored a Buddhist temple devoted to Guanyin, with three resident nuns:

All her life T'ai Ma has been a most devoted follower of the Goddess of Mercy, and after her second widowhood she took the vegetarian vow, writing it with her own blood. She was at the time threatened that "if she ever broke it the lightning would strike her dead." She visited the Hon temple daily, and the nuns taught her to recite the Buddhist scriptures, and only eighteen months ago she had two nuns occupying the very same loft which was given for our use, and it was here all the idols were assembled (since all cleared away), and T'ai Ma was taught by the nuns to worship more perfectly.[20]

Initially, Hon T'ai Ma had hoped to sponsor both Buddhist and Christian services, but before long she had been converted:

> She was led to see that her worship was vain, and that she ought to break her vegetarian vow. On the birthday of the Goddess of Mercy she came to say that for the first time she had omitted to worship her patron goddess. Mr. Beauchamp visited her house, and on that day she broke her vegetarian vow. The Bible-woman was left behind to teach her more, and had the pleasure of escorting T'ai Ma to the Hon temple to inform the nuns that the vow was broken. They were exceedingly angry to think that all their teaching had been in vain; but T'ai Ma was quite resolute.[21]

Hon had written her vow never to shed blood again in her own blood, and had entered into a mutually supportive relationship with the nuns as a sponsor. The vow and the relationship were broken under the influence of the missionaries. Becoming Christian meant stopping her obeisance to the Buddhist deity precisely on a day when, above all, she should have bowed. Note also that Hon ate meat in the presence of a European man, though it was a European woman who reported the story, and that it was a Chinese Bible-woman who "had the pleasure" of confronting the obsolete nuns.

In the missionary discourses, there were always intimate connections between diet and cultic activities. A public act of discarding or destroying non-Christian sacred images or spirit-tablets was usually required to demonstrate one's sincere repudiation of "idolatry" and to be baptized. For vegetarians converting to Christianity, meat-eating and iconoclasm were always linked. A Miss Schneider was told that old Mrs. Wang had "decided to break her fast and would be willing to take down her idols as soon as I could come down to receive them." Later in the same story: "The old woman broke her connexion with outward idolatry by partaking of a meat dinner, thus discontinuing her fast of thirty years."[22] Chewing and swallowing a piece of meat was thus a ritual action which could end "outward idolatry." Ending the vegetarian fast—the first mouthful of meat—was usually preceded and followed by a Christian religious service.

The association of Buddhism and vegetarian diet was so strong that missionaries actually encouraged meat-eating. The Rev. J. D. Valentine reported the case of a man who had been baptized in 1874 and wished his old mother to convert. She had been a vegetarian for twenty-five years and was a Buddhist. The son urged her to break her vegetarian vow. She gradually came around, giving up her use of the Buddhist rosary first:

"The next step was the breaking of her long fast — a fearful thing in the eyes of devoted, ignorant Buddhists. This took place a year ago. She took animal food."[23] The woman ate the meat at home rather than in the church, so that non-Christians could see. These actions, culminating in meat-eating, were taken as "proofs of her sincerity."[24]

After Miss Schneider had persuaded Mrs. Wang to break her vegetarian vow, there followed a kind of domino effect:

A sister of hers, living here in Chungpa, who several years ago was a catechumen but never gave up her vegetarian vow, and therefore could not be taken into membership, has taken courage and followed her elder sister in also breaking her fast. She — a Mrs. Sie — had been ill for many months. Whenever she was exhorted to put her whole trust in the Lord and give up her vow she replied that she was afraid to break it. But when she heard of her elder sister doing so she at once expressed a wish to do so too. I brought her some cooked meat, and after prayer she took the long-feared step and said she would now really trust the Lord wholly and solely. She was in such a weak condition that one felt the little remnant of life might any time be finished, and therefore we were very thankful to see her enter the fold. Only two days after breaking her fast she died quite peaceably.[25]

Mary Darley told the story of a religious seeker, unsatisfied with her Buddhist options, who became interested in Christianity when someone suggested, "Why not join the foreigners' doctrine?" The seeker began to visit the church and began to accept Christianity. Finally,

it happened that she had to make a really great decision. Fully twenty-one years ago she had very solemnly vowed to keep for the rest of her life, long and strict fasts to her goddess, at stated periods through the year. She had faithfully kept this vow, and now one of these fasts was due, one which should last for ten long weeks. She was indeed agitated. How was she to know the right thing to do? Could we suggest a compromise? What about still keeping the fast, but counting it to the Creator — God? Kwan-yin might not notice the change. Suddenly not to fast at all would most certainly offend her, and who would not tremble to meet the wrath of an offended goddess?

Despite her misgivings, the woman later broke the vow. A "beaming" Chinese worker told Darley, "The fast is broken, eggs she has eaten. I fried them myself with much lard." Darley went to check on her:

But she was not beaming, poor lady! but very thoroughly frightened. She lay at full length on a folding-chair, her face a deep peony-red. She panted and patted her portly self, and as she patted she said many times, "No, this is not sickness to death, not illness at all, or weakness, but 'she' could make me sick to death for very boldly I have defied her. I truly am trusting in God, very much am trusting in

Him; were I not trusting Him alone, those eggs I could not have eaten. Oh! I am feeling uncomfortable! Pains they are coming![26]

The story, as it is told, is quite ambiguous about the woman's faith. She feels that she has defied the bodhisattva Guanyin. There is a suggestion that Guanyin has caused her physical discomfort as punishment, though she feels the bodhisattva will stop short of actually killing her. Nonetheless, she announces her faith in the Christian God as a protection against Guanyin's wrath. The greasy eggs inside her precipitate a kind of spiritual battle which has flushed and prostrated her.

A similar story makes the explicit connection of idolatry and vegetarianism and also shows that at least some missionaries were aware of the health problems of eating meat after a long period of abstention. Mrs. Arnold Foster visited a poor sick woman who had learned of Jesus from a neighbor. She had abstained from meat to acquire merit, but "now she knew that her sins would not be forgiven because of any merit of her own, but only by trusting in the Saviour."

The next morning her neighbour called to see me, and gave me a scroll, on which there was painted a picture of the Goddess of Mercy. She said the sick woman had worshipped this for twenty years, but now she believed in Jesus, and so did not want her idol any more, but had sent it to me, as a sign that she had quite given up her idolatry. Her friend next showed me a few cash, which she said she was going to spend on a piece of pork, to make some soup for the sick woman. She wished to taste meat to show that she no longer believed that there was any merit in her vegetarianism. I could not help warning her neighbour that pork soup was not the best thing for a woman who was very ill and who had not tasted meat for many years, but she assured me that her friend thought it would do her good, and that same evening she called again to tell me she was the better for it. She did not live long, however, after my visit, and was never received into the visible Church on earth, but I believe that, ignorant and sinful though she was, the Christ Whom she trusted received her into Paradise.[27]

Though she wished for the old woman's salvation, Mrs. Foster seems to have been aware that the eating of meat after decades without it would put a strain on the digestion such that it might actually cause death, or speed it up. But questions of missionary culpability must remain ambiguous. The emphasis on diet as the very last obstacle to "entering the fold" raises many questions of religious merit and motivation. Some missionaries were uncertain about the credibility of conversion and sought at every opportunity more empirical evidence, not only of the converts' sincerity but also of their salvation. A Miss Vaughan, in 1894, noted, "In

China when a man becomes a Christian he at once sees that he cannot continue his vegetarianism. Why? Because those who are vegetarians believe that in this way they accumulate merit for the next world." And with reference to a particular case, she recounts, "Now, seeing that no merit of his own could save him, he broke his vegetarian vow by eating an egg."[28] A. E. Moule elaborated his interpretation of the vows as a form of works righteousness:

> They are not taken from ideas of mercy, i.e., the idea that it is wrong to take life for your own advantage, though this idea may have entered into the original Buddhist thought and teaching; and this, if purely a matter of conscience, however mistaken, would make the renunciation of such vows a doubtful act of Christian duty. But the vows are taken with the idea of amassing merit, not from sparing animal life, but from not sparing yourself; self-gain in fact, from the merit of self-loss, self-salvation or alleviation of self-deserved punishment from self-imposed deprivation.[29]

The real issue was not meat in itself, but the drive to convert the non-Christian from Buddhism and from notions of salvation by works. Anti-vegetarianism replicated anti-Catholicism. As long as vegetarianism was interpreted through a theology of salvation by grace alone, in contrast to "self-salvation," meat-eating was a prerequisite for baptism. As noted above, Mrs. Sie "never gave up her vegetarian vow, and *therefore* could not be taken into membership." Moule wrote that the vegetarian diet, "unless from considerations of hygiene, must be renounced when all false doctrine is given up at Baptism. I have never heard an intelligent Chinese Christian doubt the necessity of breaking a vow thus made and thus connected."[30] Here, Moule allowed one kind of exception — "hygiene" — but under the circumstances, such an exception would always be suspect.

Some missionaries lived in China for decades and undoubtedly got to know Chinese culture intimately, but the constant doubts about the sincerity of would-be converts generated a whole hermeneutics of suspicion applied to Chinese converts by Western missionaries. The cultural alienation experienced by the missionaries perhaps undermined their ability to evaluate native peoples' inner states. The persistence of these doubts suggests uncertainty about their own cultural competence to assess indigenous behavior, especially as the specifically soteriological suspicion was in turn mingled with a wide range of colonialist views of the Chinese. Nineteenth-century literature on China frequently asserted the Chinese to be *by nature* liars or "actors," to have no higher sense of Truth, and to be willing to be hypocrites. Deception was regarded as thoroughly permeating the entire culture. In a string of overlapping associations — of morality, worship, ritual, courtesy, formality, theatre, art — Chinese culture was judged a grand deceptive display, profoundly superficial (i.e., "of the surface," lacking, one is tempted to say, any meat). Chinese culture was repeatedly described as hollow or empty — or hungry.

The conversion process involved significant changes in the entire way of life, and in the mode of interacting with others, a transition between distinct devotional practices, models of community, and discursive practices. Even if a conversion had been a flash of light, the church would not have accepted the Chinese convert so quickly. Churches in the mission fields developed systems of education, examination, and probation, along with a series of specific measurements of commitment, which consisted in the giving up all worship of the idols, and (where applicable) of polygamy, foot-binding, opium, temple employment, and vegetarian vows. Hence, it was never a simple matter for a Chinese to become Christian; just saying so was not enough. As noted in Chapter 9, missionaries developed a series of instructional courses and examinations to measure the sincerity of converts. There was normally a probationary period before baptism. This distrust was perhaps inevitable, given the phenomenon of the "rice Christian" — the apparent convert who desired only the material benefits from association with the mission: food, employment, legal protection, even books (to sell).[31] (In one case, at least, rice itself was a test: when one woman came to stay at a mission, "At first she provided her own rice, as we wished to test her sincerity, but when her supply came to an end, as it did very soon, we were quite satisfied with her, and invited her to stay on with the station-class women."[32]) Missionaries extensively questioned converts on doctrinal issues and catechisms; they resisted the move to make conversion profitable; and special significance was given to acts of repudiation and destruction of ancestral tablets and images. Among these various criteria, a continued vegetarian diet was taken as a sign of insincere conversion, and under these admittedly rather exceptional circumstances, meat assumed soteriological significance.

English Appetites in China

Diplomacy on any scale in China required the ability to eat together. Hence, Chinese styles of eating were described at length: "Each one is supplied with a bowl of rice, to which he conveys the more relishable articles, by means of two small sticks, held between the thumb and fingers of the right hand; and placing the bowl in close vicinity, often in contact with the lower jaw, he shovels into his mouth as much of the rice as his distended cheeks can well contain."[33] It is a little odd that David Abeel did not use the word "chopsticks," which came to refer to Chinese dining utensils around 1700. (Previously, the term had referred to part of sea-fishing equipment.) Chopsticks presented a minor problem for foreigners, who also sometimes objected to the fact that everyone picked food from the same dish, and who were sometimes annoyed by the elaborate process of seating deference at banquets.

Diet served to differentiate foreign and native. When missionary passion drove some to go native in their diet, more experienced hands tried to dissuade them. A communication advising one group of three men and four women arriving in Shanghai, from where they would travel to their assigned mission stations, included some practical suggestions from a Mr. Wood: "Butter must be got from the coast, and cocoa. Beef, mutton, fowls, wild ducks, avoid raw fruit. Do not live on cooly food. Staple of Chinese food, rice or Chinese macaroon [noodles] with meat as relish. . . . Do not live on Chinese food when at Station. Can do so when travelling. Mr. Wood advises to live as nearly as possible in European fashion. . . . Especially with young men. Their zeal would make them wish to live in simpler style — this must be checked."[34]

While Westerners were well aware of the scarcity of meat in most Chinese diets, some had fanciful ideas about the diets of wealthier Chinese, which they knew did not exclude meat. A group of Britons invited to dine at an official's home in 1859 "supposed they would be entertained with puppy-flesh, earth-worms, rats and mice swimming in hogs'-lard; but when the time came, they were agreeably disappointed."[35] Monasteries, however, were different. A missionary named Cobbold narrated his visit to a temple: "It was breakfast-time, and we might have accepted the pressing invitation of the monks to join them in their repast, had not our heretical stomachs, still more confirmed in their prejudices by the keen morning air, craved more solid food than the kitchen of the monastery would be likely to supply."[36] In pursuit of that more "solid" food, the British were good customers for pheasants, water-fowl and other meat.[37] One finds repeated mention of shooting waterfowl.

A popular Chinese perception of this Western/Christian taste for meat was perhaps one factor in the subsequent image of the "vampiric" missionary who supposedly removed the eyes or other body parts from Chinese converts as they approached death, or from orphaned or abandoned children, in order to make medicinal potions. I use the term "vampire" here loosely, however, since it carries European (and Hollywood) associations alien to the analogous figure of Chinese tradition.[38] Whereas the European vampire was fixated primarily on blood, Chinese "vampiric" creatures, such as seductive fox-demonesses, drew semen from men. More generally, Chinese bogeymen removed and ate specific organs. For example, in an 1870 report from the Rev. F. F. Gough of the Church Missionary Society, we read, "I spoke pointedly to an aged woman (seventy-six years of age), who presently referred to the reports against us here, amongst other things, that we give 40,000 copper cash . . . to every proselyte, besides a regular allowance, on the condition that at death we take out their hearts!"[39] Hearts and other internal organs, eyes, even kneecaps, were said to have been removed from converts. Missionaries promoted surgery, and later, blood transfusions, which in hostile conditions could easily be misconstrued. Western medical knowledge (such as anatomical drawings of internal organs) was much more explicit about the dissected body. In some cases, the purported Western desire for Chinese bodies and body parts extended also to the missionaries' alleged lust for Chinese women and boys.[40] There were even hostile rumors about telegraph lines: "The blood of children was poured into the apertures made for the poles, and . . . a dead baby's tongue was required at the top of each pole to transmit the message."[41] Missionaries were sometimes nervous about any case of body mutilation when local accusations against the missionaries eating the Chinese flared up.

Recent Christian Anti-vegetarianism: Timothy Kung

This soteriology of meat has not vanished. Though this book does not deal with events after the 1930s, in this instance, it is interesting to consider a recent case to explore questions of the continuity of arguments. A recent example of this tradition of Christian anti-vegetarianism can be found in the essays and sermons of the prolific Protestant minister Timothy Kung (Gong Tianmin), and especially in the essays "Five Important Reasons Hindering the Development of Christianity: The Clash of Buddhist Doctrine and Christianity"[42] and "Eating Vegetarian Food and Eating Meat,"[43] to which we now turn. The latter essay appears in Kung's *Da Fojiao renshi shiwen* (*Answers to Ten Questions of Buddhists*), and the titles of the other essays in this work indicate the range of Kung's work on Buddhism: "Becoming Buddha and Becoming God," "Creationism and the Theory of Dependant Origination," "Is It true That You Receive the Rewards of the Causes from Previous Lifetimes?," "Ignorance [*avidya*] and Original Sin," "Can the Souls of the Deceased Attain Salvation by [the Living] Reciting Sutras and Performing Rituals of Repentance?" "Praise to Amitabha?" "Rebirth in the Pure Land or Heaven?" "A Bodhisattva Bows to a Bodhisattva!" [on superstitious devotionalism in later Buddhism], and "Who is Jesus?" Kung's essays differ from the sources previously discussed in their greater detail and in their more complex engagement with Chinese Buddhist history. Kung was born in 1926 and raised as a Buddhist in Hong Kong. At the age of twenty he rejected Buddhism and was baptized a Christian. After graduating with two bachelors degrees from Hong Kong Lutheran Theological Seminary, he studied Buddhism in Kyoto, Japan, at the Buddhist University (Bukkyo Daigaku) and at Otani University, which are affiliated with the Jodoshu and Jodoshinshu, respectively. With a total of four degrees, he worked in the Lutheran-based Christian Mission to Buddhists, which focused on converting Japanese Buddhists, and in a variety of missionary, pastoral, and academic capacities in Lutheran institutions in Taiwan, Korea, Japan, and America.

In the essay "Eating Vegetarian Food and Eating Meat" an unnamed female interlocutor explains how the pious women in her family encouraged the habit of eating vegetarian food. Now, she eats vegetarian food on special days and otherwise, when she eats meat, she feels uncomfortable, because of the idea that these animals may have been her relatives in past lifetimes. So her friends mock her as being behind the times or backward (*luowu*). It is worth noting that the interlocutor is female, and that, specifically, women are cited as encouraging vegetarianism. Is this factually accurate? Is a vegetarian diet practiced more by women than men in China? I would say it probably is the case. But, here and elsewhere in antivegetarian discourse, there may be a gender distinction operating: meat as masculine. The masculinity of meat affects not only its cultural meanings but also the distribution of protein in families, favoring men with meat. Certainly, meat is coded as a *yang* food. The woman's friends say that eating vegetarian food is "behind the times," so meat-eating also appears to be a mark of modernity and progress. During the twentieth century in China, May Fourth radicals, Christian polemicists, and Communists alike have all regarded traditional Chinese religion as part of a less than glorious past, something to be left behind in the interests of a progress which was inevitably gendered masculine.

In response to the woman's story, Kung begins by saying that he, too, used to try not eating meat, influenced (again) by his female relatives. "I even often went to the temple to burn incense!"[44] His comments move from diet to non-Christian worship with such apparent abruptness that it is clear he considers them inextricable. Christians, on the other hand, do not feel any discomfort in eating meat. Citing John 21:9–13, Kung notes that "the Lord Jesus himself did not eat vegetarian food; after his resurrection he still ate barbecued fish in front of the disciples."[45] Kung also notes the vision of Peter recorded in the book of Acts (10:9–16), in which Peter sees a host of animals and is told by a voice, "Rise, Peter, kill and eat." Kung concedes that this passage is primarily about superceding Jewish food laws and opening the mission to gentiles, but it still shows that animals are edible.[46]

Animals cannot be regarded as the equal of humans, and furthermore, Christians cannot "burn incense or bow to these things" (*shaoxiang guibai zhexie*),[47] thereby treating them as gods or as having a soul. God created these things for our use and enjoyment, though not to abuse. Kung's answer invokes creationism and also links the attempt to not kill animals with idolatry. This linkage of ritual and diet, obeisance and veg-etarianism, associates meat-eating with erect (non-bowing) posture in worship. The particular set of associations here links meat/vegetarian diet with a shift in subject position characteristic of Protestant discourses on obeisance in Chinese religion and Catholicism. Kung's campaign against what he sees as the idolatrous treatment of animals is elaborated in a series of sermons: "Do not bow to cattle as if they were divine," "Do not bow to snakes as if they were divine," ". . . plants . . . ," ". . . rocks. . . ."[48] In these sermons he criticizes the Indian tradition of the "sacred cow," the Indian *naga* cult, the bodhi tree and other uses of trees as objects of obei-sance, and various stone icons throughout Asia.

Buddhism was influenced by Brahmanism, Kung explains, and by the idea of the wheel of rebirth and the six paths: hells, *pretas* (hungry ghosts), animals, humans, *asuras* (titans) and *devas* (gods). So people see animals and think they are their parents from a previous life. Kung asks, since Buddhism has *six* paths, why do Buddhists put all the emphasis on not killing those in only *two* paths (humans and animals)? "Probably in order to promote the vegetarian movement or some other goal, and so they have gone down this heterodox path, contrary to the Buddha's teach-ings."[49] Buddhists say, "Every man on earth was my father, every woman was my mother," but how can this be possible? "Isn't it just laughable?"[50] The population of the world is increasing; but Buddhism says only good people are born as humans. With all the evil we do today, shouldn't it be just the opposite? So, transmigration makes no sense.

Such comments represent a misconstrual of the idea of animals being our relatives. Kung asks why Buddhists emphasize only the two paths of humans and animals. In doctrinal terms, one answer might be that as humans, we simply have no possibility of killing beings in hell, *pretas*, *asuras*, or *devas*. It is a moot point. If it were possible for a human to kill a *preta*, perhaps there would be injunctions against killing them; certainly there are many rituals for aiding *pretas* and those in the hells. But animals and other humans are all we *can* kill, hence the emphasis on these two paths. This seems so obvious (whether one believes in the reality of all six paths or not), one can only conclude that Kung is deliberately misconstruing the Buddhist ideas. Further, he seems to assume you only ever have one set of parents, so that it would indeed be statistically unlikely that any animal you might eat is a former parent. Again, this ignores the Buddhist conception of time as infinite (or at least inconceivably vast). Over time, all permutations are likely. A less literal version of this Buddhist idea is the cultivation of universal compassion extended to all beings *as if* they were one's parents. But Kung is not interested in the more "spiritual" aspects of Buddhist practice. Instead, he makes an odd, circular argument: Buddhists justify vegetarian food by emphasizing the two paths (human and animal) in order to promote vegetarianism.

Kung goes on: "Buddhists often criticize Christians for loving only people, not also loving animals; and they call themselves merciful, loving both people and animals; and also they say that these animals have some kind of 'Buddha nature' [*Fo xing*] just like humans have a 'spirit' [*ling xing*]."[51] He recalls two female Buddhist students who argued that even insects such as ants and bees have a spirit and are able to communicate with each other, but as humans we are unable to read their "books." "Of course this is just a kind of sophistry, and I couldn't help laughing."[52] So, Kung explains to the anonymous interlocutor, you need not worry. "And you can happily eat meat just like Christians! However, this is still just a 'theoretical' understanding that eating vegetarian food is not right, which is still not enough. If you believe in Jesus like us, it must be in your 'faith' (*xinyang*) that you become one who truly feels it. It is only in your inner heart (*neixin*) that you can get true freedom and salvation."[53]

Kung is an inheritor of the tradition of meat-eating as a proof of sincerity — not only of the acceptance of Christ but of the rejection of Buddha. Meat continues to function as a prerequisite for salvation, or at least for the acknowledgment of salvation by some members of some churches. Thus, Kung says, to become truly Christian, to be saved, you need more than a "theoretical understanding" that vegetarian practice is "not right"; you need to feel it deeply in your body (your "inner heart") and mind, in your "faith." He stops short of actually saying you cannot be saved unless you eat meat, but that is clearly the drift here.

As we have seen, earlier missionaries argued that not killing animals purely out of mercy might have been part of original Buddhism, but that a vegetarian diet as having salvific merit was a later development or degeneration. Kung takes this argument a step further, disassociating the vegetarian diet from "original" or other forms of Buddhism: "It is only the Chinese who believe this unbelievable reasoning."[54] Originally, he argues, Buddhism had nothing to do with eating vegetarian food or not. Japanese monks eat meat, and even marry and have "a hall full of children!"[55] (Note the association of meat-eating and male virility.) Or, in Thailand, the monks eat whatever they're given, including meat. Kung cites Dharma Master Leguan (1902–1987) regarding the Theravada vinaya: as long as the monk does not directly kill, it is all right. So, except for butchers, Kung says, any Buddhist can eat meat without sin. Kung also cites Leguan as saying that Chinese monks secretly buy and eat meat. Earlier missionaries had reported the same thing: "They did not pretend to keep the vegetarian vow strictly in the privacy of the nunnery, and seemed to care only for the money they could extort from the credulous."[56] In fact, Kung says, Sakyamuni himself ate bad pork, and this shows that monks used to eat meat as well. So, if Buddhists in other countries eat meat, why are Chinese Buddhists so strongly vegetarian? Some people say that the precept of dietary restriction (*zhaijie*) was originally from "an ancient Confucian method of offering to Heaven."[57] Over time, Kung says, the practices of Buddhism and Confucianism got mixed up.

According to Kung, the widespread practice of vegetarian diet in China dates from the time of Liang Wudi (502–550 C.E.), a famously pious Buddhist ruler. From the North and South Dynasties to the Sui and Tang periods (ca. 5th–8th centuries), zealous emperors (such as Sui Wendi in 583) decreed fast days. Sui Wendi had animals made out of flour to use in sacrifices, and decreed days on which hunting and fishing were banned. Hence, there is a strong tradition in China. So, Kung concludes, eating vegetarian food is really only a custom unique to Chinese Buddhism, and "originally" had nothing to do with the Buddhist faith. The idea that vegetarianism was not present in early Buddhism leads Kung to suggest it is not part of true Buddhism. Otherwise, "if we say that eating meat is breaking the precept against killing, how can we account for all the millions of Japanese monks, and monks of the Southern countries?"[58]

Kung's information is generally correct here, even if his argument assumes the priority of "original" and/or other forms of Buddhism.

Scholarly opinions differ on the diet of early Buddhists and on the idea that Sakyamuni ate meat. Amid his smorgasbord of vegetarian arguments in *To Cherish All Life,* Philip Kapleau refutes the allegation that Buddha ate meat and attributes the Buddha's words in the Pali Canon allowing meat-eating to "monks and scribes still attached to meat eating."[59] Other partisan sources on this issue similarly regard the scriptural basis for meat-eating as "self-indulgent sophistries or inventions to justify the unseemly passion of the writers for the consumption of animal flesh."[60] Japanese Buddhist clergy today indeed eat meat, although throughout much of the history of Japanese Buddhism a vegetarian diet was regarded as the proper norm for most monks and nuns. There was a gradually more lax application of this ideal, and then after the Meiji a widespread acceptance of meat-eating. Earlier, the Pure Land patriarch Shinran used meat-eating to make a point about the futility of self-effort in the age of the decline of the Dharma (*mappo*). Largely due to Japanese influence, some Korean monks eat meat, but this issue, and the problem of marriage for the clergy, is still hotly contested. As for Thailand, Kung is not entirely correct, since he neglects to mention monks of the minority Thammayut nikaya, who do not accept meat into their diet. Still, he is on basically strong ground here: a strict vegetarian emphasis is distinctive of Chinese Buddhism. Kung's attempt to isolate Chinese Buddhism from global Buddhism and from the Buddha is a project that was unknown to Ricci, who thought Buddha had got his teachings on reincarnation and diet from Pythagoras, and it was probably also irrelevant to Victorian missionaries, who saw no strategic value in such a move.

Kung's attacks on Buddhist vegetarianism are in many respects better informed than previous attacks by Ricci or by Protestant missionaries. Kung is of course Chinese, and was himself raised in the Chinese Buddhist vegetarian culture, so he articulates his criticisms from firsthand experience in his youth. His knowledge of Buddhism is more intimate, though I would not want to overstate this point—missionaries were often keen ethnographic observers (even as they added their judgments about the "heathen superstitions" they described in so much detail). However, as with previous anti-vegetarian polemics, Kung shows little inclination to give Buddhism a fair hearing. Kung pays more attention to the historical construction of Buddhist vegetarianism, which was either little known or unimportant to Western missionaries. He claims that Buddha ate meat, and tries to explain the peculiarly Chinese emphasis on a non-meat diet in historical terms, blaming it on a confusion of religious traditions and the quirks of zealous rulers. In so doing, he tries to refute the sense of a continuous lineage linking the dietary practice back to Sakyamuni. Nonetheless, the theology of Kung's arguments remains consistent with his Protestant forebears and even with Ricci.

Meat and Flesh

Several discourses have produced the confluence of anti-vegetarianism and anti-Buddhism. The theological or soteriological discourses of both Creationism and the Six Paths cosmology present diet as a response to the very nature of the universe, the nature of the human self, and its destiny after death. Many Christian missionaries attacked vegetarianism because of the strong association of Chinese Buddhism and vegetarian diet. Because of this, at least to some extent, meat-eating became associated with Christianity, as well as with the West, modernity, and virility. In addition to different conceptions of a healthy diet and many fanciful ideas about Chinese diet, there are also fundamental differences between Western and Chinese conceptions of "vegetarianism."

Discourse on the choice of meat or no meat was mingled with a wide range of other binary oppositions: male/female, modern/outdated, West/East. And Protestant/Catholic, although it must be said, the Catholic Church has had no official policy on vegetarianism, and individual Catholics, such as Ricci, have spoken against it, so it was not that Catholics were regarded as vegetarian. But Protestants opposed vegetarianism for the same reasons they opposed Catholic ritual. The "good deed" of vegetarian diet fostered works righteousness — the illusion that your own religious merit can save you. A 1915 missionary anecdote expresses the hope that a vegetarian Buddhist nun will accept the Gospel, "and so find remission of sins, which she is now seeking to obtain *by her own merits.*"[61] Though the Western missionaries and Shinran had entirely different social and historical positions, in this regard the missionaries were similar to Shinran, who ate meat as a means of repudiating the false hope of salvation by self-effort.

By definition, "vegetarianism" is a discourse against meat-eating and as such it defines itself negatively. Although vegetarian publications can phrase the issue positively — in terms of what you *can* eat — the prevalence of anti-meat rhetoric illustrates how much the identity of a group such as "vegetarians" is formed by its oppositions. Some contemporary messages in favor of meat-eating — "carnivorism" — are tied to the meat industry, but others are products of a conscious opposition to vegetarianism and its extended cultural associations (political correctness, "alternative" lifestyles, tree-hugging, cultural feminization, etc.). This formation of group identity through opposition is to a greater or lesser degree observable in all meaningful social groups. Identity is not static: changes in the opposition produce changes in the group itself. At times, a relatively marginal feature of a group's cultural resources may be suddenly emphasized and elaborated in the process of an intercultural encounter.

Meat-eating is not an incidental or isolated issue in the history of "East–West" encounters, but is one of many tangible — tasteable, smellable, edible — factors. The arguments made to support eating meat and to attack the vegetarian diet are varied and creative, coming from any number of directions: theological definitions of animals and attacks on Buddhological definitions; attempts to isolate Chinese Buddhism, as if to say that vegetarianism is not really even Buddhist; a rebuttal of the diet's health benefits; cultural assumptions about the Chinese as a passive and lethargic people; accusations that vegetarianism is idolatrous; invocations of modernity, masculinity, and colonial vigor; even apparent concern for the survival of animal species. To the extent that the doctrinal underpinnings of the Christian and Buddhist arguments have remained constant, the arguments show continuity even over four centuries. I thus regard Christian anti-vegetarianism in China as a kind of "tradition." However, to my students and colleagues in America, the idea of "Christian anti-vegetarianism" seems very strange indeed. This puzzlement is a testimony to the growth of vegetarianism based in a rhetoric of health rather than theology, and to the growth of ecological discourses articulated in Christian terms. There is in America today an active effort to convince the public that Jesus was a vegetarian. Works such as Andrew Linzey's *Animal Rights: A Christian Assessment of Man's Treatment of Animals* (1976) and *Animal Theology* (1995), or Charles Vaclavik's *The Vegetarianism of Jesus Christ* (1986), are nonetheless far from mainstream. Explicitly or implicitly, multiple anti-vegetarianisms operate in our world today. This chapter has explored one thread of anti-Buddhist anti-vegetarianism, which is quite distinct from the rhetoric about pork among Muslims and anti-Muslims, or about beef among Hindus and anti-Hindus, and distinct again from the "anti-vegetarianism" of the modern corporate meat industry.

CHAPTER II

The Other Smells

A diet of meat was one of the marks not only of Western identity but also of Christian salvation. Though it is hard to say how widespread the "baptism by meat" was, at least on certain occasions, meat-eating was one of several rituals required of Chinese who wished to join the Church of England. Though this strikes us as peculiar now, it made sense within the theology and anthropology of the missionaries, who were faced with Buddhist fasting practices, and Chinese Christians continued to assert the justification of meat-eating and the repudiation of Buddhist fasting.

One of the consequences of a higher meat intake was a difference in body odor. Let us move the meat from the mouth to the nose, to the sense of smell, and consider how Westerners smelled. Victorian missionaries, however, did not write very much about body odor — it would have been in bad taste. In general, odor is widely perceived and poorly reported. Nonetheless, testimonies of smell are worth noting, as smell can be one of the most powerful sensory experiences. Because smells are so pervasive and yet so ambiguous, descriptions of smell tend to be poetic and even fantastic.

The Odor of Westerners

The difference in the meat and alcohol content of Western and Chinese diets was apparently perceptible to the nose, judging from the remarks of Price Collier, an American traveler in 1911, who wrote: "The Chinese themselves do not smell; on the contrary they smell us, and find the odor most disagreeable. We eat strong food, and many of us drink strong drinks; the Chinese do not. On the hottest day, in a room filled with Chinese, there is no disagreeable odor from their persons. No one with a wholesome and unprejudiced sense of smell can say as much for us."[1]

It was not only Americans who noticed their own body odor. Evariste Huc wrote: "The Chinese say they perceive also a peculiar odor in an European, but one less powerful than that of the other nations with whom they come in contact."[2] Even the Chinese water buffalo, apparently, was "credited with a great aversion to what the Chinese call the 'odour' of Europeans."[3] The buffalo's hostile nose for Westerners entered popular lore and whimsy. The Chinese water buffalo is very peaceful and gentle, noted Carl Crow in 1937, but "beneath that ugly and placid exterior there lurks a savage primordial hate against some ancient enemy. Unfortunately, we foreigners appear to smell like these old foes, perhaps some ancient and odorous ape who lived in the buffalo's ancestral home in Africa."[4] Carl Crow mused at some length on the phenomenon: "The Nordic is never permanently safe in the buffalo's vicinity. Occasionally some neolithic odour arouses him and he starts to pay off an ancient grudge which has survived at least one geological period."[5] Dogs, cows, and horses were also credited with a sensitive and hostile nose for Europeans.[6]

Pearl Buck recorded the hostile thoughts of a fictional Mr. Wu: "Foreigners were rank from the bone because of the coarseness of their flesh, the profuseness of their sweat, and the thickness of their wooly hair."[7] Meat and alcohol would not have been the only source of distinctive body odor, but also the use of oils and dairy products, as Isaac Taylor Headland pointed out: "The Chinese themselves use but little, if indeed they use any, butter, and they say of us that we carry about us a butter odour. However this may be, apart from the matter of cleanliness, the Chinese do not smell like the people of Europe. This is probably due to the kinds of oils that go to make up a large portion of their foods."[8] Evaluations of Chinese personal hygiene varied, but more negative comments about Chinese body odors were probably more common. John MacGowan wrote: "The people are highly uncleanly in their persons. They never bathe."[9]

Ancestral Smells

"This was China! Oh, the thrill of it!" After Maude Boaz's joyful arrival in China, she recalled her first smell of Fujian's "clean, cool air before the dawn broke over the hills" with some affection: "The first whiff of that peculiar odour which is China's own. Where does it come from — the sun-baked soil of the cultivated plains, or from the red earth of the up-lands? Who knows? It mingles alike with the acrid smoke of the villages, and with the pleasant perfume of the pinewoods. It pervades all things, natural and material. It is neither elusive nor is it altogether intangible, but it is undoubtedly there, and it stays."[10]

Boaz associates the above thoughts precisely with her first day in her new home — the first whiff. A Westerner's first moments in China were especially finely tuned to other smells: "A new-comer is much more sen-sible of it than an old resident, as the sense of smell becomes gradually so accustomed to it as no longer to perceive it."[11] China's smell becomes the missionary's own: "China entered into us at every pore."[12] The nose goes native.

Boaz's poetic description of the smell of China seems remarkably like traditional Chinese discourse on *qi* (*ch'i*) — an all-pervasive ether, elusive yet not intangible. One wonders if she was aware of the similarity. For better or worse, the smells of bodies blended with the smells of the land. Though "China's own" odor was in the people, trees, and towns, Boaz attributes the smell of all "natural and material" things in China prima-rily to the soil. Before Boaz, Huc had suggested a similar kind of biospa-tial (or biotutelary) explanation for the territory of body odor: "Travelers in remote countries have often remarked, that most nations have an odor which is peculiar to them. It is easy to distinguish the negro, the Malay, the Tatar, the Thibetan, the Hindoo, the Arab, and the Chinese. The country itself even, the soil on which they dwell, diffuses an analogous exhalation, which is especially observable in the morning, in passing either through town or country."[13]

The less fragrant memories of China were usually urban. Thomas Blakiston wrote of "the stench from the city,"[14] as did many other visitors. Some missionaries found the cities too noisy: "But the noises were noth-ing to the *smells;* these were too pungent and evil for words!"[15] Some of the city smells, John MacGowan claimed, "seem to strike one as if with a sledge-hammer and paralyze one for the moment."[16] I noted in Chapter 3 the Victorian association of bad smells with fever-inducing "miasmas," and conversely, the moral fetishization of fresh air. Urban reformers of the Victorian period had firmly established smell as a marker and medium of disease.

The same biotutelary theme was taken to new heights in a rather strange passage by MacGowan, who gave Chinese smells a primordial lineage: "The odours . . . have nothing modern in them, but are the lineal descendants of a long line of ancestors that vanish from sight in the mist and obscurity of a remote past."[17] It is as if MacGowan is saying: Chinese smell their ancestors and the ancestors smell them — which would be consistent with the use of incense and cooked meat in Chinese ancestral cults, as the spirits were thought to have retained their sense of smell and to have enjoyed the aroma of the sacrifice. MacGowan anthropomorphized the smells of the continents, giving them positions in a class structure: "It is simply enough to say that they have the concentrated essence of the ages in them. They trace back their ancestry to the times that are lost in myth and fairy tales, and they look with disdain upon any of the modern smells, just as an aristocrat that holds his title from the times of the Conqueror would gaze with scorn upon some upstart, whose father sold soap and was knighted for the wealth he had amassed."[18]

"Ancient" smells are aristocrats; modern smells are the nouveau-riche. Chinese smells, like so much else in the Victorian imagination of China, sat on their imperial throne while the upstart shopkeepers of England "cleaned up." A similarly adventurous analogy places these ancient and modern smells into the English political system: "The Chinaman is thoroughgoing in his conservatism. . . . Even in his smells he is the rankest Tory that ever lived." [19] Conservativism was something one could even smell!

Imagined Smells

The smell of Westerners (or any smell) is normally below the historiographic radar, but surely smells conditioned social interactions in any number of ways. Ethnographers have been more receptive than historians to body odor, for reasons that seem obvious, but vision and sound continue to override the "lower senses" even in anthropological writing. The body, like food, *"reeks* with meaning."[20] We cannot assume that the Westerners' perceptions of the bad smells of "this hot smelly China"[21] (if not of Chinese bodies), or the Chinese perception of Western body odor, were only figments of their imaginations, but the smells of China have found their way into the imagination of the Other. Despite MacGowan's claim that "Never has there yet been a writer with the genius to describe these,"[22] there have been a number of literary attempts. A globe-trotting character in Earl Derr Biggers's *Charlie Chan Carries On* boasts, "Speaking of the smell of the East, I know all about it now. The odor of fetid narrow streets, vegetables rotting in the tropic sun, dead fish, copra, mosquito lotions — and of too many people trying to be in one place at one time. I'm used to it. I can look forward to China and Japan with an unconquerable nose."[23] This is hardly complementary — but it gets worse. John Hersey, who was the son of missionaries in China, created a fictionalized amalgam of missionaries, one David Treadup, in *The Call.* After a long journey to China, Treadup is disappointed by the familiar Western atmosphere in Shanghai, but he finally experiences the Otherness of China through his nose: "David, standing on the platform of Tientsin East train station, raised his nose to the evening breeze and knew he had arrived at last in some kind of China." His raised nose encountered the gruesome:

David was assaulted by the stink of great China, which came in windborne waves: the smell of nightsoil spread on fields so that the excrement of the generations would grow food to produce excrement to grow food to produce excrement in the endless cycle of a precarious agronomy; of decomposing human and animal corpses in shallow graves and floating face down in rivers; of decaying vegetation and feces in canals; of burning garbage; of the rotting guts of beasts in shambles; of garlic and sweat and menses and bad teeth and mildewed quilted garments — the hideous compacted smells of the poor.[24]

Hersey's description seems overpowering, but perhaps he was being faithful to his memories of missionary perceptions.

In addressing the "distorting factors" which created negative Western stereotypes of China, Holmes Welch complained that Westerners failed "to develop sensory check-valves. Stinks and hubbubs that the Chinese scarcely noticed, because they had learned to screen them out, became for Westerners the most striking element in a situation."[25] A deeper historical analysis of the intercultural effects of differences in smell remains to be done, but at least we have learned that one's nose can be unconquerable, as well as wholesome and unprejudiced.

CHAPTER 12

The Spectacle of Missionary Bodies

Our focus thus far has been on how Victorian missionaries and other travelers construed the Chinese in bodily terms, seeing Chinese culture as bodily rather than mental and imposing their own sets of assumptions regarding the body (and the body-mind distinction) onto their representations of China. We have been looking over the missionaries' shoulders to try to see how they saw Chinese religious activities, to imagine their imagination of the Chinese.

As we try to look through the eyes of missionaries, we should not fail to note that those eyes were blue or green, not "black" (as the Chinese call their own eye color). The gaze of the missionary was fully reciprocated. In this chapter, let us picture the missionary body itself as an object of spectacle. This body was not always suited to the heroic narrative of spreading the light of Truth in the darkened world. For example, Griffith John commented, "Sometime ago I saw a Missionary surrounded by a large crowd of heathen. He was preaching with all *his* might and they were laughing with all *their* might. I thought it was one of the saddest spectacles I had ever witnessed."[1] Obviously, it was not so sad for the crowd, entertained by this weird-looking man waving his arms around and speaking peculiar Chinese, but it was certainly a "spectacle."

Convinced as they were of the truth of their message, missionaries often interpreted their difficulties in persuading the natives as the natives' failure to fully rationalize the missionaries' message. As noted in Chapter 3, missionaries complained that the Chinese were unwilling or unable to think about the Gospel. But as the "sad spectacle" noted by John illustrates, the missionaries themselves — their visibly foreign bodies — interfered with their missions.

Body Problems Faced by Missionaries in China

In the field, missionaries are always, by definition, foreign. Their foreignness may be revealed in many ways: clothing, language, mannerism, face, hairstyle, diet, ritual practices, etiquette, legal documents such as passports, relationships to the institutions of the state, access to certain forms of power, diplomatic immunity, sources of money, sporting pastimes, aesthetic preferences, modes of transport, modes of disposal of the dead, ownership of foreign objects — the list could be more or less endless. Some signs of their foreignness could be changed very easily, others with more difficulty, and still others could not be changed at all. Clothing could easily be changed — though there were arguments about wearing native clothing — but faking a queue took a little more trouble. The local language could be acquired, to native proficiency in some cases → but more often to a lesser level of proficiency, such as fluency but always with a foreign accent, or a command of local language but only enough to get by. Itinerant preachers also traversed many linguistic zones, and fluency in one place might not work in the next town. Mannerisms could be learned, or better still, absorbed mimetically. While there were always some missionaries who never let down their guard, there were many others who had lived so long in one place and had lived so closely with the people there that they did indeed "go native." Missionaries came to *identify* with "their people."

But always with certain limitations. No matter how inconspicuous a missionary felt, as she walked the old familiar alleys and talked in fluent local dialect to natives for whom the novelty of a Westerner had long since faded, she was reminded of her foreignness every time ancestry was discussed, every time she bought a pair of shoes (so big!), and every time she looked in a mirror. Many things could help the missionary to blend in (*if* that was what she desired), but in certain fundamental ways, the missionary body was non-negotiable. The missionary body was always more or less foreign. That foreignness presented some problems as well as some advantages.

A first, but still quite abstract, problem was *foreignness* itself. It is not especially helpful to speak of Chinese "xenophobia," partly because such a term reduces all problems to the psychological category *fear* (and thus ignores such things as distaste, offense, condescension, or amusement). The Qing policy toward foreigners is often treated as a neurotic pathology rather than considered political decision-making. "Xenophobia" almost always connotes something irrational and wrong. As we survey the history of colonialism, perhaps fear of British gunboats and globalization of trade might be considered fairly rational and correct, even if the Qing response to that fear seems now self-defeating. Still, Imperial China's strong ideology of centrality is symbolized by its very name: *Zhong-guo* ("central country"). Foreigners are thus, by definition, *waiguoren*, "outer-country-people." Diplomatic custom and the legal system made the distinction of foreign and native. Official rhetoric and ritual practices promoted a strong sense of the emperor as the center of the palace, of the palace as the center of the city; of the Imperial city as the center of China; and of China as the center of the world. The assertion of centrality was also an assertion of marginality or exteriority. Yet rather than positing a rigid boundary to keep others out, the centrality of Imperial civilization was hegemonic and inclusive. In Qing rites, according to Hevia, "No absolute outside was acknowledged, only relative degrees of proximity to a center. The center was, in turn, frequently constituted anew through ritual practice. Degrees of proximity of participants to the body of the emperor were both made and displayed in rites."[2] Through ritual, abstractions such as "foreignness" became embodied experiences. Hevia's remark leads us in the right direction: to locate foreignness in the body.

Civilization and culture centered around China, and increased in refinement and profundity with proximity to the Imperium. With ritual as the crucial performance of that superiority, it is not surprising that the most serious problems of inter-cultural interaction were bodily. The refusal of Buddhist monks, Catholic missionaries or Protestants and their converts to bow to the emperor (or to parents, ancestors, or ancestral tablets) was perhaps the most intractable scandal of foreign bodies, but there were also other bodily problems generated by the fact of differences in the embodied cultures of foreigners and natives. Foreigners always have to deal with basic differences in habitus, and make decisions about what imported mannerisms they will retain despite (or perhaps because of) the problems they create. Missionaries also made decisions about which native practices could be adopted in the interest of "fitting in," and which ones native Christians must reject. The converts did not always agree with them, of course. There have always been tensions between the impulse toward indigenization and the concern that the essential Gospel will be lost or corrupted through careless nativization. At the same time, foreigners became aware of the native categories applied to them and had to negotiate with this new set of terms, and figure out which "misunderstandings" should be especially clarified. This continual negotiation of what was and was not essential to identity is what makes missionaries so interesting. Their attempts to extricate the essential from the merely cultural reveal what was most important in their lives, their conceptions of the sacred and the profane, and at the same time — for me — they highlight the inseparability of religion and culture.

During the early missions, Jesuits pursued a policy of cultural accommodation, at least in regard to "externals" such as clothing. Initially, the Jesuits dressed like Buddhist monks, but as the pitfalls of that association became clearer, they shed their Buddhist robes and identified themselves with the Confucian literati. In that case, assuming one identity involved rejecting another: Catholic missionaries in China asserted the supposed error, ignorance, and venality of Buddhist clerics as a means of distancing themselves from Buddhist monks in the eyes of both the Confucian literati in China and the anti-clerical Protestants in Europe. In doing so, Jesuit reasoning against Buddhism was largely derived from the European history of polemics against heathens. In some cases, however, missionaries drew from native Chinese anti-Buddhist rhetoric, so that we find two sometimes opposing religions (Christianity and Confucianism) sharing their hostility toward Buddhism. On the other hand, the long tradition of anti-Buddhism in China was a source for those who opposed the Catholic presence. Until the nineteenth century, Chinese anti-Catholics knew virtually nothing of European Protestant anti-Catholicism, but instead drew on a subgenre of literature which consisted of writings denouncing Buddhism, secret societies, and various heterodox teachings (*xiejiao*).

Missionaries in China, whether Buddhists in the first through eighth centuries, Catholics from the sixteenth, or Protestants from the nineteenth, experienced a wide range of problems in their efforts to spread their truths to the Chinese. There were historiographical issues, canonical issues, problems of ethnocentrism and cultural boundaries, textual and terminological issues, and ritual issues, especially regarding obeisance. There were doubts about the moral worthiness of the founders of the two religions. From the earliest times, there had been challenges to the status of Buddha: how could one admire someone who disobeyed his father and ruler by running away from home, abandoning his father, wife, and child? In failing to act upon such fundamental moral and emotional relations, Buddhism seemed to subvert both the natural and the social order. Buddha seemed to be no longer properly human.

Similarly, Jesus had not only failed to continue his family line, but was in fact executed for sedition. The incarnation was particularly preposterous. A 1727 edict by the Yongzheng emperor identified as a specific problem the idea "that heaven came down to earth and transformed itself into a man in order to save mankind. It appears that these farfetched words merely use the name of heaven in order to beguile the rash and ignorant into following their religion. This then is the heterodoxy of the West."[3] It was the incarnation, in particular, that was "farfetched." (Of course it was far-fetched: it was fetched from very far-away Europe. We will reflect on the relation of plausibility and geographical distance in the final chapter.)

More persistent than strictly doctrinal and mythological objections were objections to the bodies of missionaries and their converts. For example, there were accusations of sexual impropriety, drawn from a more widespread repertoire accusing "heterodox" groups of orgiastic behavior. The image of nocturnal, communal Christian worship (male and female together, and different classes mingling) evoked a common theme in anti-heterodox discourse: the erotic mingling of male and female, the desirous transgression of social and gender boundaries. The anti-Christian tract *Bixie jishi* included a description of a Sunday service: "The whole group mumbles through the liturgies, after which they copulate together in order to consummate their joy."[4] In the background of this image was a long history of polemic against a Daoist ritual called the *heqi* (uniting of the breaths), which involved groups of adepts in ritualized copulation. Buddhists had made lurid accusations about this ritual, which had vanished from Daoist practice long before the Jesuits arrived. But there remained a cultural precedent for religious orgies.

Though there were always some scandals involving Buddhist monks taking wives, or sexually active nuns, nonetheless, sexual intercourse among monks and nuns was usually criticized as a breaking of vows, and hence hypocrisy. There was criticism of Buddhist clerics for not getting married and having children, and criticism of them for not sticking to their vows of celibacy. Because the son's obligation to continue his family lineage was so strongly asserted, celibacy was thought to be unfilial and unnatural, as well as economically unproductive. Jesuits usually tried to evade the issue of their own celibacy because they knew of the anti-Buddhist rhetoric against celibacy as being unnatural. But Ricci argued that one could serve God and cultivate the way better if one were not married, though God has not commanded that all men be chaste.[5] However, for the most part, the celibate Jesuits made up a small number of foreigners, whereas for most of the history of Chinese Buddhism, the celibate Buddhists were all Chinese and therefore more problematic. Small groups of foreigners have a certain diplomatic immunity.

Just as Buddhist apologists took the time to justify bodily difference, so too did the Jesuits, and then the Protestants after them. The specific objections or questions shifted — for example, the Protestants had no cause to defend celibacy — but the fact of visible difference remained.

Chinese Interest in the Red-Haired Foreign Bodies

In an 1876 article John Wolfe described the attention he and his companions received when traveling through China, specifically attention to their eyes, noses, hands, fingernails, and clothes:

> Our eyes and noses seemed to be the parts which struck them as most extraordinary. They ventured frequently to touch our noses, and examined very closely our eyes. Our hands and finger-nails also underwent a close examination. Our clothes were not overlooked; they were handled by thousands of fingers. There was a repetition of this every day and night wherever we came, till we became so accustomed to it that we could quietly sleep while the operation was going on. I have frequently seen my friend fall asleep, surrounded by hundreds of Chinese examining closely each article of his dress.[6]

This last image, in particular, is very striking: a white Englishman falling asleep while "hundreds of Chinese" focus their scrutiny on his body. The image of multiple Chinese who had "ventured frequently to touch our noses" represents intercultural contact at its most direct. Such episodes appear throughout the literature of travel and itinerate preaching in China.

The appearance of Victorians in a Chinese marketplace had inescapable novelty value, and at times missionaries took their place alongside raree-shows, jugglers, storytellers, and ranters of all kinds. They often preached in the open public space in front of temples, where all kinds of marketplace behavior was accepted. Chinese curiosity about the missionaries sometimes led to questions regarding their religion but more often regarding other aspects of their culture, life histories, and especially their bodies: "If you wish to discover how indifferent the people are, you have only to stop in your address for a few moments: not one remark, probably, will be made about any thing that you have said; but the cost of your clothes, the length of your nose, the number of your fingers, the colour of your skin, will be the subjects they will observe upon."[7]

In this anecdote, curiosity about physical appearance becomes "indifference," reflecting the annoyance of the missionaries who felt they had something vastly more important to transmit. Probably any traveler could be vexed by the repetition of questions deemed trivial, or by a continual mute gaze. But missionaries had additional reasons to redirect such scrutiny. Francis M'Caw described the general hubbub wherever missionaries met publicly with Chinese. Typically, he would start talking about Jesus, and "they will listen with admiration for some time, until they are drawn aside from hearing by some inquisitive individual, who sees in our dress something which appears curious, to which he directs the attention of all present."[8] Sometimes the Chinese seemed to be obsessed with the bodies of the missionaries, and this focus on the body presented an obstacle to mission work. They were "drawn aside from hearing" the Gospel by the distractions of foreign clothing and bodily features. An 1893 account listed some of the questions female missionaries were asked while "In Chinese Villages":

"Can your eyes see treasure in the earth?" "Do you throw your deceased relations in the river instead of burying them?" (this coming with great horror from people given up to ancestral worship). "Did you work the flowers in your shoes yourself?" "Do you wash your own clothes and cook your own rice?" "What do you eat with your rice?" "Do you shave the outskirts of your head and eyebrows?" "You who have so much silver in your country, why do you not wear ear-rings and bracelets?" "How many children have you?" and then hearing we are not married, "How happy you are!" "Did you come over to this country in a sedan chair?" &c., &c.[9]

The questions are about: eyes, corpses, shoes, handicraft, household life, diet, hair, bodily ornamentation, children, and physical mobility. We can certainly discern other, underlying questions about wealth, class, and gender (since they were speaking to two unmarried and independent missionary women). "How happy you are!"

Miss Emily Garnett complained that her preaching was often interrupted by questions: "Did you make those shoes yourself?" and "Why don't you wear ear-rings?"[10] Another female missionary wrote that "a fusillade of questions was fired at me. Why was my hair short, and why were my feet long?"[11] The socially high-ranking Mrs. Taylor visited a group of women in their homes and began preaching. First, she was interrupted by someone asking if she would like a smoke. She responds, No thank you, and recommences. But then a "fresh interruption, the result of a thought regarding how much my clothes cost and how long they wear."[12] Social duties of hospitality and small talk became "interruptions" in her business.

On Mrs. Taylor's social calls, her hostesses were certainly polite, but we have noted how Chinese politeness was viewed as a barrier to the straightforward talk of Jesus which missionaries so desired. In retrospect, Mrs.

Taylor seems a bit ungracious in her irritation. Still, the questions and comments on the foreign appearance of these female missionaries were at least benign. Evariste Huc, walking through a peasant village, described a cruder interruption: "Loud remarks were made, without the smallest ceremony, on the cut of our physiognomies, our beards, noses, eyes, costume — nothing was forgotten. Some appeared pretty well satisfied with us; but others burst into shouts of laughter, as soon as they caught sight of what seemed to them our burlesque European features."[13]

Missionaries often remarked that unwanted attention to their physical appearance hindered their communication and passage in public and especially when traveling. Victorians in China were intimately aware of the long history of sporadic mob violence against foreigners in China. At the same time, Chinese with connections to Westerners were seized and killed. The *Gleaner* featured a number of articles on mob violence and missionary martyrdom. The Ku Cheng Massacre of August 1, 1895, in which dozens of missionaries were killed, was given extensive coverage, including rhetoric of "the blood of the martyrs" becoming "the seed of the church."[14] Church editorials in the wake of the Ku Cheng Massacre were unanimously against any military revenge, but the mob image remained. Many examples could be cited. There were real dangers of being a foreigner in China, dangers facilitated and exacerbated by bodily conspicuousness. They might at times have wished themselves invisible, but missionaries could not help being looked at.

Traveling in China was always potentially an adventure. A report in 1859 noted "the dread which our strange appearance sometimes excites."[15] To deal with this dread, many travelers scrupulously maintained a guise of good humor. Addressing a small crowd, Russell made the best of it by "commencing with some humoursome remarks about my own person" to break the ice.[16] Likewise, Robert Fortune made jokes about getting a pair of chopsticks for his pony to eat rice, using humor to keep the crowd happy. He wrote: "During my travels in the interior I often found the benefit of having a joke with the natives."[17] Sometimes playing the clown was the best survival strategy.

Hairy Animals

We have already seen some of the curiosities: faces, eyes, eyebrows, noses, fingers, skin, clothes, shoes, and jewelry (or lack thereof). There was also curiosity about hair. The Rev. W. A. Russell, based in Ningbo, declined to visit a rich man because he felt that the other's principal motive was just "curiosity to see one of the ong-mao-nying — red-haired men" [Pinyin: *hongmaoren*].[18] The "red" of their hair became eponymous; they were named after their supposed hair color. Sometimes red hair was ascribed specifically to the Dutch, but just as often it was ascribed to Caucasians in general. One might object that only a small percentage of the Europeans in China had red hair, although "red" could also include brown; but here, again, we see the simplifying and homogenizing of categories applied to another culture's bodies. Not only the color of head hair, but also the quantity of body hair, was isolated and grew into a stereotype. The terms *maozi* (hairy one) or *damaozi* (big hairy one) referred to Westerners in general. A term of contempt for Chinese Christians was *ermaozi* (second hairy one — i.e., one who imitates the primary hairy one, the European).

Most British men were basically clean-shaven in the early nineteenth century, but beards became more common after around 1850, suggesting rugged masculinity and the refusal to pretty oneself up. The 1850s through to the 1880s were a kind of heyday for big facial hair in England. Reginald Reynolds wrote that beards were more popular after the Crimean War (1854–56), along with smoking: "Thus did Britain begin its age of *muscular Christianity,* and in spite of the Queen's well-known objection to tobacco the typical mid-Victorian of all classes was the man with a beard and a pipe, tokens of his manliness and of his Low Church, Latitudinarian or respectable nonconformist conformity."[19]

Reynolds felt that a large beard was particularly associated with Low Church Protestants — "the lower the church, the longer the beard."[20] For some Victorian writers, a beard was a mark of Low Church Anglican or Dissenting Protestantism, in contrast to the clean-shaven look favored by Anglo-Catholic leaders, which drew mocking comment. Charles Kingsley said Catholicism was for an "effeminate shaveling."[21] The 1853 book *The Human Hair,* by hair oil salesman Alexander Rowland, argued that a bearded man was not wishy-washy or a member of the herd: "As a general rule, every man with a beard is a man of strongly-marked individuality — frequently genius — has formed his own opinions — is straightforward — to a certain degree, frequently reckless — but will not fawn or cringe to any man."[22] Nor kowtow, presumably. (The blunt frankness of the bearded man was reflected in the ejaculatory abbreviation of Rowland's grammar.) Beards were even thought to be scientifically healthier than clean-shaven faces. Rowland, and Charles Dickens, argued that they helped protect a man against chapped lips, inhaling dust and pollutants, head and throat problems, watering eyes, and toothache.[23] Dickens also thought that God and nature meant men to have beards. In the mid-

and later nineteenth century, the Chinese would have observed many especially hairy Victorians. The ethnonym *maozi* (hairy one) is therefore quite understandable, though the term dates from much earlier.

Puberty — the onset of facial hair, among other things — was also a metaphor of racial difference, according to T. S. Gowing:

As the Beard makes its appearance simultaneously with one of the most impor-tant natural changes in man's constitution, it has in all ages been regarded as the ensign of manliness. All the leading races of men, whether of warm or cold cli-mates, who have stamped their character on history — Egyptians, Indians, Jews, Assyrians, Babylonians, Persians, Arabs, Greeks, Romans, Celts, Turks, Scandi-navians, Sclaves — were furnished with an abundant growth of natural covering.[24]

It follows, then, that a people without beards cannot have "stamped their character on history," because they have not yet passed through civiliza-tional puberty. Stuck in their boyhood condition, beardless peoples — "grown-up children," as noted in Chapter 3 — also fail to develop morally. As Gowing wrote:

The rise and fall of this natural feature [beards] has had more influence on the progress and decline of nations, than has hitherto been suspected. Though there are *individual* exceptions, the absence of Beard is usually a sign of physical and moral weakness; and in degenerate tribes wholly without, or very deficient, there is a conscious want of manly dignity, and contentedness with a low physical, moral, and intellectual condition. . . . Nor is it without significance that the effeminate Chinese have signalized their present attempt to become once more free men, instead of tartar tools — by a formal resolve to have done with pigtails, and let their hair take its natural course over head and chin.[25]

Here, to fit the data to his point, Gowing switches from beards to head hair, dropping for the moment the relative absence of facial hair among "the effeminate Chinese" and instead focusing on the shortening of their head hair and the end of shaving the forehead. Gowing has refocused the critique of shaving from the chin to the upper forehead, but the associa-tions with shaving remain consistent. He takes big beards and short hair to signal physical and moral strength, manly dignity, a higher state of cul-ture, and individual freedom. By noting the natural scarcity of Chinese facial hair, there seem to be natural limits on the Chinese ability to grow into masculine adulthood. Rowland and others referred to Chinese beards as "defective" and "deficient," "nature having denied their natural growth."[26]

As also noted in Chapter 3, Westerners interpreted the long hair of

Chinese men as unnaturally feminizing, and their relative absence of facial hair was taken in the same way. Qing Chinese represented a neat inversion of this model of masculinity: instead of short hair and long beard, visitors saw long hair and very little beard. In this respect, the analogy of Chinese to women was inevitable. Facial hair marked gender. Male shaving, or a naturally hairless face on a man, threatened to blur the basic gender distinction. Women were appropriately beardless by nature. If the beard has so many health benefits, why didn't women have beards? Simply because women were not suited by nature and design to the outdoor hardships of men. Also, men's chins are unsightly and get uglier as times goes on, whereas women's and children's chins are beautiful. Dickens mused on this issue, and answered it through an appeal to feminine beauty and weakness: "For the same reason that the rose is painted and the violet perfumed, there are assigned by nature to the woman attributes of grace heightened by physical weakness, and to the man attributes of dignity and strength."[27] This feminine model of the visually attractive is part of a construction of women as natural objects of the gaze.

In China, however, great bushes of facial hair and a thick coat of hair on the forearms or chest would not have suggested virility and manly dignity. More likely, they would have been associated with the culturally marginal or remote: the wild populations beyond Chinese civilization, the ancient, the primitive, and animals. Very little has been written on the role of hair in Chinese–Western relations, but Frank Dikötter has made some suggestive remarks:

Comparable to the myth of the wild man in Europe, the hairy man was located beyond the limits of the cultivated field, in the wilderness, the mountains, and the forests: the border of human society, he hovered on the edge of bestiality. Body hair indicated physical regression, generated by the absence of cooked food, decent clothing, and proper behavior. Hair as a symbol of excessive sexuality was encapsulated in stories about the abduction of humans by hairy men.[28]

Hence, hair in profusion suggested a sub- or pre-human state, in which animal desires are acted on without the restraints which are culture: eating without even cooking, sexual intercourse without marriage, life without rituals, action without meaning. It should be noted that the Chinese word for body hair, *mao*, also denotes animal fur. In the most hostile anti-Christian broadsheets, "lord" (*zhu*) Jesus was depicted as a large pig (*zhu*), and foreigners (*yang*, literally "ocean") were shown as goats (*yang*).

Though the *Shanhaijing* (*Classic of Mountains and Seas*), *zhiguai* (accounts of anomalies), and many other texts presented a variety of hairy animal/human hybrids living in the wilderness beyond the boundaries of civilization, "hair only became a dominant symbol of otherness with the arrival of Europeans after the sixteenth century."[29] According to Frank Dikötter, the Chinese representation of the cultural Other as covered in body hair increased during the nineteenth century and especially after the Opium War. Aside from the generalization that most white men in China were actually hairier (on their bodies and chins) than most Chinese, this increasingly hirsute image articulated popular hostility toward European aggressors. With political changes in the twentieth century, the hair of the aggressor went from European to Japanese bodies: in anti-Japanese cartoons, the Japanese were depicted as hairy dwarfs raping Chinese virgins.[30]

Dikötter notes that the dominant thinking on evolution in China was neo-Lamarckian rather than Darwinian. In this view, the fetus "recapitulates" the ascending stages of evolution from animal to human during its growth in the womb. One of the most obvious signs of evolutionary progress from animals to humans is the loss of body hair. Degrees of human evolution upward from animals are indicated by body hair. Hair not only marks the line between human and animal, but also the borders between human races. Hence, "with the theory of recapitulation, absence of hair from face and body became a sign of racial development."[31] Thus, Victorians and Chinese shared some associations of body hair with aggression, but otherwise, thick, heavy beards signified entirely different values.

Whether or not Victorian travelers in China were aware of neo-Lamarckian theories, they were conscious of the animal metaphor and the sense that some humans were still close to the animals. Again, in the specific context of the crowd gaze, being watched so much and having so much attention directed to their bodies and to eating, some foreigners in China felt like May Griggs, "as though I were a wild creature in the Zoo!"[32] Griggs continued, "The people all flocked up to look at the new animal in the Zoo!"[33] Robert Fortune described himself as an animal to the Chinese, who "came from all quarters of the adjacent country to see the foreigner; and, as in the case of a wild animal, my feeding-time seemed to be the most interesting moment to them."[34] But suggesting that Europeans were like animals was only ever a joke. In this spirit of jest, Thomas Blakiston applied the animal metaphor to his own group:

On these occasions we had a fellow feeling for the latest addition to the gardens of the Zoological Society, and, while realizing that most uncomfortable sensation of being gazed at to the fullest extent, we felt equally for the hippopotamus in his bath and the black bear at the bottom of the pit. "The animals will feed at—— o'clock!" . . . To future travellers in the Central Flowery Land I would recommend a good bull-dog as a companion; he would, I think, be found most useful.[35]

With the image of a "good bull-dog" dispelling the crowds of Chinese villagers, the jest takes on a somewhat sinister tone. Some Western visitors,
though not missionaries, did bring dogs to China. (Notably, Sir Aurel
Stein took various dogs, all called Dash, on his Central Asia excursions.)

Clothing

In addition to big beards and different kinds of hair, missionaries displayed their foreignness directly on their bodies: by wearing their clothes.
What kind of clothing did Westerners present to the Chinese gaze? An
engraving depicting the colonial official and *Times* correspondent Archibald Colquhoun, a Mr. Wahab, and two Chinese identified as The Tin-
chai and Jack (see Fig. 9) shows some of the basic differences between
Victorian and Qing clothing. Compared to the local garb, the British
clothing seems more tightly fitted, with a preponderance of buttons and
pockets. Whereas the clothing of any Chinese official or gentleman
would cover his hands in long sleeves, the Westerners' hands were as visible and readily available as the workman Jack's. Western trousers were
also tighter, making a greater display of the legs all the way up to the
crotch. The trousers worn by Chinese tended to be much baggier, or half-
hidden under robes. It is thus hardly surprising that many Chinese were
curious about Westerners' clothes.

Though women's clothing changed rapidly in the nineteenth century,
men's clothing was relatively stable, changing early in the century from
quite colorful to increasingly functional, sober, and dark. Men typically
wore a coat, waistcoat, trousers of dark woolen fabrics, and a linen or cotton white shirt. Summer coats were made of poplin (a silk and worsted
mix) or alpaca (from the alpaca goat, mixed with silk or cotton). But most
coats were made of heavier fabrics composed largely or entirely of wool:
worsteds, meltons, hopsack, cashmeres, and tweed. Trousers were often
made with a strap at the end to keep the trouser leg in place. Waistcoats
were the last holdout of ornamentation, though in the 1860s even they
vanished into the dark and plain clothing of Victorian men. The 1870s has
been described as a "warmly-clad, buttoned-up decade."[36]

Victorian men's clothing showed "an increase in comfort and infor-
mality, a rejection of elegance and its tyranny . . . a suspicion of anything
ostentatious or effeminate."[37] The Victorian middle class owed its status
not to birthright but to commerce, and their clothing expressed the values of stability and seriousness. Frivolity and distraction — frilly sleeves,
festive colors, fussy fabrics — were not signs of good business, whereas the

BEFORE THE START.

1. Jack.   2. The Tin-chai.   3. Mr. Colquhoun.   4. Mr. Wahab.

FIGURE 9. "Before the Start." From Archibald R. Colquhoun, *Across Chrysê: Being the Narrative of a Journey of Exploration Through the South China Border Lands from Canton to Mandalay.* vol. 1, 27.

no-nonsense practicality of their clothing expressed their aspirations of comfort and masculinity. "The Victorian man sought above all to be inconspicuous, offending nobody by anything extreme."[38] If this generalization was valid in England, it was inverted in China, where someone dressed like Archibald Colquhoun stuck out like a sore thumb. With their theological objections to vain frivolity, missionaries were probably among the most conservative in their clothing, so it must have been jarring for them to find their clothes objects of such fascination and in some cases desire.

Though undoubtedly some concessions were made to the heat and humidity of China, conservative Victorian women's clothing was prim and proper, with full skirts and sleeves so that no skin showed other than head and hands. Hair tended to be tightly controlled, in a bun, net, bonnet or small hat, though hair styles relaxed toward the end of the century. Dresses were buttoned-up in front, with high narrow collars. Although formal dresses could be highly patterned and laden with extravagant trim, everyday public clothing was generally muted in pattern and most often dark. There was little ornamentation except for a bow, brooch, or crucifix at the collar. The dress was structured around the bodice. By pulling the waist in and supporting the volume of the skirt(s) and sometimes billowing upper dress, the bodice accentuated the hips and bosom. In the 1890s the peaked or "mutton-leg" sleeve increased the volume of the upper body. Bustles and crinolines, which further exaggerated the curvature of the female body, went in and out of fashion during the latter half of the nineteenth century, and were probably less seen in China than in England. Missionary women in China, cut off from bourgeois society and in fact little inclined to follow the frivolities of fashion, were probably unaffected by such variations in respectable wardrobe. Still, probably the most striking difference between Victorian and Qing women's clothing was the accentuation of the curvature. As stuffy as Victorian fashions may seem to us now, Chinese women wore robes which hung virtually straight down, though their lower legs in "bloomers" were visible, similar to men's legwear. While the fabric and ornaments could be gorgeous, the cut was far from voluptuous. Indeed, at a distance, women's and men's robes looked almost the same. Occasionally there were complaints, such as one in 1896 from the British consul in Fuzhou, that a haphazard mixture of Chinese and Western clothing worn by female missionaries might cause confusion or suspicion in remote villages.[39]

The general modernization of clothing after 1911 involved various fusions of Chinese and Western styles. There was a widespread change of clothing styles, especially marked by Western dress. Mary Darley remarked that by 1913 China had entered its "hat period."[40] In 1922 G. F. Saywell, describing recent changes in China, noted that young people returning from overseas study were "returning to China entirely 'modernized' — even in outward appearance. They dress immaculately, they are as fastidious about the colour of their ties and socks as any westerner."[41] Regarded as a "barbarian" fabric, wool was not popular in China, and British merchants found little market for their woolens until the end of the Qing. Soon after that, however:

Wool became an especially contested fabric in the twentieth century. Made up into a standard business men's business suit, woolen cloth could be seen as symbolizing an overt commitment to westernization and modernization, but it also was vulnerable to criticism for "foreignness." Domesticated in the form of the Sun Yat-sen suit popular from the early republican period onward, however, wool came to connote a thoroughly Chinese, and thus unimpeachable, form of modernity.[42]

Chinese first perceived the foreignness of missionary bodies as a bodily spectacle. Preaching was a display of foreign bodies with inevitable curiosity value. The power of attraction (of their bodies, if not necessarily of their words) was useful yet ambiguous and problematic. Missionaries tried to control that scrutiny, which sometimes took the form of manual fondling — touching noses, feeling cloth — but was predominantly a visual exchange. Missionaries were certainly conscious of being conspicuous, self-conscious at first, but probably inured of it quite soon after. Perhaps they even liked being looked at. Certainly, it confirmed many of their colonial assumptions about themselves and their role in the heathen world. They wanted attention in order to preach, and they bitterly resented the misdirection of that attention to the buttons and hairs of their bodies.

By being normal, they were suddenly conspicuous. They felt the discomfort of being different, and perhaps some pleasure. Their Victorian, evangelical ethos prevented them from consciously reveling in the pleasure of being the center of attention. This conspicuousness was a missiological problem, a distraction from the Gospel word; and they frowned on theatrical frivolity or vanity. Yet, as described in the following chapter, making themselves more normal (locally) meant wearing Chinese clothes (and in some rarer cases, changing their hairstyle). Such transformations were associated with disguise and provoked the missionaries' discomfort with pretense. Dressing up as Chinese opposed their values of plainness while facilitating their very mission in China.

CHAPTER 13

Under the Spotlight,
and the Disappearing Act

Missionaries were strangers in Chinese villages. No matter how well they absorbed local culture, they could never be normal enough to completely blend in. At its best, their fundamental mission was motivated by their sense of truth and compassion: they felt the spread of the Gospel was very urgent because Christ was the only way to avoid hell. This compassion led them to learn to speak Chinese and to try to understand the Chinese people. They wanted to "touch" all of China, to reach even the most remote populations. Traveling from town to town, they spoke in public, often in the tea-houses, marketplaces, and temples. To draw attention to their message, the made themselves into willing spectacles. Sometimes they were centers of the Chinese public gaze, and at other times they carefully avoided that gaze. The subtle tensions of that intense gaze wore down some of the Western visitors, but longer-term missionaries grew accustomed to it, and after a long period of residence in a town, local people got accustomed to them as well. Nonetheless, the crowd was probably one of the strongest formative experiences of missionaries arriving in China for the first time, especially if they went to live in places where few other Westerners resided.

In this chapter, we look at the high and low visibility of the missionaries — when they were surrounded by crowds of Chinese giving their full attention, and when they pursued the opposite of this intense mass scrutiny: when they tried to be invisible.

Crowds

Such crowds! In a few moments we were completely surrounded.
Nothing was to be seen but a host of olive-tinted faces, and countless,
bright black eyes, all fixed on us poor, tired mortals, the observed of all
observers! It was a good opportunity to declare our message, however.
Geraldine Guinness, *In the Far East*

The curiosity value of foreign bodies was not without its benefits. Missionaries apparently grew resolved to this curiosity — which they usually regarded as a tangential distraction from the more important business — and even made some use of it. The *Gleaner* preserved an interesting interaction between a British missionary, who couldn't speak much Chinese, and a Chinese catechist, who was speaking to a smaller crowd at length but who was attracting far less attention. As the novelty value of the Victorian dwindled, the proportions shifted: "He accordingly addressed the growing crowd, and I, standing at a little distance, spoke to a few, who manifestly paid more attention to my dress than to the speaker."[1] The missionary was someone to look at; the catechist was someone to listen to. If Chinese listened to foreigners speaking Chinese, they were not always paying attention to the argument; nor were they convinced. Matthew Yates commented, "They are often amused at hearing us speak Chinese, but are not impressed by what we say."[2] Foreign bodies could draw a crowd, meanwhile the native catechist or Bible woman could explain the Gospel. Native preachers generally had greater success in converting their fellow Chinese.

Probably all of the missionaries in China had had some experience with public speaking in Britain before their assignment to the field. Many had been active in Christian student groups and may have preached to English audiences in church. At the very least, the higher education of many of the CMS missionaries would have involved various forms of public speaking, debating, and class presentations. On the whole, this was a personally self-confident group of people. Yet down from the pulpit, the English preacher in England reverted to Everyman, no more an object of attention than anyone else. In China, the experience even of walking outside was entirely different: "On entering a city, the foreigner is soon surrounded by a crowd. If they have the opportunity, they will form themselves in a ring about him, stooping, poking out their heads, and staring very hard, more particularly if the stranger's eyes are blue — a curiosity which they will fix their eyes upon for half an hour, every now and then looking at one another and laughing heartily."[3]

Probably in the more remote villages, the novelty value of a European preacher was more pronounced. Yet treaty ports and large cities, where there were concentrations of Westerners, were also sites of busy human traffic, and there was a continual resupply of natives in transit who had never seen a foreign face. Nonetheless, for Harry Franck at least, "it was hard somehow to understand just why a town which often saw foreigners still came to stand by the hour watching with the fixed eyes of a statue our every slightest movement, be it only the tying of a shoe-lace or the buttoning of a coat."[4] How must they have felt, these foreigners suddenly subjected to mass scrutiny of their most unremarkable public appearances? It must have been a strain: "To be stared at unbrokenly hour after hour by a motionless throng becomes at times the most exasperating of experiences."[5] Foreigners remarked on the intensity of the gaze, and its relentlessness.

Contemplating the rapid formation of crowds around him, Robert Fortune imagined Chinese coming out of rock: "Indeed, I almost thought the very stones were changing into Chinamen, so rapidly did the crowd accumulate at times."[6] Others imagined Chinese turning into rock — into living "statues," rendered inert by the hypnotic power of their fascination for Western bodies:

Groups of strangers frequently visit the square, and probably having formed no correct idea of the style of the buildings, and the appearance of foreigners, gaze upon every novel object with a fixedness of posture and vision, approaching to statues. If you expose yourself in the verandah, they generally stand in full view before it, and if you walk in front of the buildings, they linger as near your track as possible, and continue to stare as though riveted by a magic spell.[7]

In another kind of effort to explain the staring, Harry Franck made an interesting analogy to the male gaze upon Latin American women.

We consider it rude to stare; the Chinese consider it almost an insult not to stare. Like the young ladies of Spanish America, who would take it as much more than a slight on their beauty not to be ogled so brazenly that it becomes almost indecency by the young men lined up on either side of their promenade, so the Chinese high official or man of wealth would be seriously hurt by a failure of the populace to flock about him wherever he appears in public. [8]

The rich and powerful Chinese consider it natural and preferable to be ogled, (supposedly) like Spanish-American women. Though in this remark the object of the gaze is the Chinese high official, clearly, foreigners felt subjected to the same gaze. The brazen ogling of young women was precisely the male gaze upon female objects — women objectified as objects of male desire — and thus the analogy suggests a feeling that the gaze of Chinese men feminized the Victorian men. Part of Victorian gender constructions was the notion that women are by nature more appropriate objects of the gaze than men. In public, the Chinese mass gaze was probably more male than female, since women's mobility and public life were restricted during the Qing. Female missionaries had greater access to private, female spaces.

Though Chinese gazing crowds were turned into statues, or into mute, zombie-like bodies, or (in jest) into spectators at a zoo, there was always a sense of vulnerability and danger in being the object of their gaze. Even Fortune, who (at least in his retelling) could be quite physically brave, emphasized the need to charm the crowd:

Alone as I now was, and surrounded by thousands of Chinese in one of their inland cities, it was absolutely necessary to keep my temper under the most complete control. In circumstances of this kind, if one laughs and jokes with the crowd, and takes everything in good part, all will generally go well, for the Chinese are upon the whole good-humoured and polite; but if he by any chance loses his temper, he will most certainly get the worst of it, and most likely will be hooted and pelted with stones. I had had some experience in the management of Chinese crowds, and therefore continued to be in the sweetest possible frame of mind in the midst of the thousands who followed me through the city as if I had been a wild animal or "white devil" indeed.[9]

Though one might consider a crowd merely as an aggregate of all the individuals in close proximity, it was common in the nineteenth century (and still today) to consider the crowd as having a mind of its own, a single consciousness not quite located in any one person. Certainly, the French Revolution provided Europeans with some specific images of the crowd as a "mob," a term derived from "mobile," though it meant much more than just a mobile crowd. This singular mob consciousness was often thought of as violent and destructive, acting on instinct rather than reason, and essentially antisocial. If there was any rationality in the crowd, it was uncritical. Crowds were also viewed as hypnotized, in a trance, as individual minds were absorbed into a herd somehow much less than the sum of its parts.

Although the behavior and true nature of the crowd was explored in many discourses throughout the nineteenth century, Gustave LeBon (1841–1931) brought the various more or less scientific developments in crowd psychology to popular readership with his 1895 tome *Psychologie des foules*. LeBon's views were very influential and were seriously challenged only in the mid-twentieth century by scholars who emphasized the positive and rational aspects of crowds. While Protestant missionaries may not have read LeBon's book, to some extent, his arguments typified popular thinking about crowds, and they may help us reconstruct some of the missionary experience at the center of crowds or as the targets of mobs.

For LeBon crowds have a terrible capacity for capricious violence and bestial savagery. Crowds are cruel and unimpressed by acts of kindness. LeBon noted the crowd's stupidity and mental deficiency. In a crowd, the individual loses personality and consciousness and becomes an automaton. As if through mass hypnosis, the crowd is body, not mind: "Its acts are far more under the influence of the spinal cord than of the brain."[10] Hence, the testimony of crowds is false and useless. Crowds exaggerate, simplify, have no sense of responsibility, and cannot discern truth. We find a correlation between LeBon's view of crowds and many of the views of the Chinese previously discussed, especially recalling the tendency of visitors to view the natives as an undifferentiated mass, as discussed in Chapter 4.

The crowd, according to LeBon, is also a regression to some earlier stage in human evolution. In a crowd, "a man descends several rungs in the ladder of civilization. Isolated, he may be a cultivated individual; in a crowd, he is a barbarian — that is, a creature acting by instinct. He possesses the spontaneity, the violence, the ferocity, and also the enthusiasm and heroism of primitive beings."[11] This regressed state is expressed in "impulsiveness, irritability, incapacity to reason, the absence of judgment and the critical spirit, the exaggeration of the sentiments, and others besides — which are almost always observed in beings belonging to inferior forms of evolution — in women, savages, and children, for instance."[12]

For LeBon the crowd is thus a woman, a child, or a savage; and furthermore, "Latin": "Crowds are everywhere distinguished by feminine characteristics, but Latin crowds are the most feminine of all."[13] LeBon's anti-religious sentiments, which were largely anti-Catholic, and his hostility to "Latin" cultures, led him to assert that crowds see in terms of "images."[14] Clearly, he did not mean only visual images but also linguistic ones, that is, *images* rather than more abstract *concepts* or *rational reasoning*. He did not mean this as a complement: crowds were idolaters, and idolatry was a crowd mentality.

A crowd was also a racial concept, since stronger races were more resistant to the dehumanizing affects of crowds: "It should be considered as an essential law that *the inferior characteristics of crowds are the less accentuated as the spirit of the race is strong.*"[15] LeBon was in agreement with

Herbert Spencer in attributing to Catholic cultures a greater authoritarianism and a corollary willingness to subordinate the individual. LeBon had almost nothing to say about Chinese crowds, in particular, except to repeat the cliché that the stagnation of China had left its people "incapable of improvement."[16] However, many other writers isolated the Chinese as especially dangerous in crowds, both for their susceptibility to manipulation, for their violence, and for their religious errors. Archibald Colquhoun wrote: "Any one knowing the grossly superstitious character of the lower classes in China, can well imagine how easily agitators, generally of the literati class, can influence the native mind. A Chinese crowd once excited is without doubt to be feared more than other crowds."[17]

LeBon described the crowd experience as religious, in the sense of inducing "the complete submission of his will, and the whole-souled ardour of fanaticism."[18] For this reason, a crowd needed and in fact preferred a strong master: "A crowd is always ready to revolt against a feeble and to bow down servilely before a strong authority."[19] Missionaries would not have recognized this "religion" as a description of their own, but they certainly viewed Chinese religions as pervaded with fanaticism, failure of willpower, herd mentality, and a docile obedience to those in power. Chinese respect for their gods was thought to have been based on fear of the gods' power rather than on any love or affection, or on any inherent moral character of the particular god. LeBon's crowd seems to have the same characteristics of the Chinese crowd (or of the Chinese *as* a crowd) in missionary reportage: bodily rather than rational, emotional, fickle, stupid, cruel, hypnotized, machine-like, incapable of telling the truth; female, childish, and metaphorically Catholic. Crowds in LeBon's vision, and Chinese culture for Victorians, represented racial throwbacks or cultural stagnations, in need of strong discipline, and actually preferring to be dominated.

Missionaries never failed to recount conversations in which Chinese, when asked why they performed certain rituals, answered that they did what their ancestors had done. The sense of going along with the crowd (a dead crowd, in fact) was also strong in these representations of the Chinese as incapable of even imagining a change from the status quo. Unable to fully die, ancestors crowded the living Chinese. The Chinese worshipped "a *host of evil spirits* and . . . a *crowd of idols*."[20] Heathenism was a crowd mentality. In Chapter 4 I noted the view of Chinese as a dense mass of bodies, more or less homogenous, the swarthy physicality of Chinese bodies melded into one body, "the lump." The density of Chinese cities was expressed as swarms of bees or ants. The solutions to the ills of this crowd existence involved individuation of personality. Missionaries saw this largely as a task the Chinese needed to accomplish by breaking the chains of the ancestral cult and unquestioned Confucian authority. But, I would suggest, the individuation of the Chinese was something that needed to happen to the Western visitors' perceptions of Chinese. If one is a foreigner, the natives are always a crowd, until mutual interactions habituate foreigners to see individual differences and personal character. Nonetheless, foreigners may differentiate only a few people and regard them as exceptions to the still unchallenged image of the racial crowd.

Only a tiny minority of Chinese ever troubled missionaries, but anti-foreign riots, official obstructions, and random harassment justified some sense of the missionaries' vulnerability. Some Westerners felt it would be easier to travel in more remote or "untouched" parts of China if they could make themselves inconspicuous.

Disguising the Western Body

Missionaries who itinerated in their Western clothes found themselves the objects of curious attention. This novelty value in their physical appearance could be useful, in drawing attention to the speaker, or it could be a hindrance, in drawing attention away from the speech. One thing missionaries could change easily was their clothing. Some found that Chinese clothing was better adapted to the climate, as well as considerably cheaper and more available. However, the most frequently expressed motivation for changing to Chinese clothing was the desire to travel among the Chinese without drawing the wrong kind of attention. In the interest of collecting tea and other plant samples from the hills of rural China, Robert Fortune effected the transformation , and Archbald Colquhoun's party also did so, in order to avoid the inevitable curiosity of crowds. Undoubtedly, many ventures into the off-limits regions of China went unrecorded. These disguises temporarily removed from view the Western identity in its outward trappings (clothes, hair, mannerisms), to a greater or lesser degree of plausibility upon inspection.

During itinerating tours in the 1830s, the free-wheeling missionary Charles Gützlaff changed his appearance, wearing Chinese clothing and wrapping his head in a turban. His call for the full adoption of Chinese clothing and hairstyles for missionaries aroused some resistance and mockery. Gützlaff was isolated from the broader missionary community in China and had a number of very influential enemies, including James Legge. Nonetheless, his example influenced William C. Burns (an English Presbyterian) and Burns's friend Hudson Taylor. The latter, as founder of the China Inland Mission, recruited a large number of missionaries and insisted on their wearing native clothing.

As a matter of practical strategy, Hudson Taylor attempted to change his appearance to that of a Chinese. His desire to identify with the Chinese was driven by his Pietist optimism about the converting power of the preached word. Like Gützlaff, he was ostracized from some of the better-funded missionary organizations, which resisted Chinese dress. In the summer of 1855, during his first visit to China and after seven preaching excursions with mixed results, Taylor decided to take the plunge: "On Thursday last at 11 P.M. I resigned my locks to the barber, dyed my hair a good black, and in the morning had a proper *queue* plaited in with my own, and a quantity of heavy silk to lengthen it out according to Chinese custom."[21] The transformation was far from pleasant for him. His head was not only "bar t'at" (as Taylor, a Yorkshireman, might have said), but furthermore exposed at the front. As was mandated for all Han Chinese males during the Qing dynasty, the hairline was extended back two or three inches. He complained:

It is a very sore thing to have one's head shaved for the first time, especially if the skin is irritable with prickly heat. And I can assure you that the subsequent application of hair-dye for five or six hours . . . does not do much to soothe the irritation. But when it comes to combing out the remaining hair which has been allowed to grow longer than usual, the climax is reached! But there are no gains without pains, and certainly if suffering for a thing makes it dearer, I shall regard my *queue* when I attain one with no small amount of pride and affection.[22]

The discomfort of head-shaving and hair-dying were placed in the framework of the heroic mission, Taylor's "cross to bear." Hardships, even the death of a fellow missionary, Taylor regarded as gifts of God, or at least part of God's larger plan.

Whereas Taylor shared the experience with his family in England, in terms of the hardships willingly undertaken by a servant of the Lord, another storyteller turned this kind of episode into comedy. Robert Fortune had his servants buy native clothing and a long false queue. He and his two Chinese assistants then sailed upriver from Shanghai, and on board the ship he could postpone the switch no longer. He put on the robes, but lacking a barber on board, one of his assistants, "the coolie," cut his hair.

[He was] a large-boned, clumsy fellow. . . . Having procured a pair of scissors, he clipped the hair from the front, back, and sides of my head, leaving only a patch on the crown. He then washed those parts with hot water, after the manner of the Chinese, and having done so, he took up a small razor and began to shave my head. I suppose I must have been the first person upon whom he had ever operated, and I am charitable enough to wish most sincerely that I may be the last. He did not shave, he actually scraped my poor head until the tears came running down my cheeks, and I cried out with pain. All he said was, "Hai-yah — very bad, very bad," and continued the operation. To make matters worse, and to try my temper more, the boatmen were peeping into the cabin and evidently enjoying the whole affair, and thinking it capital sport. I really believe I should have made a scene of a less amusing kind had I not been restrained by prudential motives, and by the consideration that the poor coolie was really doing the best he could. The shaving was finished at last; I then dressed myself in the costume of the country, and the result was pronounced by my servants and the boatmen to be very satisfactory.[23]

As with many of Fortune's anecdotes, we see both contempt for and camaraderie with his Chinese servants.

Fortune was nervous about being found in off-limits territory, and he was forced to try to stay indoors or in the boat during daylight, or to travel in a covered chair — despite his usual preference for outdoor walking. (Fortune's desire to pass undetected through technically off-limits terrain may also account for his interest in the smell of Europeans that was apparently perceptible to Chinese people and animals.) However, the joke continued, as on more than one occasion, his two Chinese helpers betrayed the secret:

I fancied I had become a very fair Chinaman; but my coolie, who was a silly, talkative fellow, imagined that he was in possession of a secret, and doubtless felt the weight of it rather uncomfortable. I observed him once or twice in close conversation with one of the boatmen, and it turned out afterwards that he told this man, as a great secret of course, that I was a foreigner — one of those *Hong-mous* who were so numerous in Shanghae. By-and-by the *secret* began to ooze out, and both boatmen and passengers were taking sly peeps at me when they thought I did not see them.[24]

The scene here, of Fortune's servants helping him in his disguise and then having fun unmasking him, and of Fortune pent up with indignation and pain yet unable to vent his irritation for fear of drawing further attention to himself, strikes me as very comical, and I suspect Victorian readers laughed as well. Fortune was certainly capable of belittling the Chinese with his sarcasm, but here at least he made himself the butt of the joke.

Having transformed their heads, these Westerners found Chinese clothing different. Taylor found his new clothes strange but not unmanageable, and the experience did not convince him of the superiority of Chinese clothing. Rather, "when you proceed to your toilet, you no longer wonder that many Chinese in the employ of Europeans wear foreign shoes and stockings as soon as they can get them." Presumably, this comment refers to the relative ease with which some Western foot- and leg-wear could be removed in the bathroom:

For native socks are made of calico and of course are not elastic . . . and average toes decidedly object to be squeezed out of shape, nor do ones heels appreciate their low position in perfectly flat-soled shoes. Next come the breeches — but oh, what unheard-of garments! Mine are two feet too wide for me round the waist, which amplitude is laid in a fold in front, and kept in place by a strong girdle. The legs are short, not coming much below the knee, and wide in proportion with the waist measurement. Tucked into the long, white socks, they have bloomer-like fulness capable, as Dr. Parker remarked, of storing a fortnight's provisions! No shirt is worn. But a white, washing-jacket, with sleeves as wide as ladies affected twenty years ago, supplies its place. And over all goes a heavy silk gown of some rich or delicate colour, with sleeves equally wide and reaching twelve or fifteen inches beyond the tips of one's fingers — folded back of course when the hands are in use. Unfortunately no cap or hat is used at this season of the year, except on state occasions, which is trying as the sun is awfully hot.[25]

Suddenly curious about their own new bodies, Westerners tended to look in the mirror and pronounce themselves Chinese — as when Matteo Ricci wrote, in 1585: "Would that you could see me as I am now: I have become a Chinaman."[26] Fortune crowed: "No one took the slightest notice of me, a circumstance which gave me a good deal of confidence, and led me to conclude that I was dressed in a proper manner, and that I made a pretty good Chinaman."[27] To be dressed properly, in this situation, was to be ignored. Yet despite these rather humorous self-congratulations, the limits to the illusion were obvious. Colquhoun admitted: "We never fancied that we should pass for Chinamen on close inspection; a certain prominence of nose, and roundness of eye, would prevent that, as well as the awkwardness of our manner. Thus dressed, however, we firmly believed that, when seated on the roof of our boat or reclining in a sedan-chair, mounted on a pony or while on foot, we should escape, to a great extent, that dangerous element in Chinese travel — curiosity."[28]

For travelers like Fortune and Colquhoun, their disguise meant keeping most Chinese at a distance, avoiding eye contact, and minimizing the movements of their foreign bodies. For missionaries, however, the disguise was always there to be unmasked, at least at the moment which defined their entire purpose in masking themselves: preaching. Even if their arrival had gone unnoticed, in standing on a box or on the steps of a temple and speaking the Glad Tidings, any trace of the illusion would vanish. Taylor noted, "Of course I am known to be a foreigner by my accent as soon as I begin to speak."[29] Missionaries were usually less concerned about passing undetected among the Chinese, and more specifically concerned that their Chinese dress should minimize unnecessary distraction and help identify them with the people.

It is hard to evaluate the success of the strategy. Certainly, many members of the China Inland Mission espoused it. On the other hand, it did not make them invisible. Robert Fortune met a missionary who had "gone native," yet continued to attract attention. "I soon found that he in his Chinese dress was a greater object of attention than I was in my English one."[30] Others admitted that Western clothing helped them command respect. Among the advantages to appearing alien was the connotation of foreign power.

Meanwhile, many Westerners reacted with shock and disdain. Undoubtedly, there was a sense of cultural superiority behind some of these objections, with the corollary that it would be demeaning to "go native." With visitors like Fortune, his Chinese dress might have struck some of the treaty port expatriates as bizarre, but in the case of missionaries, there were also religious reasons for objecting to native clothing. Walter Medhurst protested: "Disguise, although so universally and successfully employed by the Romanists, must be regarded as objectionable."[31] This reference to Catholic priests does not only refer to the wearing of Chinese clothing but also to the whole of "Romanism" being characterized by deception. Initially, Taylor's disguise included dying his hair black and wearing a queue, but he soon left off dying his hair, also feeling it was too deceptive. Though he and the China Inland Mission continued to insist on native clothing, Taylor's change of mind on dying his hair suggests a shared distrust of disguise which was linked to the Protestant construction of Catholic ritual.

Though the use of Chinese dress became a matter of policy in the China Inland Mission, as we can see in a photograph of Hudson Taylor's son and daughter-in-law (see Fig. 10), there was resistance, and not only from Taylor's enemies. In addition to his fellow laborers in the field, Taylor's mother and sister back in England found this change disagreeable. Taylor acknowledged their discomfort and embarrassment, but he was resolute: "If the Chinese costume seems so barbarous to us, our

FIGURE 10. "Mr. and Mrs. Howard Taylor in Chinese Costume." From Geraldine Guinness, *In the Far East,* 155.

English dress must be no less so to them, and . . . it cannot but be a hindrance in going amongst them in the friendly way necessary to securing their confidence and affection. . . . Without it we could not stay on here a single day. . . . It is one of those matters about which I and my devoted companion, Mr. Burns, thank God almost every day."[32] Taylor's cultural relativism — in this respect, at least — involved a forthright decision that any of the body's external trappings could be sacrificed for the goal of spiritual transformation. He saw that Western clothing could appear strange, and ridiculous.

A change from Western to Chinese clothing seems to have been much less of an issue for women. Chinese women's clothing, while not like Victorian dress, was still quite "feminine," with its flowing robes and modest cut. There would have been no problem of gender confusion, no fear of masculinized women, as there was of feminized men. Though the garments were cut very differently, Chinese clothes for men and women were relatively similar (compared to the differences in English clothing for men and women). The Victorian male would have felt as if he were putting on a dress, whereas for women the change would have seemed more like putting on a rather baggy dress, and perhaps they enjoyed the lack of a corset underneath. In either case, they would have been wearing something like a costume, at least at first, with a sense of play-acting or novelty. Though female missionaries and missionary wives were hardly party animals, it was more socially acceptable for women to dress up.

After a period of recruitment in England, Taylor sailed again for China with a group of recruits in 1866. When the recruits got there, they found a missionary community divided, with much opposition to Taylor and opposition to wearing Chinese dress. A few of the group quickly rejected the bodily regimen they had agreed to in England, and instead wore trousers, grew back their beards, and ate with a knife and fork. Taylor's biographer J. C. Pollock commented: "The C.I.M.'s unity was threatened by this battle of West and East — fork against chopstick, whisker against pigtail."[33]

For Chinese reformers, the primarily symbolic gesture against Manchu control was cutting off the queue. Many overseas Chinese had already done this. Immediately after the 1911 revolution, Sun Yat-sen had ordered that queues be cut. This order was widely put into practice in 1912, with mass rallies in cities, though the movement took longer to spread into the countryside. In general, cutting the queue and growing the hair in a shorter, Western style was seen as anti-Qing, modernist, more urban than rural, and also had Christian connotations. Samuel Woodbridge mentioned the mass queue-cutting in 1911: "Millions of queues were cut off and piled up. In some cases they were sold, and it is reported that the hair-dressers of Paris made large sums of money out of Chinese hair."[34] Mary Darley wrote in 1913, "Queues! queues! queues! nothing else was talked of."[35]

Foucault urged us to study the "microphysics of power,"[36] focusing on the apparently trivial ways that culturally meaningful bodies are crafted, so as to investigate power where it touches the body. Fork against chopstick, whisker against queue — these were bodily choices the foreign missionaries made. What other choices were involved? Trousers against robes; differences chosen in respect to medicine, travel, pastimes, and rituals. Foreignness is experienced in the body. The foreign difference is "in your face" like a big beard. The focus on food, hair, clothes — on the body — helps us to reconceive intercultural exchanges, as they so often come down to these concrete, specific choices.

That "dangerous element" in foreign travel mentioned by Colquhoun, above, was curiosity. Hence, disguise was useful but problematic. For some, it was theologically uncomfortable, a cross to bear, or an undignified sham. The illusion itself was the problem, almost as if in disguising one's body and assuming an artificial identity, one became a Chinese idol. For some, it was an objectionable action, like bowing. Where it was championed, or when the transformations were described, the change was a kind of magical transformation: Westerners conjuring themselves as Chinese. Perhaps some of the accounts of these transformations may be called *bianwen*, like the "transformation texts" of Buddhist missionary work. Samuel Woodbridge went through the same process: "And presto! A Chinese. . . . What a metamorphosis!"[37] Hudson Taylor thanked God for the chance to change his hairstyle and clothes: it opened doors and avoided obstacles to his preaching the Word.

Disguise in Chinese clothing was different according to the visitor's agenda. Travelers like Fortune or Conquhoun wanted to be unnoticed, whereas missionaries knew the disguise would become utterly transparent as soon as they began to do what they had come to do, preach. For getting from place to place without attracting attention, a disguise might have been useful. Once preaching began, the Chinese dress was intended to minimize distractions from the Gospel — it was again something *not to look at*. The disguise did not fool anyone; and this self-unmasking — in the consecrating act of preaching — coincided with a Protestant doctrinal/cultural orientation against the deceptions of vision (icons, theater, ritual). Hudson Taylor's and others' doubts about the degree of deception in their disguise — as when Taylor first dyed his hair black and then relented as it was too deceptive — are consistent with the insistence that the costumes of the "natives" (Londoners in Chinese robes) at the Great Missionary Exhibition in 1909 should not induce their wearers to frivolous pretence. Appearing to be Chinese in China was a means to invisibility requiring disengagement and distance. But at the Great Missionary Exhibition of 1909, appearing to be Chinese was a reason to be looked at, approached, and listened to.

Yet disguise required furtive movements. The illusion only worked at a distance and dissolved upon closer inspection. Disguise precluded Westerners from going out openly, or even at times from looking out of the windows of their box or boat. These imperfectly disguised Westerners had to sit in their palanquins while their native assistants roamed around freely, buying food and arranging transit. The limited view from a curtained box is a symbol of the blinkered vision we all travel with.

CHAPTER 14

Foreign Bodies

I began this book with an image of an image: "a Chinese street" recon-
structed in London, with Britons pretending to be Chinese. The sense
that Chinese culture was flawed, that its religion was wrong, was built
into that display. Probably no one objected. It is easy to stage a wrong
religion of a far-away people. But in contrast to the China of *Chinoiserie*
or the Japan of *The Mikado,* this staged version of China — and missionary publications, in general — made a claim of truth and was framed by a
narrative of ultimate value. There were consistent assertions that the exhibition was not entertainment, even though it surely was. Its "mere entertainment" value was repudiated, indicative of a piety which in many contexts stood against displays, shows, frivolous drama, illusion, and façade.
For the missionaries, such showy visual effects characterized heathenism
and Roman Catholicism.

How remote must Chinese religions have been to the visitors standing in the shuffling hubbub of the exhibition hall, looking down at the
lonely icons. How obviously false the claims of Chinese religion must
have seemed in the staged idol temple in the faked Chinese street — an
illusion created to reveal the truth about a religion of illusions.

Of course, China was represented selectively: narrow street, shops,
opium den, inn, pagoda, arches, idol temple — these stage props merged
with other elements of China in the popular imagination: bound feet,
chopsticks, queues, and "slanted" eyes. Chinese religion was a chaotic
world of heathen superstition, pagan idolatry, Babylon, Babel, and
Sodom. Though individual Chinese were described in positive terms,

especially if they converted, China as a whole was relentlessly dark, wicked, and irrational. There was a strong sense of China as an upside-down, topsy-turvy place, a society of inverted norms. China became a trope of inversion, a land of unreality, and a marker of unintelligibility. Precisely these characteristics made China so fertile as a topos of exotic fantasy — though the missionaries presented China more soberly than most popular media.

Articulating Identity

This projection of unintelligibility was confirmed when Westerners reported that the Chinese were unable to verbally articulate any reasoning (recognizable as such to Westerners) for their religious practices, an apparent inarticulacy which was taken as a species of Chinese inscrutability. Combined with an unshakable conviction that Chinese religions were fundamentally wrong, the lack of theological discourses which were recognizable as such to the missionaries led many to attribute a motiveless motion to the Chinese: literally, doing things for no reason. Answers like "Because I was taught to do this by my ancestors" or "Because it has always been done this way" were simply not acknowledged as reasons but seen as evidence of a lack of reasoning and hence evidence of a religious life of mechanical ritual without thought. Missionaries were disposed not to see any solid reasoning in acts of obeisance to icons since their basic category, "idolatry," had already judged the heathen bows. China was thought to be in the deathly grip of its own constricting tradition. Doctrinal inarticulacy (real or apparent) was treated as evidence that religious actions themselves were meaningless. Contact with those who might have articulated a more complex religious philosophy, such as educated monks or lay experts, was generally quite rare because of a disinterest in the messy details of "heathen superstition," a disbelief in any value to the investigative enterprise, or an inability to understand the subtleties of Buddhist or Daoist philosophy. Missionary accounts of Chinese religion were at times heavily larded with sarcasm and venom. A review of a Chinese compendium of religious lore prepared the reader for the interpretive task: "To understand the book thoroughly, one ought to be intimately acquainted with the absurdities suggested by a disordered fancy, one ought to study the deviations from common sense, and hear patiently the ravings of a diseased mind."[1] And there were always plenty of natives willing to confirm the missionaries' dismissive attitudes toward popular religions. Sometimes we are left with the impression that even the Chinese who practiced their religions thought them absurd.

In any culture, very few of the pious are trained theologians, and I don't doubt there were Chinese who did not think much about what they were doing. But let us note the bias in any assumption that to "know" an act is equivalent to being willing or able to talk or write about it. As Pierre Bourdieu pointed out, in treating acts which are not accompanied by doctrinal rationalization as meaningless, "the 'thinker' betrays his secret conviction that action is fully performed only when it is understood, interpreted, expressed."[2] Victorian Protestantism, with its strong orientation toward doctrinal explicitness and its self-conscious contrast to the ritual of Catholicism, would seem to have been poorly equipped to find sense in religious practices unaccompanied by doctrinal exposition. Nor were missionaries inclined to seek out Chinese doctrinal expositions, as they had already defined non-Christians religions as wrong. In general, Victorians were not well disposed to treat the Chinese as equals in many matters, such as industry, science, government, warfare, trade practices, and medicine. Missionaries did produce detailed studies of Chinese religions, but almost always explicitly geared to their repudiation.

Under such conditions, the openness to seeing reason in the Other, known as hermeneutic goodwill, was, at least, weak. Or it became instead hermeneutic ill-will — the assumption that what appears incoherent or irrational is indeed so. In contrast, a failure to understand a Bible passage would have been immediately attributed to the Christian reader's limitations, not to any textual incoherence. The fundamental shift in grammar from "I can't make sense of it" (a statement about me and my failure) to "it makes no sense" (a statement about it, about its true nature) involves a transference of a quality of perception onto the nature of the perceived. When the salient character of our media is our *inability* to understand, we tend to displace even that quality — incomprehensibility — onto the object. Nonsense is as important a cultural construct as sense, since the attribution of meaninglessness to others helps to preserve our own "common sense."

Though many activist Christians resisted the influence of some scientific discourses (such as Darwin's), they generally accepted much of the prevailing attitude toward "science," a utopian faith in the progress of science, an attitude we now label Scientism or Scientific Positivism. Even if reason could never reach as far toward Truth as revelation, the rational mind was privileged in the upward march of progress. Victorian rationality was an ascent from the "savage" or "primitive," which appear throughout Victorian intellectual life as categories applied to certain people *now* (North American Indians, Africans, Australian aborigines) and to Europeans *long ago,* so that "we" used to be primitives but through the application of intellect, racial advantages, and Christian virtues, we have "ascended" to a "higher" condition. For many evangelical Christians, the key to that ascent was the repudiation of the body (with its senses, desires, and rituals) in favor of the mind, a move rooted in Pauline rhetoric of the body as death, and one given fresh resonance by the Reformation rejection of Catholic ritual.

The rationality which allowed Victorians to imagine Chinese people as irrational or mindless assumed a particular kind of mind/body dualism. For missionaries, and pervasively throughout society, the sense of mind/body dualism was heavily informed by the Bible. The distinction was rich with religious aspects: the body was flesh, mortality, sin, and desire. While the mind could also be sinful, nonetheless, Protestant salvation was described as an inner transformation, in contrast to ritualism or works righteousness, and in contrast more broadly to the Church of Rome, which involved a more bodily participation in salvation. The oppositions of religious identity predisposed and reinforced the mind/body dualism as a common binary. This dualism was also mapped vertically onto the body, dividing it into the lower half (with its sexual organs, excrement, and mud) and the upper half (with its manual dexterity, concentration of organs of perception, and brain).

In Chapters 5 and 6, I showed the operation of mind/body categorization, even in Western representations of the language of the Chinese, which one might normally assume to be the realm of meaning par excellence. (As Frits Staal remarked, "the home of meaning is language."[3]) Yet some Chinese speech seemed meaningless to the missionaries. At first, "meaningless speech" seems an oxymoron, but actually there is no shortage: ritualized speech, foreign speech, many-times-repeated speech, Latin, mantras, grunts, animal calls, and baby wails. These various analogous cases supplied a range of metaphor to missionaries trying to describe their visceral reactions to Chinese ritual or to Buddhist mantras.

While they decried the meaningless and impotent speech of Chinese Buddhists, all missionaries experienced some years of muted or flawed speech. The difficulty and frustration of learning Chinese led easily, I think, to a view of the Chinese language as itself perversely difficult, and as intentionally or even diabolically designed to frustrate. For a group of people whose entire reason for coming to China was to *speak,* the difficulty was felt as an obstacle. Additionally, for a group accustomed to seeing divine or demonic agency in their lives — interpreting events as God or Satan acting in the world — the sense of the language as a barrier to preaching must have assumed existential significance. The act of preaching was a kind of transfiguring process, making them holy and justifying their existence — justifying their own sacrifices, and the financial support of their churches. The language, as a barrier, prevented this.

Adding to the sense of the language as obstacle were the intractable problems of translation. Missionaries were concerned sometimes with very fine distinctions between Chinese words, most notably, with the terminology of their Gospel: "God" for example. Unlike that of most visitors, their Chinese speech was not merely a matter of communicating well enough to conduct a transaction, where the true understanding is moot as long as the trade is successful or as long as the porter brings your luggage to the right address. As a strongly creed-based tradition, Christianity had a history of contentious argument over fine semantic distinctions. Given this stress on the exactly correct textual understanding, the sheer inwardness of the missionaries' project — nothing less than the transformation of souls — led some missionaries into controversial philological work as they probed deeper and deeper for a semantic anchor for "God" in Chinese. Obviously, a great deal of translation (of "ordinary" words) was unproblematic, and many missionaries left the philology to others. But the very basic and unavoidable experience of the linguistic chasm meant that all missionaries went through a long, difficult stage in which they could not speak even the Truth, and in which Chinese rationality was inaudible.

A series of underlying (or sometimes, entirely explicit) metaphors runs through Western representations of the Chinese: they were perceived as mentally or physically deficient, drugged, asleep, dead, childish, and female. Furthermore, the Chinese were depicted as a mass of homogeneous bodies, materialistic rather than spiritual, and driven by their physical senses rather than by mental discipline or willpower. These "metaphors of mindlessness" shared the insinuation that the Chinese were (in comparison to Western Christians) relatively mindless, and thus "bodiful." To Protestant missionaries, the bodifulness of the Chinese was always related to their status as heathens, living as "the children of the flesh" (Rom. 13:14). The heathen's basic weakness was sensuality, a bondage to the pleasures of the flesh, which also meant a bondage to death.

Yet in these Victorian representations, the Chinese bodifulness was not that of the idealized, "muscular" Christian (a healthy and vigorous embodiment), but rather a withered embodiment, representative of their withered culture. This Chinese, heathen bodifulness did not manifest itself in the kind of hirsute narcissism evident in the mid-Victorian cult of the "robust" and manly. For Victorian missionaries, Chinese embodiment was not masculine. The long head hair, which Victorians saw as feminine, was a matter of Qing policy and could be changed after 1911, but their facial hairlessness was considered in specifically racial terms. Differences of hair reinforced gender distinctions, us/them distinctions, and also the binary Catholic/Protestant. During much of the period under consideration, manly Protestants had short head-hair and full beards; the Anglo-Catholics stereotypically had smooth-shaven faces, and were seen as feminine; and, similarly, Chinese men had smooth faces and long hair (queues). Facial hair was a marker of masculinity, and the missionaries in China found their normal gendered hair categorization precisely inverted.

With this example and others, we can see the promiscuous, indiscriminate manner of analogies, the way in which we borrow freely among various species of "Other." The missionaries' aligning of

Protestant   Catholic,
Western   Chinese,
male   female,

and so on, reinforced the sense of Protestant-Western-male versus Catholic-Chinese-female. While this kind of homological rhetoric is evident in their writing, the homologies were also embodied in the missionaries' habitus.

Protestant/Catholic

The distinction of Catholic and Protestant, with its many permutations, was one of the most pervasive of the binary oppositions that structured Victorian Protestant perceptions of Chinese religions. Protestant missionaries were so thoroughly formed by their anti-Catholicism — by the whole range of interlocking distinctions implied by their sectarian identity — that they projected these distinctions very comfortably onto the Chinese, consistently Catholicizing the Chinese. Through the use of a postural stereotype (the bowing body), they homologized Catholics to non-Christians. In this view, the Roman church was essentially pagan: "Most of the Romish ceremonies and rites are borrowed directly from paganism."[4] It had taken the Reformation to shake that paganism off, but it also required continued vigilance, as the urge to idolatry was part of human nature since the Fall. In this view, humans always have a weakness which makes them bow down to material things as if these created things were the creator. The rejection of idolatry and Catholicism was never only a theological debate, and in Victorian life it implied not only avoidance of a posture but a whole attitude toward the self: a stoical self-control, not showing emotion, a proverbial stiff upper lip. This stylized self-control relied on the homologies embodied in missionaries' ways of thinking and behaving (their habitus).

Because Protestant reformers were attacking the obeisance of Catholics just when Jesuits were trying to excuse certain forms of non-Christian obeisance of the Chinese, the homology of bowing Catholics to bowing heathen Chinese was very obvious to some. Catholic missionaries were seen as converting the Chinese "from one form of idolatry to another."[5] In making this connection, Protestant missionaries focused on such things as monasticism, works righteousness (as they thought it), the cult of female figures such as Guanyin and Mary, but especially on obeisance to icons. Attacking the Chinese overlapped with attacking Catholicism. By coincidence, the largest numbers of Protestants, already predisposed to belittle China arrived in China in a period of decline and chaos, a low ebb brought on in large part by Western forces.

The Protestant/Catholic distinction overlapped with many of the other binary distinctions with which the missionaries structured their perceptions and representations. With their emphasis on reading the Bible in the vernacular, their (qualified) rejection of ritual, and their Industrial Revolutionary conceptions of progress and rationality, Protestants considering the West and the East aligned themselves with the mind or the soul; by contrast, Catholics, with their unintelligible liturgy operative only as "sense data" rather than meaning, their more opulent bodily rituals and obeisances, and their "Latin" emotional expressiveness, represented the body. To describe Victorian Protestant imagination in this way opens us to all of the logical problems inherent in any such generalization so far abstracted from particular examples, but I believe the point holds true. We have seen in Chapter 7 how Chinese acts of obeisance were perceived in thoroughly anti-Catholic terms: one of the basic means of establishing the similarity of Catholicism and heathenism was to point out their common ritual of obeisance.

The Kowtow

No ritual movement has been as potent in the Protestant imagination as the bow. Very few Protestants totally rejected the bow, but most abbreviated it to the kneeling position, drastically reduced the number of objects to which they bowed, and discursively reiterated the bow's meaning as non-idolatry. A great deal of Protestant discourse since the Reformation was specifically against obeisance to icons and particularly deep obeisance (to anything), which was identified variously as feminine, Catholic, pagan, and idolatrous. The relative depth of obeisance functioned as a measure of civilization. The language of obeisance was and still is heavily loaded with value judgments: grovel, debase, abject, kowtow. All these potent associations were performed in that body gesture.

Is a bow idolatry under any circumstances, or can some statement or mental state at the time of obeisance excuse the act from the accusation of idolatry? This debate, which was at the heart of the Reformation and remained a contentious issue, points us to our astounding capacity to give complex cultural meaning to a "mute" gesture, and at the same time, to the limits of our ability to make *any* meaning "stick" to an action. Certain limits were reached when Jesuits in China tried to convince their superiors that Confucian obeisance was "civil," not "religious." But it is simply not clear to an observer when a bow is an act of civil respect and when it is a religious act, especially when the "acts themselves" are nearly identical. In concrete terms, this kind of debate marks the boundaries of sacred and profane.

The Chinese were seen as particularly prone to "mere ritual" or ritual noise, and the kowtow was the quintessential Chinese act. The Chinese were imagined as very quick to fall down, a people desperate for something to bow to. Many Victorian reports noted Chinese atheistic skepticism toward religious devotions, but immediately pointed out that these skeptics still bowed to their ancestors. To convert to Protestant Christianity was to stand up (and by extension to wake up, to grow up); converts were told not to bow to icons or ancestral plaques.

The contrast of the kowtow as the quintessential Chinese act, and standing up as the posture of the West and modernity, has remained part of the cultural imagination, and reappears in dramatic ways. In the film *Shanghai Noon* (2000), Jackie Chan plays Jiang Wen (mis-heard as "John Wayne"), an agent of the Qing government sent to America in 1881 to rescue abducted Manchu princess Pei Pei. He searches for the princess, who is being held captive in a mining camp along with many Chinese laborers. As soon as he realizes he has found her in a tent, he bows his head to the ground. She says: "Please, don't draw attention! Please, stand up!" As she advances, he backs up out of the tent, and other Chinese bow as well. "Please, stand up! Don't bow! Get up!" Later, three Imperial guards find the princess in an empty church and kneel with one hand to the ground, as does Jackie (disguised now as a Catholic monk). But when an Imperial decree is unfurled, the guards and Jackie again bow their heads to the ground during the reading of the decree. All this takes place with the bad guys present and armed, and their face-to-ground posture provokes the blond cowboy good guy Roy to say, "John, get up! I thought we were past this, come on!" Finally, with music surging and in defiance of Imperial etiquette, Jackie looks up and then stands up to respond to the danger — an act of disobeisance accompanied by the solemn words: "This is the West, not the East, and the sun may rise where we come from, but here is where it sets." To break the deadlocked situation, princess Pei Pei grabs and burns the Imperial decree on a rack of votary candles. They then proceed to trash the place, in a six-shooter/kung-fu fight.

Eye to Eye with the Idolater

If holding one's face to the ground was the posture of traditional China, as it was of the irrelevant past, of Catholicism, the lower classes, subjugated peoples, and animals, the bodily performance of equality and full personhood was standing "face to face." Direct, mutual eye contact signaled equality.

A 1943 article in *Looking East* (successor to the *Gleaner*) criticized Westerners who say "these Chinese! They are so inscrutable. You can never make friends with them, for you never know where you are with them." In response to this "ignorant" view, the Reverend Rattenbury says, "I want to try to stand China face to face with you. Look into that 'inscrutable' face: look twice at it." There, in this face, you will see five characteristics: laughter-loving, home-loving, moral, religious, and kindly. Some characteristics of personality are most legible in face-to-face contact. Rattenbury attributes inscrutability to the Chinese face only to the extant that the English face is also inscrutable: "Looking at it I do not know that this Chinese face is any more inscrutable to us than our dumb, inscrutable English face is to them."[6] Foreign faces are all equally inscrutable.

In Rattenbury's article, the face-to-face contact is purely a literary evocation, which nonetheless mimics the importance of real (bodily) contact, especially eye contact. Certainly, face-to-face contact over a long period tends to complicate our stereotypes. We see exceptions to the homogeneous image of the Other, we see detail, and we understand what had previously seemed irrational. Missionaries who had lived in China for twenty years were probably less prone to the essentializing generalizations than the newly arrived, and their experience gave them authority. On the other hand, the "first impressions" genre of missionary reportage remained popular. But does physical presence actually make our stereotypes vanish? Perhaps we may say, if our stereotypes become complex, nuanced, detailed, and responsive to data which does not fit the patterns, then we are no longer talking about stereotypes, but rather, imagination. The term "stereotype" has evolved from its early use in printing and the broader meaning of faithful reproduction. In the social psychology of the 1920s, stereotyping referred to a kind of defective thinking, especially in authoritarian personalities. While this pejorative sense has remained the norm in popular usage, cognitive psychology since the 1980s has treated stereotypes as categories; as our minds always think in categories, stereotyping is fundamentally natural. More recently, this cognitive approach has been criticized as avoiding questions of power, class, and history. Consideration of stereotypes should also account for physical distance.

Since knowledge is local, there seems to be something basically natural about the fact that remote knowledge is more or less incomprehensible. As the *Daodejing* sagely noted: "The further one goes, the less one knows."[7] Remote knowledge is "far-fetched," "exotic" and "outlandish."

The sheer imbalance in numbers — the visitor and a few compatriots, contrasted to the millions of locals — and the novelty value of foreign bodies tend to individualize the self in contrast to the great mass of natives. Back home, leafing through someone's holiday snapshots or reading about the Other in a newspaper, we are further removed from the possibility of individuating the Other, as our perceptions are tied to frozen images. As Mark Harrison wrote, "We see far-away people as crowds; and in crowds people seem far away."[8]

Other people exist in crowds. Our association of differentness and foreignness — of the alien and the threatening — with the existence of frenzied and faceless faraway hordes is an aspect of human psychology with crucial implications for the formulation of social policy and foreign relations the world over. The supposed intimidation represented by mythical packs of strangers is what makes possible international and intercultural mass violence; it facilitates the process of dehumanization essential to the lifting of moral constraints against violence and persecution.[9]

How do we make it easier to kill other people? In part, we hide their faces, avert our eyes, and treat individuals as substances — distance performs these functions. Of course, the fact of distance can be mitigated in many ways. We can now move speech instantaneously around the world without apparent loss of semantic content, but moving bodies the same distance takes a lot more time and effort and money. Written text is still the primary means of communication between China and remote countries, even if the speed and volume of communications have increased since Robert Morrison's day. Our "visuals" have improved a great deal as well — snapshot camera, home video, television, film, and internet. Has this explosion of easily accessible media changed anything? Does it matter if I can find only one book about a remote place or thirty? That I can find videos, live streaming, someone to call on the phone? What does this change, what does it not change? Even with long-distance telephones, video conferencing, and the internet, there is still nothing like actual physical proximity, face to face.

But "face to face" opens up another set of problems largely absent in remote communication. First, bodily strangeness sometimes induces visceral reactions which would not be felt at a great distance. With their self-confidence about their superior diet and hygiene, educated middle-class Victorians were disposed to find Chinese peasants distasteful in person. As one missionary wrote: "It is much easier loving the souls of the heathen in the abstract in America than it is here in the concrete, encompassed as they are with such dirty bodies."[10] Being "face to face" meant dealing with many problems not encountered by armchair tourists: differences in diet and ambient bacteria; ambiguous or disturbing eye contact and personal space; unwanted attention to their bodies, and local smells, which to some noses "were too pungent and evil for words!"[11] Physical proximity generates problems which are largely absent when communication takes place at a great distance.

The contact hypothesis assumes communication is much easier in person, but in some ways the opposite is true. A scholar can take all day translating a letter surrounded by the comforts of home and carefully parse the reply, whereas spoken communication requires an unnerving immediacy. Newly arrived foreigners feel some discomfort — feelings of not being sure of oneself, of being unaware of the body-spaces around one, and so, unsure of exactly where to stand or sit. Reverent Rattenbury's "ignorant" Briton complained, "You never know where you are with them," and I read this idiom literally as well as figuratively. Some speech took place in a context of awkwardness, chronic ambiguity, and public vulnerability. This static was systematically written out of the "official" accounts sent back to England. In missionary publications, there is a tone of confidence in the author's expertise, because she has actually been there — proximity to the Chinese was a basis of authority.

Furthermore, proximity can activate the negative judgments which reinforce existing stereotypes even while revising others. Never going to a place allows us to remain naive and retain our Romantic illusions, for better or worse. On a smaller scale, sightseeing missionaries often admired Buddhist temples as features of pretty landscape, but grew harsher with proximity. In Beijing, for example, Edith Couche visited the "Llama Temple." She wrote: "Very picturesque are the temples with their curly roofs and many coloured tiles, very impressive in the distance is the chanting of several hundred voices. But the nearer one approaches to heathenism in any form, the less one is impressed. Inside the Temple the close-shaven priests kneel in rows, the eyes and attention alike are wandering, the heads are turning and twisting, while the lips babble forth sounds."[12]

Pleasant illusions are often threatened by proximity to their purported subjects. Pleasant illusions about the missionaries themselves may also have benefited from their absence. During the first half of the nineteenth century, most British missions were domestic, but in the latter half the emphasis shifted to foreign missions. Missionaries were often presented as model Christians, struggling selflessly for the greater good. The image of courageous evangelism could be better maintained when located far away and when their representations were mediated through institutional channels. The *Church Missionary Gleaner* was a highly edited document. In this sense, "far-fetched" could mean *more* plausible rather than *less*. In these and other ways, the priority of physical proximity suggested by the "contact hypothesis" was ambiguous.

This book concerns the historical problematization of bodily difference: When does difference matter? What were the historical conditions that allowed difference to be perceived, noted, categorized, and judged? These processes of perception, representation and judgment left traces for us which are predominantly textual, so that the past is legible. But the traces of "the past" are also illegible, mute, unnoticed, and forgotten. The printed word or the image is more durable than bodies, which continue after burial only in images and text; and in memory, which however lasts no longer than bodies. We are removed from our present bodily experience (to a greater or lesser degree) as we think historically. Going "further back" in our historical imagination, we lose the possibility of speaking to the authors, to eyewitnesses, to survivors. We can see their bodies no more. We lose the possibility of hearing voices and seeing images; we lose even the images of bodies, eventually even their names. Because of the distances of time and death, disembodiment is unavoidable in historical research. We lose the body in history long before we lose the word and the image.

Physical presence, on-site experience, being there — these are not cure-alls for the disadvantages of being remote. We endow the voice of one who has been there with a particular authority which in many ways seems quite justified, but foreign experience entails conditions of interpretation which are not visible to the reader. Perceptions which are unique to an experience of being there are then generalized as characteristics of the other, and once that essential image is in print, the durability of cultural products ensures its continued circulation. Bodily images gather momentum, such that to challenge them is to go against the "collective wisdom" and to contradict the obvious.

Imagination and the Obvious

Foreigners see things natives don't see, and apparently don't see things which are obvious to natives. If you are a foreigner, seeing things that "are not there," you indeed seem to be crazy at times, and in many cases you are given permission to be crazy. Foreigners have a certain diplomatic immunity to be weird, but that weirdness is only an effect of normality. The encounter with the foreign invites us to see the obvious, perhaps for the first time. "Obvious" is from the Latin for *in the way,* composed of *ob* "against" and *via* "way." The obvious is "in the way" of understanding what is beyond the immediate object of our gaze. As Wittgenstein wrote, "The aspects of things that are most important for us are hidden because of their simplicity and familiarity. (One is unable to notice something — because it is always before one's eyes.)"[13]

The *sense* which we make from the chaos of non-sense, which becomes shared or "common," gives foreign perceptions a touch of the unreal. Shorn of the restraints of (relatively) immediate verification or falsification, the faraway invites us to fantasize. While unreality is *falseness* or *lies* or *insanity,* or simply *irrelevance* in most of our lives, it is a pleasure in our play. It is sometimes called "escapism." While stereotypes have been interpreted as stemming from fear of the other, they also derive from pleasure. Hence our interest in the foreign, and at the same time a motive for our not really understanding, not really trying to understand the foreign. Until we put the time and effort into acculturating, we only see the strange surface of a foreign culture. To know a culture is also to find much of it boring, or at least unremarkable. If we learn how sensible and normal that foreign surface is — if we acquire the habitus or framework whereby the previously foreign is now just common sense, we have lost something: the invitation to dream. Dreaming takes you somewhere else, somewhere unreal.

It has been stated by many writers, in varying degrees of precision, that the gaze toward the Other is in fact a kind of gaze toward a mirror. Colonizing cultures constructed their images of the colonized in ways which confirmed their right to conquer and possess. Most famously, Edward Said's *Orientalism* (1978) described nineteenth-century Euro-American representations of Islam and Arab cultures — the "Orient" — as products of a particular set of oppositional and imbalanced power relations. In furthermore rejecting the possibility of solving the problem by simply creating new and true representations to replace the old false ones, Said served as a pioneer for many studies, including this one. Such critiques are important, but in many cases have a quality of indignation which presumably stems from the association of such colonizing discourses with the violence they seemed to justify. It is also clear that all cultures form "stereotypes" of others, more or less exotic or inhuman as the case may be. Yet the capabilities for violence have never been evenly distributed, so that a Chinese racist image of Westerners seems less offensive than the Western racist image of Chinese. (Or, a woman's anti-man joke passes by where a man's anti-woman joke would bring condemnation.) There are reasons why some hostile stereotypes seem offensive while others seem merely quaint, irrelevant, sour grapes, or therapeutic. But this difference has little to do with accuracy. The anger which runs through Sheng-mei Ma's *The Deathly Embrace,* for example, is fueled by Emperor Ming the Merciless from *Flash Gordon* and the New Age ethnic mysticism of Amy Tan, but comes out most stridently when Ma discusses the 1982 murder of Vincent Chin. Since stereotypes were so clearly involved in that murder, as in other racist violence and the massive violence of colonialism, it seems justified to present the downward gaze toward the Other as a violent act in itself, an appropriation of perceived elements of the Other for the purposes of justifying one's own violence or of confirming one's own superiority. The "construction of the Other" has been a catch phrase for talking about self-serving, mostly Western, fantasies or theodicies which are the commentaries to violence. Given the world history of colonialism, this "bias" seems justified. Critiques of "Orientalism" have at times been marked by an anger which borders on simple demonization of "the West." Ziauddin Sardar's *Orientalism,* for example, presents Orientalism as a Western sin primarily against Islam, but finally notes a series of stereotypes about Britons in two episodes of the television series *Friends* — Big Ben, funny accent, envy of American wealth, silly social pretensions — and concludes that even England has been "Orientalized."[14] If England can be "Orientalized," it is clear that we must separate the specific history of power imbalance under colonialism from the universal tendency toward stereotyping (simplifying, homogenizing, appropriating, etc.). Similarly, Zhang Longxi has shown how translations of Said's *Orientalism* in China have been associated with "cultural conservatism, narrow-minded nationalism, and sinocentrism, and thus have the radical significance of their challenge to hegemony and domination seriously compromised."[15]

At times, dehumanizing stereotypes have been partially exorcised by bringing the self and the Other face to face, by giving the opportunity for the silenced Other to speak. Stereotyping is sometimes treated as a kind of incorrect thinking, and it follows that correct thinking will dissolve the threats of violence — this is a variation of the contact hypothesis. Bring alienated peoples together for mutual learning on an even ground and each side's stereotypes will disappear. Those who see the Other as real individuals will be less likely to attack them. In practice, this is probably not a bad strategy, though we have seen that physical coexistence harbors its own dangers. And where is there truly even ground? But if stereotyping is thought of as a natural mode of thinking, as is more common now in cognitive psychology, it becomes absurd to imagine thought without stereotyping. Given the limiting and mostly negative associations with the word "stereotype," however, it is more fruitful to think of this construction of the Other in terms of imagination.

The mediating processes whereby we learn about the Other seem to present an obstacle or barrier to a less mediated version of the narrative — or even to the events themselves, reality, "what really happened." As a historian, one might lament that we always have less documentation, or the "wrong kind" of documentation to establish a sense of verity in our imaginative reconstructions of "the past," according to the specific questions we ask. But these obstacles are also the conditions of our knowledge, and therefore also enabling. We always, only, imagine the past. We imagine names and dates, and subtle *longue-durée* shifts in the Weltenschaung.

The Perceivability of Bodies

The foreigner is more or less excluded from linguistic communication, and so relies heavily on "body language." But is body language a "language"? Bodies have always been interpreted either as texts or through the metaphors of language. This transformation of the body into text is highly problematic. While very occasionally a direct gesture-to-word correlation is fairly clear, in almost all cases the body simply does not create "language." The body creates meaning — though "meaning" may still be the wrong word — but not language. Because the body is meaningful yet mute, bodily images of other peoples — sometimes grotesque, sometimes superhuman — persist in culture, flying under the radar of language. An image of Others is not a proposition, and in not arguing for anything, it is more impervious to debate than an explicit proposition. It is not as if every picture of a Chinese were accompanied by the note, "all Chinese look like this."

Most of the time, bodies are not directly translated to language nor to any linguistically expressed rationality. But the *perceivability* of the body is immediate, at least as immediate as vision, once the foreigner has stepped off the boat. The body *seems* to be a straightforward expressive signifier, and so contrasts with the more obvious obscurity of alien language and rationality. In fact, the immediacy of perceptions of Other bodies is also illusory, or imagined. Vision is not neutral.

Wittgenstein wondered about the bodily limits to communication with the alien: "Suppose you came as an explorer into an unknown country with a language quite strange to you. In what circumstances would you say that the people there gave orders, understood them, obeyed them, rebelled against them, and so on?"[16] He was willing to grant at least the possibility of making such judgments, given that, in fact, people do deduce these moves in alien language games, and often correctly so. In the absence of common speech, we figure out these moves through observation of bodily behavior. Hence, Wittgenstein posited the possibility of a universal mode of communication independent of language: "The common behavior of mankind is the system of reference by means of which we interpret an unknown language."[17] But does any such "system of reference" really exist? What bodily behavior is actually universally meaningful? How would one do historical research on such a "system" — the system of common human meaning? What can be said about pre- or non-discursive meaning?

Pointing to the inseparability of word and gesture, Wittgenstein described the process of understanding as being "tossed to and fro" between language and embodiment: "How curious: we should like to explain our understanding of a gesture by means of a translation into words, and the understanding of words by translating them into a gesture. (Thus we are tossed to and fro when we try to find out where understanding properly resides.)"[18]

Abbreviations Used in the Notes

CMG	*Church Missionary Gleaner*
CMS	Church Missionary Society
HE	*Homes of the East*
IWCD	*India's Women and China's Daughters*
LLSWW	*The Life and Letters of Samuel Wells Williams, LL.D.: Missionary, Diplomatist, Sinologue*
RGC 1877	*Records of the General Conference of the Protestant Missionaries of China, Held at Shanghai, May 10–24, 1877*
RGC 1890	*Records of the General Conference of the Protestant Missionaries of China, Held at Shanghai, May 7–20, 1890*

Notes

Preface

1. Ma, *The Deathly Embrace*, xi.

Chapter 1

1. *Church Missionary Gleaner* [hereafter *CMG*], February 1909, 31.
2. "A Forecast by One behind the Scenes," *CMG*, June 1909, 92.
3. Sir John Kennaway, M.P., President of the Church Missionary Society, was the opening speaker for the June 10, 1909 proceedings (*Times* [London], 11 June 1909, 9). The estimate of 200,000 visits is from *CMG*, August 1909, 113; the 250,000 estimate is from CMS, *Proceedings, 1909–1910*, 14.
4. *Times* (London), 8 June 1909, 10.
5. *CMG*, March 1909, 48. A later version of the poster placed India in the center (*CMG*, June 1909, 92).
6. *CMG*, February 1909, 31; also *CMG*, April 1909, 63.
7. *CMG*, June 1909, 94.
8. *Times* (London), 9 June 1909, 9.
9. Missions leaders included the American Methodist John Raleigh Mott, secretary of the International Committee of the YMCA and future Nobel Peace Prize winner; Eugene Stock, secretary of the CMS; the Rev. A. K. Taylor of the British and Foreign Bible Society; the Rev. Dr. Ralph Wardlaw Thompson, foreign secretary of the London Missionary Society; and prominent missions supporter Lord Kinnaird. Retired colonial administrators in attendance were Sir Andrew Fraser, former lieutenant-governor of Bengal; Sir William Mackworth Young, the former lieutenant-governor of Punjab and current vice-president of the CMS; Sir James A. Bourdillion; and Sir Thomas Fowell Buxton, the former

governor of South Australia. Naturally, a series of high-ranking church dignitaries spoke. These included Bishop Mongomery, the Dean of Norwich; as well as the Lord Bishops of London, Down, Southwark, St. Albans, and Ely. Other speakers were Albert Carless, King's College Professor of Surgery; and the Irish aristocrat Sir Algernon Coote.

10. *Times* (London), 31 May 1909, 4.

11. *CMG*, April 1909, 62–63. The *CMG* for June 1909 (p. 96) shows a picture of four adult "Chinese" and a child, posing. *The Round World*, June 1909, 92, shows a more mixed group, including Britons dressed as Chinese and the magazine's editor wearing a *bhoorka*. Most of those costumes were made in England in consultation with missionaries on furlough or even in the field. Ninety-four garments were sent from China (see *CMG*, May 1909, 80; *CMG*, June 1909, 94; *The Round World*, June 1909, 91).

12. *CMG*, August 1909, 127. The Bible verse is adapted from Luke 10:2 and Matthew 9:38.

13. World Missionary Conference, *Report of Commission VI*, 116; see also, CMS, *Proceedings, 1909–1910*, 12.

14. *CMG*, March 1909, 46; *CMG*, June 1909, 95.

15. *CMG*, December 1908, 191.

16. *CMG*, April 1909, 63. And: "No pains will be spared to add to the spectacular attractions a spiritual tone and educative value" (*CMG*, December 1908, 191).

17. *CMG*, March 1909, 47.

18. *CMG*, November 1909, 175. CMS, *Proceedings, 1909–1910*, mentions only five hundred pounds in stock and costumes (14).

19. See *CMG*, July 1909, 111; *CMG*, December 1909, 191; and CMS, *Proceedings, 1909–1910*, 14.

20. "It consists of a stiff cartridge paper model of a city gate; a street containing three shops, an opium den, an idol shrine, and a Christian Day School; tables of merchandise, furniture, a sedan chair; and thirteen figures, all to be coloured and cut out" (*India Women's and China's Daughters* [hereafter *IWCD*], July 1909, 104–5). The miniature came with an explanation by Zenana missionary Miss. A. B. Cooper, of Lo-nguong. The prototype for these models may have been a set of miniatures created for planning purposes before the exhibition (see *The Round World*, June 1909, 88).

21. Darley, *Cameos of a Chinese City*, 172–73.

22. W. E. Hipwell, "Union in Face of the Foe; or, Co-operation in Evangelistic Effort in China," *CMG*, December 1907, 185.

23. Darley, *Cameos of a Chinese City*, 175.

24. Ibid., 176. "And they took the bullock which was given them, and they dressed it, and called on the name of Baal from morning even until noon, saying, O Baal, hear us. But there was no voice, nor any that answered. And they leaped upon the altar which was made" (I Kings 18:26). For a similar reference to the prophets of Baal in a competition between Christians and non-Christians in China, see Dunch, *Fuzhou Protestants*, 9–11.

25. Darley, *Cameos of a Chinese City*, 182.

26. Boaz, *"And the Villages thereof,"* 28.

27. Edith Couche, "East and West," *IWCD,* January 1916, 21. As the lonely private detective Phillip Marlowe once said, "Eyes looked at us in that dead, alien silence of another race" (Chandler, "Try the Girl," 110).

28. MacGowan, *Sidelights on Chinese Culture,* 1.

29. Conger, *Letters from China,* 289–90.

30. Ibid., 35.

31. Selden, *The Cricket in Times Square,* 54.

32. Ibid., 55.

33. Ibid., 84.

34. Moy, *Marginal Sights,* 66–81. On the exoticism of and hostility toward American Chinatowns, see also McClellan, *The Heathen Chinee,* 31–68.

35. Moy, *Marginal Sights,* 68.

36. Barthes, *Empire of Signs,* 3. See also Zhang Longxi's comments on this text, in his *Mighty Opposites,* 48–51.

37. Barthes, *Empire of Signs,* 3.

38. Ibid., 4.

39. Ibid., 10.

40. For overviews of Western images of China, see Spence, *The Chan's Great Continent*; MacKerras, *Western Images of China*; and Isaacs, *Images of Asia.*

41. Conger, *Letters from China,* 289.

42. Thomas, "Foreign Missions and Missionaries," 114.

43. Staal, *Rules without Meaning,* 3.

Chapter 2

1. Franck, *Wandering in Northern China,* 57.

2. On chinoiserie, see Zhang, *Mighty Opposites,* 27–36; Spence, *The Chan's Great Continent,* 62–80.

3. Peyrefitte, *The Collision of Two Civilizations,* xviii.

4. Louis Byrde, "China's Awakening," *CMG,* February 1907, 23.

5. Boardman, *Christian Influence,* 4.

6. "The Society's Missions: V. — The Fu-Kien Mission," *CMG,* May 1889, 67. On the mingled hostility toward missionaries and foreigners in general, see Liao, *Anti-foreignism and Modernization in China,* 39–52.

7. "Resolutions of the CMS General Committee, August 13, 1895," *CMG,* September 1895, 142.

8. Maud Boaz, "Days of Reform in China," *IWCD,* November 1912, 216.

9. For a general overview, see Girardot, "Chinese Religion and Western Scholarship," 83–111; for a more detailed study, see Girardot, *The Victorian Translation of China.*

10. Adrian Fortesque, "Iconoclasm," *Encyclopaedia of Religion and Ethics,* ed. James Hastings (Edinburgh: T & T Clark, 1913–22), 7:201.

11. Ernst Boerschmann wrote a good study (1911) of Putuoshan, in German.

Reginald Johnston wrote a sympathetic *Buddhist China* (1913), which was hostile to the dismissive attitudes of missionaries. William Edward Soothill and Lewis Hodous compiled *A Dictionary of Chinese Buddhist Terms,* published in 1937 and still in use today despite its flaws. Johannes Prip-Møller spent time in Chinese monasteries doing research for his superb *Chinese Buddhist Monasteries: Their Plan and Its Function as a Setting for Buddhist Monastic Life* (1937).

12. Harlan P. Beach, *A Geography and Atlas of Protestant Missions,* vol. 2 (New York: Students Volunteer Movement for Foreign Missions, 1903), 31.

13. Young, "The Politics of Evangelism," 99.

14. "C.M.S. Probation Form C," in *Church Missionary Society Archive,* (Marlborough: Adam Matthew Publications, 1999), sect. 1, part 14, reel 297.

15. Letter, Arthur E. Moule to Rev. G. Furness Smith, 16 November 1910, in *Church Missionary Society Archive* , sec. 1, pt. 14, reel 297.

Chapter 3

1. M. Fearnley, "A Missionary's First Arrival in China," *CMG,* March 1856, 34.

2. Morgan, *Manners, Morals and Class in England,* 69–70; compare this view to the nineteenth-century practice of phrenology.

3. Wittgenstein, *Philosophical Investigations,* 178.

4. Foster, *In the Valley of the Yangtse,* 115.

5. "China — Distress of Nations with Perplexity," *CMG,* July 1862, 77.

6. Huc, *A Journey through the Chinese Empire,* 1:xiii.

7. C. Goodrich, "Importance of a Vernacular Christian Literature, with Special Reference to the Mandarin," *RGC 1877,* 213.

8. "Chinese Justice," *CMG,* March 1853, 33.

9. Williams, *LLSWW,* 91

10. Ibid., 394

11. Ibid., 257. "I am sure that the Chinese need harsh measures to bring them out of their ignorance, conceit, and idolatry" (ibid., 325). On the notion that the Chinese understand only force and actually need violence for their own good, see Miller, "Ends and Means."

12. "The Movement in China," *CMG,* October 1853, 110.

13. "A Hopeful Effort — Bing-oo, China," *CMG,* January 1857, 14; with a picture, ibid., 13.

14. Nelson, "Entire Consecration Essential to Missionary Success," *RGC 1877,* 48.

15. "Difficulties of Missionary Work — Polite Insincerity," *CMG,* March 1851, 136.

16. "Buddhist Idolatry in China," *CMG,* August 1847, 92. On a visit to a Buddhist cave-temple, a priest was found "moaning his ritual" ("Buddhism of China," *CMG,* August 1859, 90).

17. R. H. Graves, "How Shall the Native Church be Stimulated To More Aggressive Christian Work," *RGC 1877,* 340.

18. Ibid., 341–42.

19. Miss Rodd and Miss Bryer, "In Chinese Villages," *IWCD*, December 1893, 556.

20. "Missionary Labours at Ningbo," *CMG*, July 1851, 183. George Smith wrote, "Fresh air is not at all required by the Chinese, but it is very precious to us foreigners" ("The Vicinity of Fuh-chau," *CMG*, March 1861, 27).

21. Mabel Pantin, "Modern Miracles at Dong-kau," *IWCD*, October 1903, 235–36.

22. MacGowan, *Sidelights on Chinese Culture,,* 177.

23. Ibid., 178.

24. Nightingale, *Notes on Nursing*, 10.

25. Ibid., 12. "The very first canon of nursing . . . is this: TO KEEP THE AIR HE BREATHES AS PURE AS THE EXTERNAL AIR, WITHOUT CHILLING HIM" (ibid., 8). See also, pp. 9–10, on opening windows.

26. May Griggs, "Forward in Service," *Looking East*, June 1943, 94.

27. Blakiston, *Five Months on the Yang-tsze*, 232. "A Chinaman never walks when he can possibly find any other mode of conveyance, and these persons were consequently much surprised to see us apparently enjoying our walk" (Fortune, *Two Visits to the Tea Countries*, 1:137).

28. Darley, *Cameos of a Chinese City*, 146.

29. Fortune, *Two Visits to the Tea Countries*, 1:37. On Robert Fortune, see Thurin, *Victorian Travelers*, 27–53; and MacKerras, *Western Images of China*, 50–52.

30. Nightingale, *Notes on Nursing*, 49. She endorsed architectural plans with wide open spaces surrounding the buildings.

31. "The Movement in China," *CMG*, October 1853, 110.

32. "Difficulties of Missionary Work — Polite Insincerity," *CMG*, March 1851, 136.

33. MacGowan, *Sidelights on Chinese Culture*, 6.

34. Ibid., 7.

35. "The Shing-wong-min of Canton," *CMG*, November 1861, 127 (emphasis added).

36. Williams, *LLSWW*, 80.

37. W. Brereton, "Our Peking Mission," *CMG*, August 1879, 96. Fortune, who was certainly capable of very sympathetic views of Chinese religion, regarded the missionary enterprise as noble but rather futile: "The Chinese as a people are cold and indifferent to religion of any kind: humanly speaking, nothing less than a miracle will convert them to Christianity" (Fortune, *A Residence among the Chinese*, 134).

38. Fortune, *Two Visits to the Tea Countries*, 1:154. Note that Fortune uses "race" to mean merely "group of people," not intending any of the hereditary or genetic senses of "race" which became common later in the nineteenth century. "The countenances of many of the priests who swarm in the temples around Hangchow are merely expressive of vacant idiocy" (Woodbridge, *Fifty Years in China*, 63).

39. Fortune, *A Residence among the Chinese*, 268–69. And: "All the men were apparently imbecile, but the superior seemed to be in a state approaching to insanity" (269).

40. "The Tien-Doong Monastery, Near Ningpo," *CMG*, December 1859, 135.

41. "Buddhism of China," *CMG*, August 1859, 91.

42. Gützlaff, *Journal of Three Voyages*, 382.

43. Davis, *The Chinese*, 2:87.

44. Foster, *In the Valley of the Yangtse*, 116.

45. "Chinese Life," *CMG*, May 1867, 50–51.

46. E[dith] Couche, "The Kwangsi-Hunan Mission," *IWCD*, October 1915, 187.

47. "The Hospital in Lo-Nguang City," *IWCD*, August 1902, 190.

48. Edith Couche, "The Opportunity in China," *CMG*, June 1913, 91.

49. "National Feasts and Processions in China," *CMG*, October 1851, 220. The Chinese were described as "a population intelligent on every subject save one, the most important of all [religion], and yet, on that, blind, foolish, and deceived, 'groping in the dark without light'" ("Cases of Conversion to Christianity at the Cities of Lo-nguong in the Provinces of Fuh-chau, China," *CMG*, July 1867, 79).

50. "Chinese Missionary Work," *CMG*, January 1851, 112.

51. "T'in Dong," *CMG*, January 1863, 13–14.

52. *CMG*, October 1850, 73.

53. "Opium and Its Victims," *CMG*, October 1850, 78.

54. A. E. Hamilton, quoted in "A Contrast," *CMG*, January 1919, 13.

55. W. C. White, "Three Weeks with 'Opium Fiends,'" *CMG*, January 1907, 7. For more on Christian anti-opium activities, see Dunch, *Fuzhou Protestants*, 49–55. Interestingly, public rituals to burn opium paraphernalia, such as in the photograph that appears on page 53 of Dunch's book, resemble the rituals for burning the idols of converts.

56. Abeel, *Journal of a Residence in China*, 46.

57. "The Opium Traffic," *CMG*, August 1856, 90. A 1906 *CMG* editorial noted past discussion in the House of Commons, with the common view that "morality and religion and the happiness of mankind were very fine things in their way, but that we could not afford to buy them at the cost of the Indian revenue" ("E. S.," "The Opium Question," *CMG*, July 1906, 97).

58. "E. S.," "The Opium Question," *CMG*, July 1906, 97. See also Lodwick, *Crusaders against Opium*, 27–71.

59. "Opium and Its Victims," *CMG*, October 1850, 77.

60. "The Great Stumbling-Block to Xty in China," *CMG*, December 1855, 138.

61. "China — Distress of Nations with Perplexity," *CMG*, July 1862, 77–78.

62. Louis Byrde, "China's Awakening," *CMG*, February 1907, 23.

63. A. E. Moule, in "T'in Dong," *CMG*, January 1863, 15.

64. Fortune, *Three Years' Wanderings*, 5.

65. Abeel, *Journal of a Residence in China*, 78–79.

66. Fortune, *Two Visits to the Tea Countries*, 1:94.

67. Fortune, *A Residence among the Chinese*, 406–7. Contemplating these monks, Fortune concluded that "Buddhism must surely have greatly degenerated since the days when it was first promulgated" (ibid., 407).

68. Mary Darley, "Kien-Ning Prefecture and its Needs," *IWCD*, April 1905, 84.

69. Williams, *LLSWW*, 180.

70. Griffith John, "The Holy Spirit in Connection with Our Work," *RGC 1877*, 44.

71. H. Grattan Guinness, "The Voice of the Brother's Blood," in Geraldine Guinness, *In the Far East*, 6.

72. "China — Its Need of Christianity," *CMG*, 1845, 38.

73. Fortune, *A Residence among the Chinese*, 332.

74. "China — Distress of Nations with Perplexity," *CMG*, July 1862, 78–79.

75. Llewelyn Lloyd, "Fuh-chow, the Banyan City," *CMG*, June 1899, 85.

76. Ellis, Introduction to *Journal of Three Voyages*, xxx.

77. "Revolting Scenes in the Beggars' Square, Canton — Cruelty of Heathenism," *CMG*, December 45, 137.

78. Conger, *Letters from China*, 5. See also "Chinese Worship of the Spirits of the Dead at Singapore," *CMG*, October 1858, 119–120; "Superstitions of the Chinese," *CMG*, June 1867, 63–64; E. Davys, "A Chinese Mountain Tomb," *CMG*, August 1881, 87.

79. Abeel, *Journal of a Residence in China*, 119.

80. Fortune, *Two Visits to the Tea Countries*, 1:256; see also 1:78–79, 101–2, 254–56.

81. Robert Henry Cobbold, "Ningpo, and Our Missionary Prospects There," *CMG*, July 1852, 83.

82. MacGowan, *Sidelights on Chinese Culture*, 74.

83. "The Chinese," *CMG*, July 1854, 75.

84. Peyrefitte, *The Collision of Two Civilizations*, 147. Peyrefitte clearly thinks this condition is as true now as ever; he freely jumps between late-seventeenth-century discourse and his personal experiences in China as a French diplomat in the 1980s.

85. S. Wells Williams, quoted in Williams, *LLSWW*, 338.

86. Cohen, *China and Christianity*, 81.

87. Abeel, *Journal of a Residence in China*, 48.

88. "Sketches of Idol-worship: IV. — The Strength of Idolatry as an Agency of Priestcraft," *CMG*, October 1874, 117–18. And: "Although the Chinese have long considered themselves the wisest people in the world, their religious rites and customs are most foolish and trifling. Their religion is more like child's play than any thing serious. A mere baby, playing with its doll, could scarcely act more childishly than they do toward their gods" ("Missions to China," *Church Missionary Juvenile Inquirer*, December 1844, 363–64).

89. G. W. Coultas, quoted in "Along the Hang-chow River," *CMG*, October 1900, 156.

90. Edith Couche, "The Kwangsi-Hunan Mission," *IWCD*, October 1915, 187. "We have had to teach and lead them as little children" (J. W. Lambuth, "Standard of Admission to Full Church Membership," *RGC 1877*, 245).

91. "Sketches of Idol-worship: IV. — The Strength of Idolatry as an Agency of Priestcraft," *CMG*, October 1874, 117.

92. W. E. Hipwell, "Union in Face of the Foe; or, Co-operation in Evangelistic Effort in China," *CMG*, December 1907, 185.

93. "Buddhism of China," *CMG,* August 1859, 91.

94. Franck, *Wandering in Northern China,* 277. Others described the men of Shandong as "finer in appearance, and more manly in character, than those of the south" ("The Shan-tung Province," *CMG,* August 1861, 89).

95. See Hall, *Muscular Christianity.* On Victorian constructions of masculinity and physical force, see Houghton, *The Victorian Frame of Mind,* 201–9. On the American variants of the movement, see Putney, *Muscular Christianity.*

96. Wee, "Christian Manliness and National Identity," 74.

97. *RGC 1877,* 338.

98. Williams, *LLSWW,* 106.

99. Bailey, *Leisure and Class in Victorian England,* 73. See also McLeod, *Religion and Society in England,* 149–54, 199–200; and Mangan, *Athleticism.*

100. Henty, *With the Allies to Pekin,* 15–22.

101. Ibid., 84.

102. Arnold, *Held Fast for England,* 20.

103. R. Nelson, "Entire Consecration Essential to Missionary Success," *RGC 1877,* 53.

104. In addition to *Character* (1871), *Thrift* (1875), and *Duty* (1887), Smiles best-known work is *Self-Help; with Illustrations of Character and Conduct* (1859). Subsequent editions had slightly varying subtitles.

105. Smiles, *Self-Help,* 310.

106. R. H. Graves, "How Shall the Native Church be Stimulated To More Aggressive Christian Work," *RGC 1877,* 339.

107. Reed, *Glorious Battle,* 211.

108. Smiles, *Character,* 51. See also Knight, "'Male and Female He Created Them,'" 23–57.

109. "A Week at Lo-nguong," *CMG,* March 1874, 33. For a similar reason, it is customary to admire an infant by saying how ugly it is. In fact, dressing little boys in girls' clothing was also a common practice in Victorian England, and it had more to do with hygiene than with the devil (Mitchell, *Daily Life in Victorian England,* 136).

110. Woodbridge, *Fifty Years in China,* 112. Sarah Conger described the long hair of her "house boys" (i.e., her adult male servants), who "seem more like well-bred girls than men" (Conger, *Letters from China,* 36).

111. Stock, *The Story of the Fuh-Kien Mission,* 79. Cf. Genesis 13:10.

112. "The Difficulties of the Chinese Language," *CMG,* November 1860, 131.

Chapter 4

1. Mrs. Taylor (wife of B. Van Someren Taylor), "Gleanings from Chinese Homes," *CMG,* May 1889, 77.

2. Huc, *A Journey through the Chinese Empire,* 1:176 (emphasis added). Griffith John viewed the heathen as utterly this-worldly: "The people are as hard as steel. They are eaten up, both soul and body, by the world. They don't seem

to feel that there can be reality in anything beyond sense" (Cohen, *China and Christianity*, 79).

3. Llewelyn Lloyd, "A Journey to Kiong Ning Fu," *CMG*, November 1878, 124. "Wealth is the 'summum bonum' in the estimation of a Chinese" (Thomas M'Clatchie, "Chinese Missionary Work," *CMG*, January 1851, 112).

4. Thomas M'Clatchie, "Chinese Missionary Work," *CMG*, January 1851, 112. Also: "Their thoughts and desires are completely taken up with what may be for their interest and happiness in this life, and the concerns of eternity have no place in their minds" ("The Chinese," *CMG*, July 1854, 74).

5. "Chinese Missionary Work," *CMG*, January 1851, 111.

6. Darley, *Cameos of a Chinese City*, 175. Regarding the "most miserable" town of Fu-ning, whose name means "Happiness and Peace," one missionary in 1900 felt that the name "might again be very nearly interpreted 'Laziness and Plenty to eat.'" (Miss E. M. K. Thomas, "A Most Miserable Fu City," *CMG*, August 1900, 121). So Chinese happiness is laziness.

7. Abeel, *Journal of a Residence in China*, 101.

8. Ibid., 171.

9. J. W. Lambuth, "Standard of Admission to Full Church Membership," *RGC 1877*, 241.

10. Abeel, *Journal of a Residence in China*, 107

11. Williams, *LLSWW*, 174.

12. Samuel Wells Williams, quoted in ibid., 289.

13. Samuel Wells Williams, quoted in ibid., 338. Robert Fortune wrote: "Crowds of people were going in and coming out of the temple exactly like bees in a hive on a fine summer's day" (Fortune, *A Residence among the Chinese*, 252). "They pressed about us like bees" ("Fuh-Chau Fuh," *CMG*, February 1856, 17). And in "human swarms" ("A Missionary's First Arrival in China," *CMG*, March 1856, 33). See also McClellan, *The Heathen Chinee*, 45.

14. "Pekin," *CMG*, July 1858, 87.

15. Fraser, *Round the World on a Wheel*, 382.

16. Blakiston, *Five Months on the Yang-tsze*, 116.

17. Mabel Pantin, "A Brief Review of C.E.Z.M.S. Work in Dongkau," *IWCD*, September 1925, 168.

18. Fortune, *Two Visits to the Tea Countries*, 2:16.

19. Spence, *The Memory Palace of Matteo Ricci*, 114.

20. Stock, *The Story of the Fuh-Kien Mission*, 60–61.

21. "From Kwan-Yin to Christ," *Homes of the East* [hereafter *HE*], January 1921, 2 (emphasis added).

22. Yates, "Ancestral Worship," *RGC 1877*, 386.

23. Quoted in Moy, *Marginal Sights*, 51.

24. MacGowan, *Sidelights on Chinese Culture*, 20.

25. "Commencement of Missionary Labours at Shanghai," *CMG*, September 1846, 102.

26. "Contrast between Idolatry and Christianity in China," *CMG*, December 1848, 126.

27. Stock, *The Story of the Fuh-Kien Mission*, 7.

28. Smiles, *Self-Help*, 339.

29. Huc, *A Journey through the Chinese Empire*, 1:34.

30. S. Wells Williams, in Williams, *LLSWW*, 385. A Catholic writer in 1869 described the literati thus: "These Pharisees of China, irreconcilable enemies of the Christian faith, completely eaten up with pride, are neither able to nor wish to understand a religion of humility and penitence" (Cohen, *China and Christianity*, 80–81).

31. Abeel, *Journal of a Residence in China*, 57.

32. Ibid., 140.

33. Blakiston, *Five Months on the Yang-tsze*, 318.

34. Sing Tsae-seng, "A Letter from Bishop Sing, Assistant Bishop of Chekiang," *CMG*, May 1929, 95.

Chapter 5

1. Mrs. Sturge, "A Trip to China," *HE*, October 1913, 31–32. Also: "Here we are back again in this topsy-turvy land of China, which is like nothing on earth except Ireland" (Miss E. Couche, "Yungchow Once More," *IWCD*, October 1928, 182).

2. Ernst Faber, "The Advisability, or the Reverse, of Endeavoring to Convey Western Knowledge to the Chinese Through the Medium of their Own Language," *Journal of the China Branch of the Royal Asiatic Society* 21 (1886): 15. For a good general overview of problems of translation of foreign knowledge into Chinese, see Wright, "The Chinese language and Foreign Ideas."

3. Williams, *LLSWW*, 344.

4. Fraser, *Round the World on a Wheel*, 275.

5. Ibid., 303.

6. Davis, *The Chinese*, 2:140.

7. Bush, *Five Years in China*, 107

8. "The Rev. 'O Kwong-Yiao's Report on Z-Ky'I," *CMG*, June 1881, 62.

9. Trigault, *The China That Was*, 45.

10. Davis, *The Chinese*, 2:140.

11. C. Goodrich, "Importance of a Vernacular Christian Literature, with Special Reference to the Mandarin," *RGC 1877*, 214.

12. Woodbridge, *Fifty Years in China*, 51.

13. Ibid., 61 (emphasis added).

14. "Chinese Missionary Work," *CMG*, January 1851, 111.

15. "The Advisability, or the Reverse," 14.

16. Ibid. In this respect, according to Alfred J. Bamford, there were nations worse off than China: "Savage nations have been found in whose languages Christian missionaries could not speak of the Christian virtues. They had no names for them in their vocabulary because they had no ideas of them in their minds" (ibid., 12).

17. C. Maud Bettersby, "China's Darkness and Dawn," pt. 1, *IWCD,* December 1897, 250. S. Wells Williams conceded that his perceptions might be culturally subjective: "Such is Chinese literature, for it is (to our taste) destitute of imagination" (quoted in Williams, *LLSWW,* 360).

18. Colquhoun, *Across Chrysê,* 1:200.

19. Davis, *The Chinese,* 2:171–72. Davis commented, "The fact is, that the confusion of the originals has occasionally, by means of uncouth translation, been made 'confusion worse confounded.'" (2:172).

20. Quoted in Drake, "Protestant Geography in China," 92.

21. R. H. Cobbold, "A Letter from Ningpo, China," *CMG,* June 1856, 73.

22. Huc, *A Journey through the Chinese Empire,* 2:359; see also Blakiston, *Five Months on the Yang-tsze,* 180.

23. Holm, *Pidgins and Creoles,* 2:514.

24. Leland also published widely on ballads and folklore, including the following works: *A dictionary of slang, jargon & cant embracing English, American, and Anglo-Indian slang, pidgin English, tinker's jargon and other irregular phraseology,* comp. and ed. Albert Barrère and Charles G. Leland (London: Ballantyne Press, 1889–90); and *Fusang; or, The discovery of America by Chinese Buddhist priests in the fifth century* (New York: J. W. Bouton, 1875).

25. "Mary Coe," in Leland, *Pidgin-English Sing-Song,* 25.

26. Ibid., 26; n.b.: "he" means "the."

27. Leland, *Pidgin-English Sing-Song,* 2.

28. Ibid., 9.

29. Mühlhäusler, *Pidgin and Creole Linguistics,* 96–102. "In the early days of Pidgins and Creoles, the distinction between expatriate foreigner talk and indigenous versions of a language was considerably less than it is today, the former being perfectly acceptable as a means of communication. Thus the language of early writings is usually the version of the socially dominant group" (ibid., 313).

30. Ferguson, "Absence of Copula and the Notion of Simplicity," 144.

31. Parker, "The Comparative Study of Chinese Dialects," 20.

32. Leland, *Pidgin-English Sing-Song,* 7.

33. Decamp, Introduction to *Pidginization and Creolization of Languages,* 21–22; also Whinnom, "Linguistic Hybridization and the 'Special Case' of Pidgins and Creoles," 104.

34. Parker, "The Comparative Study of Chinese Dialects," 19. Papuan Pidgin English was referred to as "vile gibberish" and "horrible jargon" (Mühlhäusler, *Pidgin and Creole Linguistics,* 244–55).

35. Leland, *Pidgin-English Sing-Song,* 131.

36. Holm, *Pidgins and Creoles,* 1:2.

37. Blakiston, *Five Months on the Yang-tsze,* 119. As Mühlhäusler commented: "The general idea conveyed to the readers of Mickey Mouse is that most members of exotic races speak some childish primitive jargon. The idea is reinforced by the extravagant clothing and use of ridiculous gestures or postures of these Pidgin speakers. In some instances, similar language is also spoken by monkeys, dogs or dwarfs" (Mühlhäusler, *Pidgin and Creole Linguistics,* 310).

38. Abeel, *Journal of a Residence in China*, 110. Earlier, Trigault had passed judgment on Chinese music, and many Victorian writers agreed: "The whole art of Chinese music seems to consist in producing a monotonous rhythmic beat as they know nothing of the variations and harmony that can be produced by combining different musical notes. However, they themselves are highly flattered by their own music which to the ear of a stranger represents nothing but a discordant jangle" (Trigault, *The China That Was*, 35–36).

39. Sae Gaussen, "Evangelism in Nienow," *Looking East*, September 1948, 136.

40. Franck, *Wandering in Northern China*, 478. Long after they had left the site, "the charivari of droning priests and misused instruments drifted to our hearing" (ibid., 479). Note the definition of *charivari* in the *Oxford English Dictionary:* "A serenade of 'rough music', with kettles, pans, tea-trays, and the like, used in France, in mockery and derision of incongruous or unpopular marriages, and of unpopular persons generally; hence a confused, discordant medley of sounds; a babel of noise."

41. Hagspeil, *Along the Mission Trail*, 30.

42. Ibid., 319.

43. Fortune, *Two Visits to the Tea Countries*, 1:111.

44. *CMG*, June 1856, opposite p. 73. Similarly, see the picture captioned: "A Chinese burning paper to appease the spirits of his ancestors," which shows two barefooted men, one burning paper, the other sitting smoking a long pipe ("Pseudo-Chinese Writing on the Wall," *CMG*, May 1867). The frontispiece from the March 1853 *Church Missionary Gleaner* illustrated "A Chinese Court of Justice," with a judge above a man in a cangue and another man kneeling in supplication. Garbled Chinese characters appear on signs and above persons (*CMG*, 3 March 1853, 25). And: Mrs. Sturge, "A Trip to China" (*HE*, October 1913, 32) includes a line of Chinese, identified as John X.16 but obviously reproduced by someone who knows no Chinese since the characters are seriously garbled. As an example of Chinese rendered literally topsy-turvy, see the name Xibao ("Little Precious") written upside-down (cf. the notion that the Chinese do everything upside-down) to illustrate an essay by a Miss Jackson ("Little Precious," *HE*, January 1916, 7). Further examples could easily be supplied.

Chapter 6

1. Huc, *A Journey through the Chinese Empire*, 1:185–86.

2. Fortune, *Two Visits to the Tea Countries*, 1:105. "No dependence can be placed upon the veracity of the Chinese. I may seem uncharitable, but such is really the case" (ibid., 2:5). Or Huc, again: "The Chinese have so elaborately developed their system of lying and deceit, that it is very difficult to believe them, even when they do speak the truth" (Huc, *A Journey through the Chinese Empire*, 1:286).

3. Blakiston, *Five Months on the Yang-tsze*, 5. ". . . those shams so constantly seen in China, from the government down to the religion" (ibid., 4). The decep-

tions of local mandarins, Gützlaff wrote, were "political popery" (Gützlaff, *Journal of Three Voyages*, 183). Chinese courts were regarded as hopelessly corrupt and unjust, yet "there is a great *show* of justice" ("Chinese Justice," *CMG*, March 1853, 31). "Gardening rarely engages their attention, for, though fond of flowers, they prefer the artificial to the natural" (Gützlaff, *Journal of Three Voyages*, 229).

4. MacGowan, *Sidelights on Chinese Culture*, 11.

5. Blakiston, *Five Months on the Yang-tsze*, 5. "Among all the Chinese I have come in contact with, there is a want of two very precious qualities — veracity and gratitude" (ibid., 318).

6. MacGowan, *Sidelights on Chinese Culture*, 11.

7. Dingle, *Across China on Foot*, 250–51.

8. "Visit to a Buddhist Temple in China," *CMG*, June 1845, 70. Regarding the Mongolians in their religious practices, an American missionary wrote: "There was one thing which struck me — the very apparent heartlessness with which they went through the whole service. And no wonder. All their chants and prayers are in an unknown tongue" ("A Tour in Mongolia," *CMG*, August 1866, 95).

9. William Milne, quoted in Davis, *The Chinese*, 2:98.

10. Milne, quoted in ibid., 2:97–98. The Chinese character *fan* can refer to Brahma, and hence Sanskrit, or it can refer generally to India or Buddhism.

11. "Buddhist Idolatry in China," *CMG*, August 1847, 93.

12. Fortune, *Two Visits to the Tea Countries*, 2:281.

13. Milne, quoted in Davis, *The Chinese*, 2:98.

14. Milne, quoted in ibid., 2:96–97.

15. Gützlaff, quoted in ibid., 2:89.

16. Gützlaff, quoted in ibid.

17. Milne, quoted in ibid., 2:97.

18. Abeel, *Journal of a Residence in China*, 90.

19. May Griggs, "Forward in Service," *Looking East*, June 1943, 95.

20. "Contrast between Idolatry and Christianity in China," *CMG*, December 1848, 127.

21. Huc, *A Journey through the Chinese Empire*, 1:271–72.

22. Smith, *To Take Place*, 102–3. Talal Asad takes a similar approach, looking at the term as it evolved in the *Encyclopedia Britannica* from 1771 to 1910 (see Asad, *Genealogies of Religion*, 56–60). He notes that the word "ritual" referred to a text, a book containing instructions on religious services, through to the 7th edition in 1852; and that the 9th and 10th editions have no entries under "ritual" or "rite," which might be considered the calm before the anthropological storm, since the 11th edition, published in 1910, treats "ritual" in a profoundly different way — as a cultural phenomenon crucial to all religions but not confined to religion: "a type of practice that is interpretable as standing for some further *verbally definable*, but tacit, event" (ibid., 37). In other words, "ritual" was considered culturally and historically important in so far as it signified (something else).

23. Jensen, *Myth and Cult among Primitive Peoples*, 4. The human agent is passive in this mystical moment: "New aspects of reality have revealed themselves to man" (4–5). See also Smith, *Imagining Religion*, 42–43. And for sug-

gestive discussions of the priority of "experience," see Benavides, "Guiseppe Tucci," 165; and Sharf, "Buddhist Modernism," 228–30.

24. Jensen, *Myth and Cult among Primitive Peoples*, 3.

25. Ibid., 5.

26. Ibid., 6

27. Smith, *To Take Place*, 103.

28. Quoted in Zito, "Ritualizing *Li*," 321.

29. Ibid.

Chapter 7

1. Evans, *The Case of Kneeling*, 1–2.

2. Burton, *Jesu-Worship Confuted*, 1.

3. Stillingfleet, *Several Conferences*, 38. The host was fed to goats and dogs, cast on the ground, eaten, and hung around a horse's neck (see Eire, *War against the Idols*, 113, 121, 128, 138, 146. For a rich treatment of the ritual and politics of the host in the late Medieval period, see Zika, "Hosts, Processions, and Pilgrimages." In particular, Zika treats the host as a clerical instrument of control: "It served as a demonstration of priestly power" (60). See also Kibbey, *The Interpretation of Material Shapes*, 44–59.

4. Wandel, *Voracious Idols and Violent Hands*, 195. This study of iconoclasm in the 1520s shows how "iconoclasts called attention to the ways the objects in the churches enabled a certain form and manner of worship and participated in a particular conception of divinity: Images were an essential medium of medieval Roman theology" (ibid.). For a discussion of the sociopolitical dimensions of iconoclasm, see also Eire, *War against the Idols*, 151–65. For sources on sixteenth-century German iconoclasm, see Mangrum and Scavizzi, *A Reformation Debate*.

5. Davis, *The Chinese*, 2:187. "Tinsel" is used also in Gützlaff, *Journal of Three Voyages*, 58, 441.

6. Andreas Karlstadt, in Mangrum and Scavizzi, *A Reformation Debate*, 23.

7. Stillingfleet, *Several Conferences*, 44.

8. Ibid., 37.

9. Ibid., 224.

10. Quoted in Pelikan, *Obedient Rebels*, 78.

11. "E.S.," "A Letter from Rome," *CMG*, January 1892, 6; see also "E. S.," "Another Letter from Rome," *CMG*, February 1892, 22–23.

12. Rosa, "Seventeenth-Century Catholic Polemic," 95.

13. Ibid., 97.

14. Heber, "From Greenland's Icy Mountains," 90. This hymn is briefly discussed in Mitchell, *Daily Life in Victorian England*, 274; and Thomas, "Foreign Missions and Missionaries," 116–17.

15. Peyrefitte, *The Collision of Two Civilizations*, 251.

16. Huc, *A Journey through the Chinese Empire,*,1:xvi.

17. Ibid., 1:xvii.

18. Ibid., 1:xviii.

19. Rodd and Bryer, "In Chinese Villages," *IWCC,* December 1893, 556. The quotation "wholly given to idolatry" is from Acts 17:16, in reference to the people of Athens.

20. Burder, *The History of All Religions,* 679. W. Gilbert Walshe upholds this view: the later developments of Buddhism and Daoism "served to degrade the primitive simplicity and purity" of an original monotheism (Walshe, "China," 550). Among the "new inventions" was, for example, the ledger of merit, prompting Davis to remark: "This method of keeping a score with heaven is as foolish and dangerous a system of morality as that of penances and indulgences in the Roman church" (Davis, *The Chinese,* 2:171).

21. Gützlaff, *Journal of Three Voyages,* 371–72. John MacGowan had a similar view: "The best days for China were in the ancient past, according to the sacred books of the nation, when God and heaven were the predominant words in the religious life of the people, and when the idols had not yet come from India to lower the conceptions of the Divine" (MacGowan, *Sidelights on Chinese Culture,* 338).

22. Louis Byrde, "China's Awakening," *CMG,* February 1907, 23.

23. "Cyril," *A Flower of Asia,* 349.

24. "The Great False Religions of the World," *CMG,* April 1899, 57.

25. E. S. K., "Oriental Religions," *IWCD,* August 1909, 121.

26. R. Lechler, "On the Relation of Protestant Missions to Education," *RGC 1877,* 168.

27. Ibid., 162.

28. Smith, *Chinese Characteristics,* 119.

29. "Our Illustrations" (comments attached by an "eye witness"), *CMG,* October 1877, 118. See also, e.g., Davis, *The Chinese,* 2:163, 170, 174–78; Burder, *The History of All Religions,* 687, 691. See also Staunton, *An Authentic Account,* 2:100. S. Wells Williams links ideals of chastity in Chinese and "Romanist" monasticism in *The Middle Kingdom* (193). See also Hallisey, "Roads Taken and Not Taken," 46.

30. "Our Illustrations," *CMG,* October 1877, 119.

31. Grueber, *China and France,* 109–10. See also Jensen, *Manufacturing Confucianism,* 55.

32. Davis, *The Chinese,* 2:83.

33. Gerard Smith, "How the Heathen Pray: V. — Helps to Prayer," *CMG,* December 1875, 137 (one of a series of "How the Heathen Pray" columns).

34. "Great Activity of Romish Missions," *CMG,* October 1843, 109.

35. "Romish Procession at Macao," *CMG,* April 1856, 43.

36. "Romanism at Chusan," *CMG,* January 1852, 12.

37. "Missionary Excursion from Shanghai," *CMG,* August 1846, 90.

38. S. Wells Williams, quoted in Williams, *LLSWW,* 387.

39. "Visit to a Buddhist Temple in China," *CMG,* June 1845, 70.

40. "Romanism at Chusan," *CMG,* January 1852, 11 (emphasis added). "It is the working of the same corrupt principle which leads the Chinese to worship

the ancestral tablet, and the corrupt Romanist or Greek Christian to bow themselves before images and pictures, and invoke the aid of the Virgin and the Saints" ("The Chinese," *CMG,* July 1854, 75).

41. "Chinese Missionary Work," *CMG,* January 1851, 111.

42. S. Wells Williams, quoted in Williams, *LLSWW,* 409.

43. Morgan, *Manners, Morals, and Class in England,* 82–83.

Chapter 8

1. "Buddhism of China," *CMG,* August 1859, 90.

2. "Kwan-Yin," *HE,* January 1921, 2.

3. L. Fleming, "In Heathen China," *IWCD,* April 1905, 93.

4. Mary Darley, "Kien-Ning Prefecture and its Needs," *IWCD,* April 1905, 84. Twenty-five years later, Darley inspected a great heap of images destroyed by soldiers: "Idols great and small, whole and in pieces, lying about in the various halls. The King god himself prostrate, half of his face hacked off, his red, embroidered satin robe on the ground near by. It was indeed the moment in which to point the awed and wondering onlookers from the 'dead idols' around them, to the 'Living Creator God.'" (Darley, "To-day in Kienning," *IWCD,* March 1930, 47).

5. W. A. P. Martin, "The Worship of Ancestors — A Plea for Toleration," *RGC 1890,* 628.

6. Ibid., 626.

7. Ibid.

8. Ibid., 629.

9. H. V. Noyes, "How Far Should Christians Be Required to Abandon Native Customs?" *RGC 1890,* 612. The "same word" Noyes was referring to was probably *bai,* or possibly *li.*

10. *RGC 1890,* 659.

11. "Praying for Rain in China," *CMG,* April 1874, 40.

12. "The Story of the Fuh-Chow Mission: II. — Sowing the Seed," *CMG,* April 1876, 44.

13. W. Ellis, quoted in Gützlaff, *Journal of Three Voyages,* xxvi.

14. Blakiston, *Five Months on the Yang-tsze,* 179; see also 183.

15. "Chinese Missionary Work," *CMG,* January 1851, 113.

16. "Cyril," *A Flower of Asia,* 267.

17. Ibid.

18. Ibid., 268.

19. Ibid.

20. "Good News from Fuh-chau," *CMG,* February 1866, 17.

21. "Persecution in China," *A Quarterly Token for Juvenile Subscribers,* April 1868.

22. Henry Blodget, quoted in *RGC 1877,* 84.

23. Miss K. M. Griggs, "Part of a Five Weeks' Tour in the Loyuan District," *IWCD,* September 1925, 170–71.

24. Haliburton, *Wise Saws*, 130.

25. Cary and Cary, *Poetical Works*, 329.

26. Adam Smith quoted in Bryce, *Lectures on Rhetoric and Belles Lettres*, 198. See also Thomas, Introduction to *A Cultural History of Gesture*, 9.

27. Morgan, *Manners, Morals, and Class in England*, 67.

28. Smiles, *Character*, 271.

29. Arnold, *Held Fast for England*, 33.

30. Ibid., 34. Henty also criticized the French, who pulled hair during fights. "Why, in England even girls would hardly pull each other's hair" (ibid.).

31. Spencer, *The Principles of Sociology*, 2:118.

32. Ibid, 2:141–42.

33. Quoted in Peyrefitte, *Collision of Two Civilizations*, 325.

34. Quoted in Smiles, *Self-Help*, 400. Smiles wrote: "It is good for men to be roused into action and stiffened into self-reliance by difficulty, rather than to slumber away their lives in useless apathy and indolence" (Smiles, *Character*, 378). A garbled metaphor — being moved to action is related to becoming "stiffened." (but stiff has other meanings, e.g. a stiff drink is "strong" drink, a stiff fine, etc.).

35. Bourdieu, *The Logic of Practice*, 72.

36. Hevia, *Cherishing Men from Afar*, 73–74.

37. Smiles, *Character*, 154.

38. Hsü, *The Rise of Modern China*, 211; also, Peyrefitte, *The Collision of Two Civilizations*, 513–16.

39. Doyle, *The Return of the Guards*, 105–7. See also Fraser, *Flashman and the Dragon*, for a satirical take on these mythic events.

40. Hevia, *Cherishing Men from Afar*, 79.

41. Ibid.

42. Ibid., 234.

43. Mangrum and Scavizzi, *A Reformation Debate*, 35.

44. Stillingfleet, *Several Conferences*, 37. The same Fanatick voice says: "What the cup of fornication means, that is Idolatry, and to bow at the name of Jesus, and to bow to the Altar, that is Idolatry" (ibid., 35).

45. Peyrefitte, *Collision of Two Civilizations*, 251. Peyrefitte then comments: "Macartney's frequent antipapist flourishes were typical of the time. It was the age of Voltaire" (ibid.).

46. S. Wells Williams, in Williams, *LLSWW*, 319. "It has never been easy to impress upon Western minds the genuine apprehensions which agitated the imperial counsellors as to the disturbing effect which a concession of audience without prostration would produce upon a people educated to regard its ruler as a divinity. It is hardly too much, indeed, to say that a slight to a Roman Augustus, or to a Pope in the middle ages, might have been allowed with less danger to the dignity of the potentate than this act of approach without low obeisance to the 'Dragon Throne.'" (Frederick Wells Williams, in ibid., 318).

47. S. Wells Williams, in ibid., 405.

48. Spencer, *Principles of Sociology*, 2:220.

49. Ibid., 2:122.

50. Ibid. Also, 2:118, 140–43, 223–24.

51. Ibid., 143.

52. Lakoff and Johnson, *Metaphors We Live By*. See also Stallybrass and White, *The Politics and Poetics of Transgression*, 144–45.

53. R. Nelson, "Entire Consecration Essential to Missionary Success," *RGC 1877*, 54.

54. Ibid., 53.

55. The phrase is Foucault's. See his "Technologies of the Self," 16–49; and his "Political Technology of Individuals," 145–62.

56. Schopen "Archaeology and Protestant Presuppositions," 1–23.

57. Crawley, "Kneeling," 746.

58. Ibid. On Martin Luther's assertion of the propriety of kneeling in worship, see Pelikan, *Obedient Rebels*, 84–85; Luther also saw kneeling as becoming less necessary as Christian faith became more earnest. Liturgical forms were thus a "concession" (93).

59. Blakiston, *Five Months on the Yang-tsze*, 318.

Chapter 9

1. MacGowan, "Goon," 8–18. Unless otherwise noted, all quotations in this chapter are from this text. John MacGowan arrived in Shanghai in 1860 and spent much of his time in Amoy until his retirement in 1910. He spent a great deal of his time publishing magazines and books on Chinese dialects, history, culture, and the missions; these included *Christ or Confucius, Which?* (1889) and *A History of China: From the Earliest Days Down to the Present* (1897).

2. Lao Tzu, *Tao Te Ching*, 57, 91.

3. Confucius, *The Analects*, 88, 107.

4. MacGowan, *Sidelights on Chinese Culture*, 83–84.

5. Ibid., 51–52. Also: Icons have to be propitiated, but idol worship does not reform character (ibid., 80–81).

6. Elsewhere, MacGowan described a procession to Heaven (MacGowan, *Sidelights on Chinese Culture*, 84–85).

7. Fortune, *A Residence among the Chinese*, 32.

8. The original text reads "was to appear to Him," but I believe the capitalized "Him" is a typographic error, since the sentence makes sense only if "him" refers to Goon.

9. G. W. Coultas, quoted in "Along the Hang-chow River," *CMG*, October 1900, 156.

10. For some interesting remarks on conversion processes, see Dunch, *Fuzhou Protestants*, 5–11.

11. Spiritualism provided for some a scientific quality to metaphysical beliefs such as the afterlife, but as a movement it tended to push the boundaries of religious orthodoxy and was associated with certain radical agendas such as women's rights. Victorian communication with "the other side" included rap-

ping (typology), table-turning, the use of the planchette or Ouija board, clair-voyance, clairaudience, spirit photography, automatic writing, possession, and trance-speaking, in addition to communication methods used in the wider field of divination, including palmistry, crystal-gazing, Tarot, dowsing, and reading tea-leaves.

12. MacGowan, *Sidelights on Chinese Culture*, 92.

Chapter 10

1. For example, "The Chinese live largely on vegetables; they are the usual accompaniment of rice with the great majority of the people. As a rule, the poor-er people only eat meat twice a month" (W. Munn, "Street Scenes in Western China," *CMG*, October 1911, 153). For other examples, see Peyrefitte, *The Colli-sion of Two Civilizations*, 344; Bird, *The Yangtze Valley and Beyond*, 143 (on the Chinese diet of rice), 297 (on the scarcity of livestock). The Protestant mission-ary C. Maud Bettersby noted, "Rice forms the staple food, and beef is rarely eaten, but fowls, fish, and pork make up for the deficiency" (C. Maud Betters-by, "China's Darkness and Dawn," pt. 2, *IWCD*, December 1897, 272). Note the lack of red meat, which is here a "deficiency." Also: Conger, *Letters from China*, 7–8; Fortune, *A Residence among the Chinese*, 42.

2. Spence, *The Chan's Great Continent*, 38.

3. Crow, *Four Hundred Million Customers*, 233–35.

4. Stevenson, *Collected Poems*, 379.

5. Wu, "Vegetarianism," 73.

6. Ohnuki-Tierney, "McDonald's in Japan166–67. Not all of her generaliza-tions about Japan can be applied to China, however; Japan has a distinct dietary history.

7. Miss Johnson, "Nangwa: The Women's Hospital, Nangwa-ke," *IWCD*, December 1894, 555.

8. Letter, Ignatius of Loyola to the Jesuit Patriarch of Ethiopia, February 1555 (no. 143), in Ignatius of Loyola, *Obras*, 911. Ignatius's *Spiritual Exercises* includ-ed rules for moderation in eating and against "delicacies," but meat is conspicu-ously absent in these prohibitions (*Ejercicios espirituales*, "Reglas para ordenarse en el comer para adelante," in ibid., 239–40). My thanks to Mark Jordan for his help with the contexts of the Jesuit polemics.

9. Ricci, *The True Meaning*, 265.

10. Ibid., 261.

11. Ibid., 253.

12. Ibid., 267.

13. Ibid., 255.

14. Ibid., 259.

15. Robert Palmer, "A Day's Preaching in the Shaou-hing Plain," *CMG*, Octo-ber 1877, 113. The leader of the Taiping rebellion (and self-proclaimed younger brother of Jesus) Hong Xiuquan (1813–1864) agreed with this view: "Hong argued that such a practice could not be meritorious, for God had provided ani-

mals to be used as food by man" (Rudolph Lechler, quoted in Lutz and Lutz, *Hakka Chinese*, 123.

16. "Good News from China," *CMG*, July 1868, 74. See Jones, *Buddhism in Taiwan*, 14–30, on the categories of *zhaijiao* and Buddhism.

17. Ritson, *An Essay on Abstinence*, 184. A report from Bishop 'O Kwong-yiao describes a Buddhist monk who converts and then breaks his vegetarian fast ("The Rev. 'O Kwong-Yiao's Report on Z-Ky'i," *CMG*, June 1881, 62). A picture captioned "Vegetarian Buddhists at Ning-Tiak, converted to Christianity" recalls an earlier conversion of three "Buddhists of the Vegetarian sect" ("Vegetarian Converts in China," *CMG*, September 1885, 99.) "The Buddhists are vegetarians, and consider it an act of great merit to preserve the life of animals. . . . Food was being prepared for the monks, but no meat, as they are all strict vegetarians" ("Kushan and Kuliang — A Contrast," *CMG*, August 1906, 120, 121). See also Stock, *The Story of the Fuh-Kien Mission*, 101, 307–8; and A. E. Moule, "The Chinese Vegetarian Vow," *CMG*, November 1914, 174.

18. A. E. Moule, "The Chinese Vegetarian Vow," *CMG*, November 1914, 174.

19. "The Fuh-Kien Mission," *CMG*, September 1884, 105; "Vegetarian Converts in China," *CMG*, September 1885, 99. A female convert named Lin, "the ladies' woman servant," and another convert named Sie "gave up her idols, broke her vegetarian vow and in consequence of her intercourse with the missionaries has had considerable persecution" (O. M. Jackson, "The Story of Mien-Cheo," *CMG*, March 1897, 42–43).

20. Mrs. Edward Horder, "A Visit to the Hon Uk," *CMG*, September 1902, 138–39.

21. Ibid., 139.

22. Miss Schneider, "Broken Vows," *CMG*, May 1914, 77.

23. Jarvis Downman Valentine, "Converts at Shaou-hing," *CMG*, December 1877, 138.

24. Ibid.

25. Miss Schneider, "Broken Vows," *CMG*, May 1914, 77. One can't help think that eating meat after so many years of a vegetarian diet — long after the stomach had lost the enzymes to digest meat — must have pushed her over the edge!

26. Mary Darley, "Mrs. Liu's Choice," *HE*, January 1921, 3–4.

27. Mrs. Arnold Foster, *In the Valley of the Yangtse*, 158–59.

28. Miss Vaughan, "At Home in China," *CMG*, July 1894, 99.

29. A. E. Moule, "The Chinese Vegetarian Vow," *CMG*, November 1914, 174. The selfish accumulation of merit was the standard missionary explanation for the Chinese vegetarian diet. Another example is T. P. Tindall, "A Thorough Break with the Past," *CMG*, July 1922, 147. In contrast, in a 1929 missionary account an unnamed former Buddhist nun had been set free from both the meatless diet and the fallacy of salvation by self-effort: "For a long time she kept her vegetarian vow, but now she loves to tell others who are seeking salvation by that road, of her own futile efforts and the true Way she has found at last" (Mrs. Marshall, "The Story of a Buddhist Nun," *Church Missionary Outlook*, March 1929, 53).

30. A. E. Moule, "The Chinese Vegetarian Vow," *CMG*, November 1914, 174.

31. Given my argument, it is ironic that the term "rice Christian" was used; perhaps "meat Christian" would be more accurate. However, in Chinese, "rice" tends to mean simply "food." On the mood of distrust of any material reward for converts, see Hyatt, *Our Ordered Lives Confess*, 25–62.

32. H. R. Rodd and L. J. Bryer, "After Furlough: At Ciong-Bau Once More," *IWCD*, August 1906, 125.

33. Abeel, *Journal of a Residence in China*, 47–48.

34. "Memo of conversation between G. G. T. and the Revd J. H. Horsburgh, October 12, 1891," in *Church Missionary Society Archive*, sec. 1, pt. 13, reel 278.

35. "Domestic Manners of the Chinese," *CMG*, May 1859, 61–62. This writer did not like that they all picked food from the same dish, but noted that spoon and fork were provided for those unable to use chopsticks. Collier remarks on the unpleasantness of seeing dogs, cats, rats, hawks, reptiles, and grasshoppers as food (Collier, *The West in the East*, 400). On the supposed consumption of rats, see also McClellan, *The Heathen Chinee*, 92–93.

36. "Missionary Tours in the Interior of China," *CMG*, August 1856, 98.

37. Fortune, *Two Visits to the Tea Countries*, 1:115.

38. See Cohen, *China and Christianity*, 31. See also Bird, *The Yangtze Valley and Beyond*, 215, 246, 254, 269. On the specifically Western concept of the vampire and its inappropriateness in other cultures, see White, *Speaking with Vampires*, 27–30.

39. "Missionary Itinerancy in the Neighbourhood of Ningpo," *CMG*, November 1870, 123. S. Wells Williams noted: "The best part of the community really believe that the stories about plucking out children's eyes, etc., are entirely true" (quoted in Williams, *LLSWW*, 385). H. M. Eyton-Jones reported a translation of a placard hung on the city walls, which said: "Followers of Jesus become akin to the beasts, their conscience is dead, their lives become injured, their end is certain. Even in death their bodies are maltreated. Their eyes are torn from their sockets, their hearts from their bodies, and the knee-caps wrenched off" (H. M. Eyton-Jones, "How the Chinese Are Incited," *CMG*, July 1895, 107).

40. See Cohen, *China and Christianity*, 49–51, 54–55, 89–92.

41. Woodbridge, *Fifty Years in China*, 72.

42. Kung, *Gong Tianmin xinwenji sanshipian*, 29–44.

43. Kung, *Da Fojiao renshi shiwen*, 7–12.

44. Ibid., 8.

45. Kung, *Gong Tianmin xinwenji sanshipian*, 41.

46. Ibid. Kung also cites a similar scriptural case from Mark 7:19.

47. Kung, *Da Fojiao renshi shiwen*, 8.

48. Kung, *Gong Tianmin dengdaoji*, 123–46.

49. Kung, *Da Fojiao renshi shiwen*, 9; and Kung, *Gong Tianmin xinwenji sanshipian*, 41.

50. Kung, *Da Fojiao renshi shiwen*, 9.

51. Kung, *Gong Tianmin xinwenji sanshipian*, 42.

52. Ibid.

53. Kung, *Da Fojiao renshi shiwen*, 11.

54. Kung, *Gong Tianmin xinwenji sanshipian*, 41.

55. Ibid., 40.

56. Mrs. Marshall, "The Story of a Buddhist Nun," *CMG,* March 1929, 52. This echoes a description of a "theatrical performance" witnessed by a missionary in 1908: "Scene 1. A temple. Buddhist priest poorly dressed, evidently dissipated, stands before his idols. Worshipper enters. Priest (aside), 'A little business at last, now I'll be able to get some meat to eat' [a splendid hit, as the priests are *supposed* to be vegetarians]" ("Changing China," *CMG,* June 1908, 88–89, square brackets in original).

57. Kung, *Da Fojiao renshi shiwen*, 10.

58. Ibid., 11.

59. Kapleau, *To Cherish All Life*, 39–40.

60. Gregerson, *Vegetarianism*, 21.

61. Miss K. E. White, "New Year's Day in a Chinese City," *CMG,* January 1915, 6 (emphasis added).

Chapter 11

1. Collier, *The West in the East*, 400. See also Blakiston, *Five Months on the Yang-tsze*, 310–11.

2. Huc, *A Journey through the Chinese Empire*, 1:46.

3. Bird, *The Yangtze Valley and Beyond*, 231.

4. Crow, *Four Hundred Million Customers*, 148–49.

5. Ibid.,149.

6. "Chinese dogs are very anti-foreign, and smell Europeans from afar" (Foster, *In the Valley of the Yangtse*, 143). "First of all Mr. Conger's pony had to be eaten [during the 1900 siege of Beijing], as he hated foreigners as bitterly as do the Chinese. He would snort, strike, kick, and jump at foreigners, and would not touch a proffered morsel that the other ponies would eagerly eat" (Conger, *Letters from China*, 117).

7. Buck, *Pavilion of Women*, 159.

8. Headland, *Home Life in China*, 174. In Japan, the distinctive odor of Europeans has been identified as butter, as in the expression *bata kusai* (butter smell).

9. MacGowan, *Sidelights on Chinese Culture*, 181.

10. M. E. Boaz, "Fragments that Remain," *IWCD,* January 1931, 15.

11. Huc, *A Journey through the Chinese Empire* 1:45–46.

12. Ibid., 1:47.

13. Ibid., 1:45.

14. Blakiston, *Five Months on the Yang-tsze,* 310. On the reports of strong smells in San Francisco Chinatown, see McClellan, *The Heathen Chinee,* 32–33.

15. F. I. Codrington and A. M. Robinson, "Birds on the Wing" (a continuing story), *HE,* May–June 1934, 39. Deaconess Wade, back after a furlough in England, had to pinch her nose: "The streets, excepting for a few semi-foreign houses, appear the same as ever: just as dirty and evil-smelling!" (A. J. Wade, "Back

in 'Old-Field' (Kutien)," *IWCD*, July 1936, 125). Miss Baring-Gould, returning to China in 1913 after some time away, noted, "The dirt looked the same — filth beyond description — and the smells smelt the same!" ("The C.M.S. Delegation to the Far East," *CMG*, April 1913, 61).

16. MacGowan, *Sidelights on Chinese Culture*, 177.

17. Ibid., 260

18. Ibid., 177.

19. Ibid., 260

20. Stoller, *The Taste of Ethnographic Things*, 25 (emphasis added).

21. V. Mander, "A Junior Missionary in China," *IWCD*, March 1914, 58.

22. MacGowan, *Sidelights on Chinese Culture*, 177.

23. Biggers, *Charlie Chan Carries On*, 179.

24. Hersey, *The Call*, 111.

25. Welch, *The Buddhist Revival in China*, 242.

Chapter 12

1. *RGC 1877*, 93.

2. Hevia, *Cherishing Men from Afar*, 23. See also Zito, *Of Body and Brush*, 29–30, 182–84.

3. Spence, *Emperor of China*, 13–14. The Emperor went on: "Some of their words were no different from the wild or improper teachings of Buddhists and Taoists, and why should they be treated differently? One of my censors wrote that the Western god fashioned a man with a human soul from the blood of a virgin, Mary; and they claimed that Jesus was born in the reign of Han Ai-ti [reigned 6 B.C.–A.D. 1], that he was killed on a cross for man's sins, and that they had meetings in which slaves and masters, men and women, mixed together and drank some holy substance. I had asked Verbiest why God had not forgiven his son without making him die, but though he had tried to answer I had not understood him" (ibid., 84).

4. Cohen, *China and Christianity*, 49.

5. Ricci, *The True Meaning*, 413. He also used the analogy of Confucian praise of chaste widows (ibid., 417).

6. "The Story of the Fuh-Chow Mission: V," *CMG*, July 1876, 80. Similarly, Robert Fortune reported that villagers "wanted to see how and in what manner I went to bed. My temper was unusually sweet at this time, and therefore I had no objection to gratify them even in this, providing they remained quiet and allowed me to get to sleep" (Fortune, *A Residence among the Chinese*, 270).

7. "Ningpo, and our Missionary Prospects There," *CMG*, July 1852, 83.

8. "Missionary Labours at Fuh-Chau," *CMG*, April 1857, 41.

9. Miss Rodd and Miss Bryer, "In Chinese Villages," *IWCD*, December 1893, 557.

10. Miss E. Garnett, "Chinese Visitors in Sz-Chuen," *CMG*, August 1893, 122.

11. W. C. White, "Jottings from a Journal," *CMG*, January 1903, 13.

12. Mrs. Taylor, "Gleanings from Chinese Homes," *CMG*, May 1889, 77.

13. Huc, *A Journey through the Chinese Empire*, 1:42.

14. "Resolutions of the CMS General Committee, Aug 13, 1895," *CMG*, September 1895, 142. An 1857 article in the *Gleaner* described missionaries escaping a violent mob: "This immediately aroused the cupidity of the worst portion of the community" ([S. Wells Williams], "Canton — Yeh and his Cruelty," *CMG*, September 1857, 103). In the same year, the governor of Canton issued a proclamation "offering 200 dollars for every English head brought to him" ("Latest Intelligence from Missionaries in China," *CMG*, May 1857, 57). H. M. Eyton-Jones described "how the Chinese are incited," and even presented a translation of an incendiary placard hung on the Funing city walls (*CMG*, July 1895, 107). "A Local Riot in Mid China" described rioters looting and burning down a church earlier that year (E. Thompson, *CMG*, October 1900, 148–50).

15. "Missionary Labours at Ningpo, China," *CMG*, March 1859, 29.

16. "The Great Stumbling-Block to Christianity in China," *CMG*, December 1855, 137.

17. Fortune, *Two Visits to the Tea Countries*, 1:183.

18. "The Great Stumbling-Block to Christianity in China," *CMG*, December 1855, 137. In Pinyin: *hongmaoren*. The term was transcribed variously — e.g., *hong-mow-jin*, or *hong-mou-jin* — according to dialect differences and unstandardized transliteration methods.

19. Reynolds, *Beards*, 285–86.

20. Ibid., 290.

21. Reed, *Glorious Battle*, 220; see also 80–81. On the association of Anglo-Catholicism and effeminacy, see also Knight, "'Male and Female He Created Them,'" 34.

22. Rowland, *The Human Hair*, 106.

23. Ibid., 101–7. See also Charles Dickens, "Why Shave?" quoted in ibid., 201–2; and Gowing, *The Philosophy of Beards*, 5–10.

24. Gowing, *The Philosophy of Beards*, 4. Charles Dickens wrote: "In the world's history the bearded races have at all times been the most important actors" (quoted in Rowland, *The Human Hair*, 197).

25. Gowing, *The Philosophy of Beards*, 5.

26. Rowland, *The Human Hair*, 112.

27. Quoted in Rowland, *The Human Hair*, 200.

28. Dikötter, "Hairy Barbarians," 52.

29. Ibid.

30. Ibid., 54–64.

31. Ibid., 60.

32. K. M. Griggs, "The Story of Ching Kang," *IWCD*, August 1923, 117.

33. Miss K. M. Griggs, "Part of a Five Weeks' Tour in the Loyuan District," *IWCD*, September 1925, 170. Blakiston made humor of it: "Granted, but the animal wears clothes . . ." (Blakiston, *Five Months on the Yang-tsze*, 157).

34. Fortune, *Two Visits to the Tea Countries*, 1:142–43.

35. Blakiston, *Five Months on the Yang-tsze*, 117.

36. Cunnington and Cunnington, *Handbook of English Costume*, 266.

37. Walkley and Foster, *Crinolines and Crimping Irons*, 128.

38. Ibid., 132.

39. Wehrle, *Britain, China, and the Antimissionary Riots*, 60.

40. Mary Darley, "God's Over-Rulings in Kienning," *IWCD*, February 1913, 33.

41. G. F. Saywell, "The Missionary's Background in China," *CMG*, January 1922, 3.

42. Steele and Major, *China Chic*, 23. See also Cheng, "Politics of the Queue," 131–32.

Chapter 13

1. "Missionary Labours at Ningpo, China," *CMG*, March 1859, 31.

2. *RGC 1877*, 111.

3. "Chinese Life," *CMG*, April 1859, 50.

4. Franck, *Wandering in Northern China*, 296.

5. Ibid., 295. While he was eating, wrote Fortune, "the doors and windows were completely besieged with people. Every little hole or crevice had a number of eager eyes peeping through it, each anxious to see the foreigner feed" (Fortune, *A Residence among the Chinese*, 270).

6. Fortune, *Two Visits to the Tea Countries*, 1:36.

7. Abeel, *Journal of a Residence in China*, 78–79.

8. Franck, *Wandering in Northern China*, 296.

9. Fortune, *A Residence among the Chinese*, 351–52.

10. LeBon, *The Crowd*, 56.

11. Ibid., 52.

12. Ibid., 55–56.

13. Ibid., 59.

14. Ibid., 89, 124ff.

15. Ibid., 180.

16. Ibid., 105.

17. Colquhoun, *Across Chrysê*, 1:40.

18. LeBon, *The Crowd*, 94.

19. Ibid., 75.

20. "From Kwan-Yin to Christ," *HE*, January 1921, 2 (emphasis added).

21. Taylor and Taylor, *Hudson Taylor in Early Years*, 319.

22. Ibid.

23. Fortune, *Two Visits to the Tea Countries*, 2:8.

24. Ibid., 2:33–34; also, 2:16.

25. Taylor and Taylor, *Hudson Taylor in Early Years*, 319–20.

26. Spence, *Memory Palace*, 114.

27. Fortune, *Two Visits to the Tea Countries*, vol. 2, 16.

28. Colquhoun, *Across Chrysê*, vol. 1. p. 24.

29. Taylor and Taylor, *Hudson Taylor in Early Years*, 318.

30. Fortune, *Two Visits to the Tea Countries*, 1:64. Murray Rubinstein makes

a similar conclusion about Robert Morrison's short-lived adoption of native dress in 1808, namely that it made him more, not less conspicuous, and that it alienated his compatriots (Rubinstein, *The Origins of the Anglo-American Missionary*, 80).

31. Pollock, *Hudson Taylor and Maria*, 51; also 157, 163–64. Blakiston wrote, "It may be said that to disguise oneself in native clothes and travel through the country would be a species of deceit incompatible with the sacred office" (Blakiston *Five Months on the Yang-tsze*, 180).

32. Taylor and Taylor, *Hudson Taylor in Early Years*, 371.

33. Pollock, *Hudson Taylor and Maria*, 167.

34. Woodbridge, *Fifty Years in China*, 107. See also Cheng, "Politics of the Queue," 123–42.

35. Mary Darley, "God's Over-Rulings in Kienning," *IWCD*, February 1913, 33. See also Dunch, *Fuzhou Protestants*, 142–45.

36. Foucault, *Discipline and Punish*, 28.

37. Woodbridge, *Fifty Years in China*, 113.

Chapter 14

1. "Review of the Shin Seën Tung Keën, — A General Account of the Gods and Genii," *The Chinese Repository* 7, no. 10 (February 1839): 506.

2. Bourdieu, *The Logic of Practice*, 36.

3. Staal, *Rules without Meaning*, 3.

4. Davis, *The Chinese*, 2:83.

5. "Romanism at Chusan," *CMG*, January 1852, 11.

6. H. B. Rattenbury, "On Being Friends with China," *Looking East*, June 1943, 81.

7. Lao Tzu, *Tao Te Ching*, 108.

8. Harrison, *Crowds and History*, 321.

9. Ibid., xiii.

10. Williams, *LLSWW*, 174.

11. F. I. Codrington and A. M. Robinson, "Birds on the Wing" (a continuing story), *HE*, May–June 1934, 39.

12. Edith Couche, "Yungchow via Siberia," *IWCD*, March 1917, 32.

13. Wittgenstein, *Philosophical Investigations*, 50.

14. Sardar, *Orientalism*, 115.

15. Zhang, *Mighty Opposites*, 195.

16. Wittgenstein, *Philosophical Investigations*, 82.

17. Ibid.

18. Wittgenstein, *Zettel*, 41.

Bibliography

Abeel, David. *Journal of a Residence in China, and the Neighboring Countries, from 1829 to 1833*. New York: Leavitt, Lord and Co., 1834.

"The Advisability, or the Reverse, of Endeavouring to Convey Western Knowledge to the Chinese Through the Medium of their Own Language." *Journal of the China Branch of the Royal Asiatic Society* (1886): 1–21.

Anderson, Olive. "The Growth of Christian Militarism in Mid-Victorian Britain." *English Historical Review* 86, no. 338 (January 1971): 46–72.

Argyle, Michael, and Mark Cook. *Gaze and Mutual Gaze*. Cambridge: Cambridge University, 1976.

Arnold, Guy. *Held Fast for England: G. A. Henty, Imperialist Boys' Writer*. London: Hamish Hamilton, 1980.

Asad, Talal. *Genealogies of Religion: Discipline and Reasons of Power in Christianity and Islam*. Baltimore: John Hopkins University Press, 1993.

Bailey, Peter. *Leisure and Class in Victorian England: Rational Recreation and the Contest for Control, 1830–1885*. London: Routledge and Kegan Paul; Toronto and Buffalo: University of Toronto Press, 1978.

Barnett, Suzanne Wilson, and John King Fairbank, eds. *Christianity in China: Early Protestant Missionary Writings*. Cambridge, MA: Harvard University Press, 1985.

Barthes, Roland. *Empire of Signs*. Translated by Richard Howard. New York: Noonday Press, 1970.

Bays, Daniel H. ed., *Christianity in China: From the Eighteenth Century to the Present*. Stanford, CA: Stanford University Press, 1996.

Beach, Harlan P. *A Geography of Protestant Missions*. New York: Students Volunteer Movement for Foreign Missions, 1903.

Bell, Catherine. *Ritual Theory, Ritual Practice*. Oxford: Oxford University, 1992.

Benavides, Gustavo. "Guiseppe Tucci, or Buddhology in the Age of Fascism."

In *Curators of the Buddha: The Study of Buddhism under Colonialism,* edited by Donald S. Lopez, Jr., 161–96. Chicago: University of Chicago Press, 1995.

Biggers, Earl Derr. *Charlie Chan Carries On.* Indianapolis: Bobbs-Merrill, 1930.

Bird, Isabella. *The Yangtze Valley and Beyond: An Account of Journeys in China, Chiefly in the Province of Sze Chuan and Among the Man-tze of the Somo Territory.* Boston: Beacon Press, 1987.

Blakiston, Thomas W. *Five Months on the Yang-tsze; with a Narrative of the Exploration of Its Upper Waters, and Notices of the Present Rebellions in China.* London: John Murray, 1862.

Boardman, Eugene Powers. *Christian Influence upon the Ideology of the T'ai-P'ing Rebellion, 1851–1864.* Madison: University of Wisconsin, 1952.

Boaz, Maud Elizabeth. *"And the Villages thereof."* London: Morgan and Scott, for the Church of England Zenana Missionary Society, 1926.

Bourdieu, Pierre. *Distinction: A Social Critique of the Judgement of Taste.* Translated by Richard Nice. Cambridge, MA: Harvard University Press, 1984.

———. *Language and Symbolic Power.* Edited by John B. Thompson, translated by Gino Raymond and Matthew Adamson. Cambridge, MA: Harvard University, 1991.

———. *The Logic of Practice.* Translated by Richard Nice. Stanford, CA: Stanford University, 1990.

Bremmer, Jan, and Herman Roodenburg, eds. *A Cultural History of Gesture: From Antiquity to the Present Day.* Ithaca, N.Y.: Cornell University Press, 1992.

Buck, John Lossing. *Land Utilization in China.* Nankang: University of Nankang, 1937.

Buck, Pearl S. *Pavilion of Women.* New York: John Day, 1946.

Burder, William. *The History of All Religions of the World: with Accounts of the Ceremonies and Customs, or the Forms of Worship, Practiced by the Several Nations of the Known World, from the Earliest Records to the Present Time.* New York: Gay Brothers, 1870.

Burton, Henry. *Jesu-Worship Confuted, or, Certain Arguments Against Bowing at the Name Jesus, Proving it to be Idolatrous and Superstitious, and so utterly unlawfull, with Objections to the contrary fully Answered.* London: H.C., 1660.

Bush, Charles P. *Five Years in China: or, The Factory Boy made a Missionary. The Life and Observations of Rev. William Aitchison, Late Missionary to China.* Philadelphia: Presbyterian Board of Publication, 1865.

Cary, Alice, and Phoebe Cary. *The Poetical Works of Alice and Phoebe Cary.* Boston and New York: Houghton Mifflin, 1882.

Chandler, Raymond. "Try the Girl." In *Killer in the Rain,* 109–41. London: Hamish Hamilton, 1964.

Cheng, Weikun. "Politics of the Queue: Agitation and Resistance in the Beginning and End of Qing China." In *Hair: Its Power and Meaning in Asian Cultures,* edited by Alf Hiltebeitel and Barbara D. Miller, 123–42. Albany: State University of New York, 1998.

Church Missionary Society [CMS]. *Proceedings of the Church Missionary Society for Africa and the East, 1909–1910.* London: Church Missionary Society, 1910.

Church Missionary Society Archive. Marlborough: Adam Matthew Publications, 1999.

Cohen, Paul A. *China and Christianity: The Missionary Movement and the Growth of Chinese Antiforeignism, 1860–1870.* Cambridge, MA: Harvard University Press, 1963.

Collier, Price. *The West in the East: From an American Point of View.* London: Duckworth, 1911.

Colquhoun, Archibald R. *Across Chrysê, Being the Narrative of a Journey of Exploration Through the South China Border Lands from Canton to Mandalay.* 2 vols. London: Sampson Low, Marston, Searle, and Rivington, 1883; reprint, Taipei: Ch'eng Wen, 1972.

Confucius. *The Analects.,* Translated by D. C. Lau. New York: Penguin, 1979.

Conger, Sarah Pike. *Letters from China: With Particular Reference to the Empress Dowager and the Women of China.* Chicago: A. C. McClurg, 1909.

Crawley, Alfred Ernest. "Kneeling." *Encyclopaedia of Religion and Ethics,* edited by James Hastings, vol. 7, 745–47. Edinburgh: T & T Clark, 1913–22.

Crow, Carl. *Four Hundred Million Customers.* New York: Harper and Brothers, 1937.

Cunnington, C. Willett, and Phillis Cunnington. *Handbook of English Costume in the Nineteenth Century.* London: Faber and Faber, 1959.

"Cyril" [Henry E. Dennehy]. *A Flower of Asia: An Indian Story.* London: Burns and Oates, 1901.

Darley, Mary. *Cameos of a Chinese City.* London: Church of England Zenana Missionary Society and Marshall Brothers, 1917.

Davis, John Francis. *The Chinese: A General Description of the Empire of China and its Inhabitants.* 2 vols. London: Charles Knight, 1836–40.

Decamp, David. Introduction to *Pidginization and Creolization of Languages,* edited by Dell Hymes, 13–39. Proceedings of a Conference held at the University of the West Indies, Mona, Jamaica, April 1968. Cambridge: Cambridge University Press, 1971.

Dikötter, Frank. "Hairy Barbarians, Furry Primates, and Wild Men: Medical Science and Cultural Representations of Hair in China." In *Hair: Its Power and Meaning in Asian Cultures,* edited by Alf Hiltebeitel and Barbara D. Miller, 51–74. Albany: State University of New York Press, 1998.

Dingle, Edwin J. *Across China on Foot.* New York: Henry Holt, 1911.

Doyle, Sir Francis Hastings. *The Return of the Guards and Other Poems.* London: Macmillan, 1866.

Drake, Fred W. "Protestant Geography in China: E. C. Bridgman's Portrayal of the West." In *Christianity in China: Early Protestant Missionary Writings,* edited by Suzanne Wilson Barnett and John King Fairbank. (Cambridge, MA: Harvard University Press, 1985).

Dunch, Ryan. *Fuzhou Protestants and the Making of a Modern China, 1857–1927.* New Haven, CT: Yale University Press, 2001.

Eire, Carlos M. N. *War Against the Idols: The Reformation of Worship from Erasmus to Calvin.* Cambridge: Cambridge University Press, 1986.

Ellis, William. Introduction to *Journal of Three Voyages along the Coast of China, in 1831, 1832, & 1833, with Notices of Siam, Corea, and the Loo-Choo Islands,* by Charles Gützlaff. London: Frederick Westley and A. H. Davis, 1832; reprint, Taipei: Ch'eng-Wen, 1968.

Evans, John. *The Case of Kneeling at the Holy Sacrament, Stated and Resolved.* London: Fincham Gardiner, 1683.

Fairbank, John K., ed. *The Missionary Enterprise in China and America.* Cambridge, MA: Harvard University Press, 1974.

Fasick, Laura. "Charles Kingsley's Scientific Treatment of Gender." In *Muscular Christianity: Embodying the Victorian Age,* edited by Donald E. Hall, 91–113. Cambridge: Cambridge University Press, 1994.

Faure, Bernard. *Visions of Power: Imagining Medieval Japanese Buddhism.* Translated by Phyllis Brooks. Princeton, NJ: Princeton University Press, 1996.

Ferguson, Charles A. "Absence of Copula and the Notion of Simplicity." In *Pidginization and Creolization of Languages,* edited by Dell Hymes, 141–50. Cambridge: Cambridge University Press, 1971.

Fortune, Robert. *A Residence among the Chinese: Inland, on the Coast, and at Sea.* London: John Murray, 1857.

———. *Three Years' Wanderings in The Northern Provinces of China, Including a Visit to the Tea, Silk, and Cotton Countries: with an Account of the Agriculture and Horticulture of the Chinese, new Plants, etc.* London: Mildmay, 1847.

———. *Two Visits to the Tea Countries of China and the British Tea Plantations in the Himalaya.* 2 vols. London: John Murray, 1853.

Foster, Mrs. Arnold. *In the Valley of the Yangtse.* London: London Missionary Society, 1899.

Foucault, Michel. *Discipline and Punish: The Birth of the Prison.* Translated by Alan Sheridan. New York: Vintage Books, 1979.

———. "Political Technology of Individuals." In *Technologies of the Self: A Seminar with Michel Foucault,* edited by Luther H. Martin, Huck Gutman, and Patrick H. Hutton, 145–62. Amherst: University of Massachusetts Press, 1988.

———. "Technologies of the Self." In *Technologies of the Self: A Seminar with Michel Foucault,* edited by Luther H. Martin, Huck Gutman, and Patrick H. Hutton, 16–49. Amherst: University of Massachusetts Press, 1988.

Franck, Harry A. *Wandering in Northern China.* New York: Century, 1923.

Fraser, George Macdonald. *Flashman and the Dragon.* London: Collins Harvill, 1985.

Fraser, John Foster. *Round the World on a Wheel.* Thomas Nelson and Sons, 1899; reprint, London: Futura, 1989.

Gay, Peter. "The Manliness of Christ." In *Religion and Irreligion in Victorian Society,* edited by Richard W. Davis and Richard J. Helmstadter, 102–16. London: Routledge, 1992.

Gentzler, J. Mason. *Changing China: Readings in the History of China from the Opium War to the Present.* New York: Praeger, 1977.

Gernet, Jacques. *China and the Christian Impact: A Conflict of Cultures.* Translated by Janet Lloyd. Cambridge: Cambridge University Press, 1985.

Gill, Sam. "The Academic Study of Religion." *Journal of the American Academy of Religion* 62, no. 4 (Winter 1994): 965–75.

Girardot, Norman J. "Chinese Religion and Western Scholarship." In *China and Christianity: Historical and Future Encounters,* edited by James D. Whitehead, Yu-ming Shaw, and N. J. Girardot, 83–111. Notre Dame, IN: University of Notre Dame, 1979.

——. *The Victorian Translation of China: James Legge's Oriental Pilgrimage.* Berkeley: University of California Press, 2002.

Goffman, Erving. "The Nature of Deference and Demeanor." In *Interactional Ritual: Essays on Face-to-Face Behavior,* 47–96. Garden City, NJ: Anchor, 1967.

Goforth, Rosalind, and Jonathan Goforth. *Miracles Lives of China.* New York: Harper and Bros., 1931.

Gowing, T. S. *The Philosophy of Beards: A Lecture Physiological, Artistic, and Historical.* Ipswich: J. Haddock, 1850.

Gregerson, John. *Vegetarianism: A History.* Fremont, CA: Jain Publishing, 1994.

Grosz, Elizabeth. *Volatile Bodies: Toward a Corporeal Feminism.* Bloomington: Indiana University Press, 1994.

Grueber, Johann. *China and France, or Two Treatises.* London: Samuel Lowndes, 1676.

Guinness, Geraldine, ed. *In the Far East.* 3rd ed. Totonot: Inland China Mission, 1901 [1st ed., 1889].

Gützlaff, Charles. *Journal of Three Voyages along the Coast of China, in 1831, 1832, & 1833, with Notices of Siam, Corea, and the Loo-Choo Islands.* London: Frederick Westley and A. H. Davis, 1832; reprint, Taipei: Ch'eng-Wen, 1968.

Hagspeil, Bruno, S.V.D. *Along the Mission Trail.* Vol. 4, *In China.* Techny, IL: Mission Press, S.V.D., 1927.

Haliburton, Thomas Chandler. *Wise Saws, or, Sam Slick in Search of a Wife.* New York: Dick and Fitzgerald, 1855.

Hall, Donald E. "Muscular Christianity: Reading and Writing the Male Social Body." In *Muscular Christianity: Embodying the Victorian Age,* edited by Donald E. Hall, 3–13. Cambridge: Cambridge University Press, 1994.

——, ed. *Muscular Christianity: Embodying the Victorian Age.* Cambridge: Cambridge University Press, 1994.

Hallisey, Charles. "Roads Taken and Not Taken in the Study of Theravada Buddhism." In *Curators of the Buddha: The Study of Buddhism under Colonialism,* edited by Donald S. Lopez, Jr., 31–61. Chicago: University of Chicago Press, 1995.

Harrison, Mark. *Crowds and History: Mass Phenomena in English Towns, 1790–1835.* Cambridge: Cambridge University Press, 1988.

Headland, Isaac Taylor. *Home Life in China.* London: Methuen, 1914; reprint, Taipei: Ch'eng Wen Publishing, 1974.

Heber, Reginald. *The Poetical Works of Reginald Heber.* London: John Murray, 1842.

Henty, George A. "A Brush with the Chinese." In *Tales of Daring and Danger*, 119–60. London: Blackie and Sons, 1890.

———. *With the Allies to Pekin: A Tale of the Relief of the Legations.* London: Blackie and Sons, 1904.

Hersey, John. *The Call.* New York: Alfred A. Knopf, 1985.

Hevia, James L. "The Archive State and the Fear of Pollution: From the Opium Wars to Fu-Manchu." *Cultural Studies* 12, no. 2. (April 1998): 234–64.

———. *Cherishing Men From Afar: Qing Guest Ritual and the Macartney Embassy of 1793.* Durham, NC: Duke University Press, 1995.

———. "The Scandal of Inequality: *Koutou* as Signifier." *Positions: East Asia Cultures Critique* 3, no. 1 (1995): 97–118.

———. "Sovereignty and Subject: Constituting Relations of Power in Qing Guest Ritual." In *Body, Subject, and Power in China,* edited by Angela Zito and Tani E. Barlow, 181–200. Chicago: University of Chicago Press, 1994.

Hinton, Perry R. *Stereotypes, Cognition, and Culture.* Hove: Psychology Press, 2000.

Holm, John. *Pidgins and Creoles.* 2 vols. Cambridge: Cambridge University Press, 1989.

Houghton, Walter E. *The Victorian Frame of Mind, 1830–1870.* New Haven, CT: Yale University Press, 1957.

Howard, Anne. *Mary Spencer: A Tale for the Times.* London: Seeley, Burnside, and Seeley, 1844.

Hsü, Immanuel C. Y. *The Rise of Modern China.* New York: Oxford University Press, 1970.

Huc, Evariste Régis. *A Journey Through the Chinese Empire.* 2 vols. New York: Harper and Bros., 1855.

Hyatt, Irwin T., Jr. *Our Ordered Lives Confess: Three Nineteenth-Century American Missionaries in East Shantung.* Cambridge, MA: Harvard University Press, 1976.

Hymes, Dell, ed. *Pidginization and Creolization of Languages.* Proceedings of a Conference held at the University of the West Indies, Mona, Jamaica, April 1968. Cambridge: Cambridge University Press, 1971.

Ignatius of Loyola, Saint. *Obras completas de San Ignacio de Loyola.* 2nd ed. Edited by Ignacio Iparraguirre. Madrid: Editorial Católica, 1963.

Isaacs, Harold R. *Images of Asia: American Views of China and India.* New York: Capricorn Books, 1962.

Jensen, Adolf E. *Myth and Cult among Primitive Peoples.* Chicago: University of Chicago Press, 1963.

Jensen, Lionel M. *Manufacturing Confucianism: Chinese Traditions and Universal Civilization.* Durham, NC: Duke University Press, 1997.

Jones, Charles Brewer. *Buddhism in Taiwan: Religion and the State, 1660–1990.* Honolulu: University of Hawai'i Press, 1999.

Kapleau, Philip. *To Cherish All Life: A Buddhist Case for Becoming Vegetarian*. San Francisco: Harper and Row, 1982.

Kibbey, Ann. *The Interpretation of Material Shapes in Puritanism: A Study of Rhetoric, Prejudice, and Violence*. Cambridge: Cambridge University Press, 1986.

Kipnis, Andrew. "(Re)inventing *Li: Koutou* and Subjectification in Rural Shandong." In *Body, Subject, and Power in China*, edited by Angela Zito and Tani E. Barlow, 201–23. Chicago: University of Chicago Press, 1994.

Knight, Frances. "'Male and Female He Created Them': Men, Women, and the Question of Gender." In *Religion in Victorian Britain*, Vol. 5, *Culture and Empire*, edited by John Wolffe, 23–57. Manchester: Manchester University Press, 1997.

Kung, Timothy [Gong Tianmin]. *Da Fojiao renshi shiwen* [Answers to Ten Questions of Buddhists]. Taipei: Guizhu chubanshe, 1998.

——. *Gong Tianmin dengdaoji* [Christian Sermons of Rev. Timothy Kung]. Taipei: Published by the Author, 1993.

——. *Gong Tianmin xinwenji sanshipian* [Thirty Selected New Works of Timothy Kung]. Taipei: Published by the Author, 1993.

Lai, Whalen, and Michael von Brück. *Christianity and Buddhism: A Multi-Cultural History of Their Dialogue*. Maryknoll, N.Y.: Orbis, 2001.

Lao Tzu. *Tao Te Ching*. Translated by D. C. Lau. New York: Penguin, 1963.

Lakoff, George, and Mark Johnson. *Metaphors We Live By*. Chicago: University of Chicago Press, 1980.

LeBon, Gustave. *The Crowd*. New Brunswick: Transaction Publishers, 1995.

Leland, Charles G. *Pidgin-English Sing-Song: or, Songs and Stories in the China–English Dialect*. London: Kegan Paul, Trench, Trübner and Co., 1897.

Liao, Kuang-sheng. *Anti-foreignism and Modernization in China, 1860–1980*. Hong Kong: Chinese University Press, 1984.

Lincoln, Bruce. "Of Meat and Society, Sacrifice and Creation, Butchers and Philosophy." *L'Uomo* 9, no. 1–2 (1985): 9–29.

Lodwick, Kathleen L. *Crusaders against Opium: Protestant Missionaries in China, 1874–1917*. Lexington: University Press of Kentucky, 1996.

Lopez, Donald S., Jr., ed. *Curators of the Buddha: The Study of Buddhism under Colonialism*. Chicago: University of Chicago Press, 1995.

Lurie, Alison. *The Language of Clothes*. New York: Vintage Books, 1981.

Lutz, Jessie G., and Rolland Ray Lutz. *Hakka Chinese Confront Protestant Christianity, 1850–1900: With the Autobiographies of Eight Hakka Christians, and Commentary*. Armonk, NY: M. E. Sharpe, 1998.

Ma, Sheng-mei. *The Deathly Embrace: Orientalism and Asian American Identity*. Minneapolis: University of Minnesota Press, 2000.

MacGowan, John. "Goon." In *Some Typical Christians of South China*, edited by William Sandford Pakenham-Walsh, 8–18. London: Marshall Brothers, 1905.

——. *Sidelights on Chinese Culture*. London: Kegan Paul, Trench, Trübner and Co., 1907.

MacKerras, Colin. *Western Images of China*. New York: Oxford University Press, 1989.

Mancoff, Debra N., and Dale J. Trela, eds., *Victorian Urban Settings: Essays on the Nineteenth-Century City and Its Contexts*. New York: Garland, 1996.

Mangan, J. A. *Athleticism in the Victorian and Edwardian Public School: The Emergence and Consolidation of an Educational Ideology*. Cambridge: Cambridge University Press, 1981.

Mangrum, Bryan D., and Giuseppe Scavizzi, intro. and trans. *A Reformation Debate: Karlstadt, Emser, and Eck on Sacred Images: Three Treatises in Translation*. Toronto: Victoria University Press, 1991.

McClellan, Robert. *The Heathen Chinee: A Study of American Attitudes Toward China, 1890–1905*. Columbus: Ohio State University Press, 1971.

McLeod, Hugh. *Religion and Society in England, 1850–1914*. London: Macmillan, 1996.

Miller, Stuart Creighton. "Ends and Means: Missionary Justification of Force in Nineteenth-Century China." In *The Missionary Enterprise in China and America*, edited by John K. Fairbank, 249–82 (Cambridge, MA: Harvard University Press, 1974).

Mitchell, Sally. *Daily Life in Victorian England*. Westport, CT: Greenwood Press, 1996.

Morgan, Marjorie. *Manners, Morals, and Class in England, 1774–1858*. New York: St. Martin's Press, 1994.

Moy, James S. *Marginal Sights: Staging the Chinese in America*. Iowa City: University of Iowa Press, 1993.

Mühlhäusler, Peter. *Pidgin and Creole Linguistics*. Exp. and rev. ed. London: University of Westminster Press, 1997.

Nightingale, Florence. *Notes on Nursing: What it is, and What it is not*. London: Harrison, 1859.

Norman, Edward. *The English Catholic Church in the Nineteenth Century*. Oxford: Clarendon, 1984.

Ohnuki-Tierney, Emiko. "McDonalds in Japan: Changing Manners and Etiquette." In *Golden Arches East: McDonalds in East Asia*, edited by James L. Watson, 161–82. Stanford, CA: Stanford University Press, 1997.

Oliphant, Nigel. *A Diary of the Siege of the Legations in Peking during the Summer of 1900*. London: Longmans, Green, and Co., 1901.

Pakenham-Walsh, William Sandford. *Some Typical Christians of South China*. London: Marshall Bros., 1905.

Parker, E. H. "The Comparative Study of Chinese Dialects." *Journal of the China Branch of the Royal Asiatic Society* 12 (1878): 19–50.

Pelikan, Jaroslav. *Obedient Rebels: Catholic Substance and Protestant Principle in Luther's Reformation*. New York: Harper and Row, 1964.

Peyrefitte, Alain. *The Collision of Two Civilizations: The British Expedition to China in 1792–4*. Translated by Jon Rothschild. London: Harvill, 1993.

Pollock, John Charles. *Hudson Taylor and Maria: Pioneers in China*. New York: McGraw-Hill, 1962.

Putney, Clifford. *Muscular Christianity: Manhood and Sports in Protestant America, 1880–1920.* Cambridge, MA: Harvard University Press, 2001.

Records of the General Conference of the Protestant Missionaries of China, Held at Shanghai, May 10–24, 1877 [*RGC 1877*]. Shanghai: Presbyterian Mission Press, 1879.

Records of the General Conference of the Protestant Missionaries of China, Held at Shanghai, May 7–20, 1890 [*RGC 1890*]. Shanghai: American Presbyterian Mission Press, 1890.

Reed, John Shelton. *Glorious Battle: The Cultural Politics of Victorian Anglo-Catholicism.* Nashville: Vanderbilt University Press, 1996.

Reinders, Eric. "The Iconoclasm of Obeisance: Protestant Images of Chinese Religion and the Catholic Church." *Numen* 44, no. 3 (September 1997): 296–322.

Reynolds, Reginald. *Beards: Their Social Standing, Religious Involvements, Decorative Possibilities, and Value in Offence and Defence Through the Ages.* New York: Doubleday, 1949.

Ricci, Matteo, S.J. *The True Meaning of the Lord of Heaven (T'ien-chu Shih-i).* Translated by Douglas Lancashire and Peter Hu Kuo-chen, S.J.; Chinese–English edition edited by Edward J. Malatesta, S.J. Variétés Sinologiques, n.s., no. 72. Taipei: Ricci Institute, 1985.

Ritson, Joseph. *An Essay on Abstinence from Animal Food as a Moral Duty.* London: Richard Phillips, 1802.

Rogers, Nicholas. *Crowds, Culture, and Politics in Georgian Britain.* Oxford: Clarendon, 1998.

Rosa, Susan. "Seventeenth-Century Catholic Polemic and the Rise of Cultural Rationalism: An Example from the Empire." *Journal of the History of Ideas* 57, no. 1 (January 1996): 87–107.

Rosen, David. "The Volcano and the Cathedral: Muscular Christianity and the Origins of Primal Manliness." In *Muscular Christianity: Embodying the Victorian Age,* edited by Donald E. Hall, 17–44. Cambridge: Cambridge University Press, 1994.

Ross, Alexander. *Pansebeia: or, A View of all Religions in the World: With the several Church-Governments, from the Creation, to these Times. Also, a Discovery of all known Heresies in all Ages and Places: And choice Observations and Reflections throughout the whole.* London: John Saywell, 1655.

Rowland, Alexander. *The Human Hair, Popularly and Physiologically Considered with Special Reference to its Preservation, Improvement and Adornment and the Various Modes of its Decoration in all Countries.* London: Piper, Bros., and Co., 1853.

Rubinstein, Murray A. *The Origins of the Anglo-American Missionary Enterprise in China, 1807–1840.* Lanham, MD: Scarecrow Press, 1996.

Said, Edward W. *Orientalism.* New York: Pantheon Books, 1978.

Sardar, Ziauddin. *Orientalism.* Buckingham: Open University Press, 1999.

Schopen, Gregory. "Archaeology and Protestant Presuppositions in the Study of Indian Buddhism." *History of Religions* 31, no. 1 (August 1991): 1–23.

Schwartz, Barry. *Vertical Classification: A Study in Structuralism and the Sociology of Knowledge*. Chicago: University of Chicago Press, 1981.

Selden, George. *The Cricket in Times Square*. Illustrations by Garth Williams. New York: Farrar, Straus, and Giroux, 1960.

Sharf, Robert H. "Buddhist Modernism and the Rhetoric of Meditative Experience." *Numen* 42, no. 3 (1995): 228–30.

Shi Zhuyun. *Fojiao yu Jidujiao debijiao* [A Comparison of Buddhism and Christianity]. Gaoxiong: Qinglian yinjinghui, 1983.

Simoons, Frederick J. *Eat Not This Flesh: Food Avoidances from Prehistory to the Present*. Madison: University of Wisconsin Press, 1994.

Smiles, Samuel. *Character*. Chicago: Belford, Clarke and Co., 1884.

——. *Self-Help; with Illustrations of Character and Conduct*. Philadelphia: J. B. Lippincott, 1880.

Smith, Adam. *Lectures on Rhetoric and Belles Lettres,* edited by J. C. Bryce. Oxford: Clarendon Press, 1983.

Smith, Arthur H. *Chinese Characteristics*. New York: Fleming H. Revell, 1894.

Smith, Jonathan Z. *Imagining Religion: From Babylon to Jonestown*. Chicago: University of Chicago Press, 1982.

——. *To Take Place: Toward Theory in Ritual*. Chicago: University of Chicago Press, 1987.

Spence, Jonathan D. *The Chan's Great Continent: China in Western Minds*. New York: W. W. Norton, 1998.

——. *Emperor of China: Self-portrait of K'ang-hsi*. New York: Vintage Books, 1975.

——. *God's Chinese Son: The Taiping Heavenly Kingdom of Hong Xiuquan*. New York: W. W. Norton, 1996.

——. *The Memory Palace of Matteo Ricci*. New York: Penguin, 1984.

Spencer, Herbert. *The Principles of Sociology*. 3 vols. New York: D. Appleton, 1900.

Staal, Frits. *Rules without Meaning: Ritual, Mantras, and the Human Sciences*. New York: Peter Lang, 1989.

Stalleybrass, Peter, and Allon White. *The Politics and Poetics of Transgression*. Ithaca, NY: Cornell University Press, 1986.

Standaert, Nicolas, S.J. *The Fascinating God: A Challenge to Modern Chinese Theology Presented by a Text on the Name of God Written by a 17th Century Chinese Student of Theology Inculturation*. Working Papers on Living Faith and Cultures, no. 17. Rome: Editrice Pontifica Universita Gregoriana, 1995.

Staunton, George. *An Authentic Account of an Embassy from The King of Great Britain to the Emperor of China*. 3 vols. London, 1797.

Steele, Valerie, and John S. Major. *China Chic: East Meets West*. New Haven, CT: Yale University Press, 1999.

Stevenson, Robert Louis. *Collected Poems*. Edited by Janet Adam Smith. New York: Viking, 1971.

Stillingfleet, Edward. *Several Conferences Between a Romish Priest, A Fanatick Chaplain, and a Divine of the Church of England, Concerning the Idolatry of the*

Church of Rome: being a Full Answer to the Late Dialogues of T. G[odwin]. London, 1679.

Stock, Eugene. *The Story of the Fuh-Kien Mission of the Church Missionary Society.* London: Seeley, Jackson and Halliday, 1890.

Stoller, Paul. *The Taste of Ethnographic Things: The Senses in Anthropology.* Philadelphia: University of Pennsylvania Press, 1989.

Taylor, Dr., and Mrs. Howard Taylor. *Hudson Taylor in Early Years: The Growth of a Soul.* London: China Inland Mission, 1936.

Thomas, Kieth. Introduction to *A Cultural History of Gesture: From Antiquity to the Present Day,* edited by Jan Bremmer and Herman Roodenburg, 1–4. Ithaca, N.Y.: Cornell University Press, 1992.

Thomas, Terence. "Foreign Missions and Missionaries in Victorian Britain." In *Religion in Victorian Britain.* Vol. 5, *Culture and Empire,* edited by John Wolffe, 101–34. Manchester: Manchester University Press, 1997.

Thurin, Susan Schoenbauer. *Victorian Travelers and the Opening of China, 1842–1907.* Athens, OH: Ohio University Press, 1999.

Trigault, Nicholas, S.J. *The China That Was: China As Discovered by the Jesuits at the Close of the Sixteenth Century.* Translated by Louis Joseph Gallagher, S.J. Milwaukee: Bruce Publishing Co., 1942.

Turner, Bryan S. *Orientalism, Postmodernism, and Globalism.* London: Routledge, 1994.

Uhalley, Stephen, Jr., and Xiaoxin Wu, eds. *China and Christianity: Burdened Past, Hopeful Future.* Armonk, NY: M. E. Sharpe, 2001.

Walkley, Christina, and Vanda Foster. *Crinolines and Crimping Irons: Victorian Clothes: How They Were Cleaned and Cared For.* London: Peter Owen, 1978.

Walshe, W. Gilbert. "China." In *Encyclopaedia of Religion and Ethics,* edited by James Hastings, vol. 3, 549–52. Edinburgh: T & T Clark, 1913–22.

Wandel, Lee Palmer. *Voracious Idols and Violent Hands: Iconoclasm in Reformation Zurich, Strasbourg, and Basel.* Cambridge: Cambridge University Press, 1995.

Wee, C. J. Wan-Ling. "Christian Manliness and National Identity: The Problematic Construction of a Racially "Pure" Nation." In *Muscular Christianity: Embodying the Victorian Age,* edited by Donald E. Hall, 66–88. Cambridge: Cambridge University Press, 1994.

Wehrle, Edmund S. *Britain, China, and the Antimissionary Riots, 1981–1900.* Minneapolis: University of Minnesota Press, 1966.

Welch, Holmes. *The Buddhist Revival in China.* Cambridge, MA: Harvard University Press, 1968.

Whinnom, Kieth. "Linguistic Hybridization and the 'Special Case' of Pidgins and Creoles." In *Pidginization and Creolization of Languages,* edited by Dell Hymes, 91–115. Proceedings of a Conference held at the University of the West Indies, Mona, Jamaica, April 1968. Cambridge: Cambridge University Press, 1971.

White Unto Harvest in China: A Survey of the Lutheran United Mission, the China Mission of the N.L.C.A., 1890–1934. ["Written by the missionaries."] Minneapolis: Board of Foreign Missions, 1934.

White, Luise. *Speaking with Vampires: Rumor and History in Colonial Africa*. Berkeley and Los Angeles: University of California Press, 2000.

Wierzbicka, Anna. "Kisses, Handshakes, Bows: The Semantics of Nonverbal Communication." *Semiotica* 103, no. 3–4 (1995): 207–52.

Williams, Frederick Wells. *The Life and Letters of Samuel Wells Williams, LL.D.: Missionary, Diplomatist, Sinologue*. New York: G. P. Putnam's Sons, 1889.

Williams, S. Wells. *The Middle Kingdom: A Survey of the Geography, Government, Literature, Social Life, Arts, and History of the Chinese Empire and its Inhabitants*. New York: Charles Scribner's Sons, 1907.

Wittgenstein, Ludwig. *Philosophical Investigations*. Translated by G. E. M. Anscombe. 2nd edition. Oxford: Blackwell, 1958.

———. *Zettel*. Edited by G. E. M. Anscombe and Georg Henrik von Wright; translated by G. E. M. Anscombe. Berkeley and Los Angeles: University of California Press, 1967.

Wolffe, John, ed. *Religion in Victorian Britain*. Vol. 5, *Culture and Empire*. Manchester: Manchester University Press, 1997.

Woodbridge, Samuel Isett. *Fifty Years in China*. Richmond, VA and Texarkana, AK-TX: Presbyterian Committee of Publication, 1919.

World Missionary Conference. *Report of Commission II: The Church in the Mission Field*. Edinburgh and London: Oliphant, Anderson, and Ferrier; New York, Chicago, and Toronto: Fleming H. Revell Co., 1910.

———. *Report of Commission VI: The Home Base of Missions*. Edinburgh and London: Oliphant, Anderson, and Ferrier; New York, Chicago, and Toronto: Fleming H. Revell Co., 1910.

Wright, Arthur F., "The Chinese Language and Foreign Ideas." In *Studies in Chinese Thought*, edited by Arthur F. Wright, 286–303. Chicago: University of Chicago Press, 1953.

Wu, Hsien. "Vegetarianism." Pts. 1 and 2. *Journal of Oriental Medicine* 10, no. 6 (June 1929): 65–74; 11, no. 1 (July 1929): 1–11.

Young, Earnest P. "The Politics of Evangelism at the End of the Qing: Nanchang, 1906." In *Christianity in China: From the Eighteenth Century to the Present*, edited by Daniel H. Bays. Stanford, CA: Stanford University Press, 1996.

Zhang, Longxi. *Mighty Opposites: From Dichotomies to Differences in the Comparative Study of China*. Stanford, CA: Stanford University Press, 1998.

Zika, Charles. "Hosts, Processions, and Pilgrimages: Controlling the Sacred in Fifteenth-Century Germany." *Past and Present* 118 (February 1988): 25–64.

Zito, Angela. *Of Body and Brush: Grand Sacrifice as Text/Performance in Eighteenth-Century China*. Chicago: University of Chicago Press, 1997.

———. "Ritualizing *Li* : Implications for Studying Power and Gender." *positions: east asia cultures critique* 1, no. 2 (Fall 1993): 321–48.

Zito, Angela, and Tani E. Barlow. Introduction to *Body, Subject, and Power in China*, edited by Angela Zito and Tani E. Barlow, 1–19. Chicago: University of Chicago Press, 1994.

Index

Compositor: BookMatters, Berkeley
Text: 10/13 Galliard
Display: Galliard
Printer and Binder: Maple-Vail Manufacturing Group